A TWISTED HISTORY OF THE UNITED STATES 1450-1945

GARY RICHIED

WITH CHARLIE WESTERMAN

First trade paperback edition July 2022.
First trade e-book edition July 2022.

Produced by Brett Hoffstadt. Manufactured in the United States of America

Paperback ISBN 979-8-9863894-0-0
eBook ISBN 979-8-9863894-1-7

Dedications

For Sarah, A.L.E.S., Jude, Emily and Linus

– GR

And to Pope Francis, *for pissing Gary off*

– CW

Contents

Reconstruction, Industrialization, Empire and Depression, 1865-1939

World War II, The Cold War, and the Warfare-Welfare State, 1939-1945

Introduction

This is not your grandparents' nor your parents' U.S. History book (no offense to Grandma, Pau-Pa, Mom or Dad). Too bad for them; lucky for you. Instead of the boring, drab and sleep-inducing texts to which your elders were subjected and to which you have become accustomed (by state and teacher mandates nonetheless), ***A Twisted History of the United States*** is designed in such a way as to maximize your appreciation of United States History in the proven format of modern social media networks, thus the ***TW-IST*** which is a combination of a tweet and historical allusion. What follows therefore is a creative—dare we say even crafty—history book that lacks none of the narrative style, scholarship, analysis and accuracy already found in the best works in the field but features an attractive and accessible layout and medium by which to convey historical arguments. You're welcome.

The fact is that no one really likes reading large pages of largely uninterrupted text with integrated photos and an occasional primary source block along the margin. Major history text publishers assert that such formats do indeed pique readers' attention, but in reality, anyone who has been in a history course for, I don't know, any of the last 20-odd decades or so (we may be addressing more of the dead than the living at this point, but you get our drift...) knows quite well that skimming is done more than actual deep reading and furthermore, despite Eric Foner, David Kennedy, and Lizabeth Cohen's best efforts, attempting to attentively read their texts is akin to overdosing on Lunesta, eating turkey with heavy gravy, and watching the senior golf tour or worse, a Jerome Powell speech on "the dual mandate" of the Federal Reserve. In other words, they put us into a deep sleep only after our necks are strained because of the violent nods of slumber leading to nappy time.

No more. No more of that.

This book is a remedy meant to function as the best damn supplement to a standard United States History curriculum. For those liberated from the yoke that is school, this book is a fix and a filler for all of the holes left over from the incomplete and Swiss cheese sense of history granted to us by hacks, corporate media types, our college professors, and establishment politicians... I apologize for the redundancy there.

We humans seek meaning in our world. We wonder. It is in our nature to ask why and seek the truth. This book is not one for the comfortable nor those comforted by fictitious history that renders people pliant and placated. It is for the truth-seekers. It is for wonderers.

Beyond the novel format, what you will realize very quickly in actually reading this book is that we pull no punches. This is an utterly opinionated, incredibly biased, and yes, truly ***twisted*** history of the United States. It is not meant to be comprehensive. What we have attempted and succeeded in doing here is to highlight the major focus points and hinges upon which the development of the United States has turned. As good (great?) historians, we recognize that objectivity is an elusive goal that in the worst cases is used as both a cudgel and a veil of authority by which indoctrinators, instead of true teachers of history, force a vision of the past upon their susceptible audiences. History in its classic, best and truest sense is an investigation of the past filled with dynamic interpretation of evidence, analysis of human action, and evaluation of its effects. While the purpose of the historian is to tell the truth, the whole truth, and nothing but it, only the most idiotic and pretentious feign to be able to access it in its purity. The evidence itself is adulterated, messed with, incomplete, biased, and skewed so engaging it without proper application of the tools of historians renders us hook-winked, bamboozled, led-astray, run-amuk... Note here: I'm channeling my inner Malcolm X, who I happen to like a great deal. That is to say both the real Malcolm X and my tiny, internal version of him. Forgive the digression. In short, to do good historical work is to aim and strive for objectivity while being engaged simultaneously in an unrelenting process of self-evaluation and a continual assessment of the lenses through which we view the past. My (Richied's) lenses and approaches include the facts that I am an anarcho-capitalist libertarian who favors personal freedom and agency and is biased against states, i.e. governments. In fact, I loathe them. Yes, all of them. My experiences as a professor of history at both the collegiate and high school levels and work with the AP College Board for two decades aid me in determining the very best ways to impart historical information and to engage students and audiences. My (Westerman's) lenses and approaches on the other hand include being a former student of (Richied) as well as favoring liberty/capitalism over government and having an overall skeptical outlook on external information. My stance on liberty was further radicalized after having a morbidly obese guy mandate me with regards to public health. So there. Most if not all of our cards are there for you, out on the table. Be aware of them, because they necessarily color our vision and understanding.

Regarding use of this text, no one likes reading through instruction manuals (ok, maybe that brown-nose, conventional history A-student who really did deserve to be stuffed in his locker proves the exception), so we'll keep this as brief as possible. We suggest flipping to a section or segment in which you already have interest. See how much your perspective is affirmed, challenged or altered. In any of those cases, the book will entice you to read on. We suspect that, whatever your initial take from your first read, that will change as you continue the plunge into the rest of the work.

The ***twists*** have certain identifying characteristics. Just like regular tweets, the time and place of the twists are included so as to give you historical, geographic, and chronological points of reference. Any twists that are in quotes represent the actual words of the author or historical person. Should the ***twist*** not have quotes, then this is our creative injection of what the subject would (or should) have said. Some of them are funny. Many are ingeniously creative. All are revealing and well-situated within the text. If you don't find any of the ***twists*** to match those qualities, then you have no sense of humor or appreciation of historical genius. Just saying...

In addition to the *twists*, poignant analytical asides can be found in the "Well, How 'Bout That?!" boxes. As much as we wrote in the regular text, unfettered by concerns of mainstream reprobation, in those boxes, we really let it loose.

The book comes in both paper and e-book formats.

About what might appear to be an abrupt end to this tome: There is a clear and purposeful reason for concluding it in 1945. This is not because your average American high school and undergraduate survey course is lucky to get there, though that is all too commonly and unfortunately true. It is because of what seems to us to be an undeniable fact: There was an all-encompassing revolution that concluded in 1945, the finality of which ensured the creation of a new America. Indeed, as you'll discover at the end of this book, the revolution *was*, and its completeness is easily observed once we remove the scales of the establishment narrative from our eyes.

So as to make this experience as interactive as possible, we invite you to interact with us. We are active in the social media spaces—the free and slavish ones alike. We do the latter for our dear fans. We will see your commentary, critiques, suggestions, insights, and questions, and we will respond. Compliments are especially welcome.

Wow, a history text that is informative, interactive and responsive! No more naps in the middle of reading about Jacksonian democracy or the Progressive Era?! Take that, Eric Foner et. al!

Enjoy the experience. We certainly are.

Dive in.

1
Pre-Colonial America

Native American Societies Prior to the Arrival of that Famous Son of Genoa

That famous or infamous son of Genoa, of course, was Christopher Columbus.

Native, indigenous Americans by 1492 lived on a continent like no other in the world. North America's geography features all of the biomes of the globe. Glacier movements thanks to melting that began approximately 10,000 years ago carved into the landmass. These movements formed vast networks of lakes and rivers extending well into the interior of the continent. These waterways would later facilitate European exploration and colonization of the interior of the continent, as the rivers, streams and lake systems existed as the only arteries and by-ways upon which inhabitants could bypass thick forests and in some areas quite rough terrain.

The numerous tribes of Native Americans/American Indians formed civilizations that, from the historical and archeological evidence we are able to gather today, were **adept** at **adapting** to the geographical space in which they found themselves, often through **adoption** of neighboring communities' technologies and innovations. See what I did there? I just changed the vowels in the middle of three words in order to convey a central point in the history of all civilizations, the Native American ones included.

For example, take the Pueblo peoples from what is today the Southwestern United States and Northwestern Mexico. Having settled in an arid region and already reliant on agriculture for sustenance, the Pueblo constructed intricate irrigation systems to transform previously dry land into arable, productive farms. The Sioux, sometimes referred to as the Lakota, inhabited the Great Plains region in the center of the United States today, engaged in hunter-gatherer activities and utilized every part of the buffalo upon which they depended for survival.

Aside from notable examples like the Iroquois in the Northeast (think New England, Upstate New York and Southeastern Canada), most American Indian tribes lived itinerant, mobile lifestyles—some as farmers, some as hunter-gatherers—with little to no institutional or governmental development so often seen in more stationary societies. The lack of stability and tendency to be on the move due to environmental challenges or territorial, rival tribes meant that Native Americans lacked opportunities to form lasting, durable institutions. This includes aspects found in other civilizations such as a class of scribes, recorded language, trade systems, and uniform religious rituals and rites.

Another notable feature of North American indigenous societies that often surprises people today: The total population of North America by the end of the 15th century was around 4 million. That's it. 4 million. That's about the size of today's Detroit metropolitan area—in the entirety of North America! This means that in demographic (population studies) terms, the continent was very sparsely populated.

These demographic factors could have contributed to some even more revealing and frankly controversial facts about Native American societies. First, though many Indians had natural-sounding names when translated into European languages—Red Cloud, Crazy Horse, Turtles Run, and (forgive me as I'm a child of the 80s and 90s) Dances with Wolves (yes, I know in the Kevin Costner movie that he technically was not an Indian)—Native Americans, despite what you were taught in school, were not conscientious environmentalists to any greater or lesser degree than say contemporary Europeans, Africans or Asians.

An Eden-like America prior to European arrival in the late 15th century represents the first of many prominent myths of American history deconstructed in this book. Just wait until we get to the causes of the Civil War, the nature of the Great Depression, or who in reality won World War II.

About how advanced, scientifically and technologically speaking, Native American societies were prior to the Genovese mariner's arrival in 1492: well, relative to Chinese, European, African and Islamic civilizations at the time, the answer is that Native Americans were rather primitive. In some areas, the Native Americans (especially the Central American tribes) fared comparably, such as in architecture, astronomy and botany. However, they did not use the wheel. They had no written language. In the case of Central American tribes such as the Maya and Aztec, ritualistic human sacrifice was commonplace in scope and genocidal in nature. The rate of human sacrifice accelerated during times of drought or plague as it was thought that the gods might be satisfied with the human offerings and relent from their punishment.

None of this of course justifies the intentional exploitation of Native Americans by Europeans themselves and then the generally unplanned decimation of Native American populations thanks to the introduction of foreign pathogens. The geographic, demographic, economic, and social conditions of North America rendered Native American societies prone to European conquest and later colonization. Indeed, it is important then to transition into what was transpiring across the Atlantic in order to more fully appreciate how the New World would not just serve as a point of novel, exotic fascination for Europeans, but rather become an area of competitive conquest and a bubbling cauldron of civilizational exchange.

The Real Wild, Wild West: Europe in the Late 15th-Early 16th Centuries

Think the famous shootouts at the OK Corral or in Tombstone, Arizona—even the U.S. Army's decades-long campaigns against Western Indian tribes—were dramatic episodes of violence? They were pop-gun occasions compared to the almost constant conflict and warfare that afflicted Europe as it transitioned from the High Middle Ages to the Early Modern Period (as historians term them today), 1450-1550. First, it was a united Christian Europe, especially kingdoms and nations in Eastern Europe, that warred with the formidable and ever-advancing forces of the real global superpower of the age, the Ottoman Turks. After the fall of the last Byzantine stronghold of Constantinople in 1453, Turkish advancement into Eastern Europe extended beyond the banks of the Danube River as Vienna itself was threatened. Those wars would continue as then Europe itself would implode thanks to the really big and transformative revolution that was the Protestant Reformation.

The very natures of both European New World exploration and then settlement and colonization were defined by these developments. The dominance of Islamic civilization in North Africa and the Eastern Mediterranean effectively severed the former connections that had linked European traders with their Asian counterparts and thus their highly prized goods. Yes, spices were included in this category, but luxury materials such as rare woods and jewels, precious metals including silver, and Chinese silk belong as well. Back to the spice thing for a moment: Imagine how incredibly bland European fare was without the variety of spices found in your sure-to-be-taken-for-granted home spice rack. Sure, the Europeans had salt and some other basics from places like the Levant and North Africa, but cinnamon, nutmeg, black pepper, and a multitude of other spices were only native to the Indian subcontinent, China, and the rest of Southeast Asia. Merchants acquired them to be sold in desirous European markets. The sailors who worked as the UPS and FedEx of the day were extremely skilled and highly experienced mariners from coastal regions throughout Europe, especially Northern Italian port cities and the Iberian Peninsula, inhabited by two growing, Christian kingdoms—Spain and Portugal.

The Portuguese led the way in establishing new trade routes to Asia via the Cape of Good Hope at the southernmost tip of Africa and then into the Indian Ocean. Spain soon followed suit, but the new Spanish monarchs, Ferdinand and Isabella, were intrigued by their hired mariners who insisted that a new route was available.

★ ! ★ ! ★

Well, How 'Bout That?

No one—and I mean no one at all aware of basic geography or sea-faring—believed the world to be flat. This a rabidly anti-Catholic myth that Da Gama, Columbus and his ilk held that the world existed on an utterly flat plane. Cf. Henry Charles Lea, A History of the Inquisition of Spain: And the Inquisition in the Spanish Dependencies, *1907.*

On to that pivotal year of 1492. If you were able to go back in time and travel to, let's say New Year's Eve, December 31, 1492 and ask a random person on the street in Madrid, Seville, or Bilbao what the most important event of the year was, invariably he would exclaim, "La Reconquista!" or the Reconquest of Spain from Muslim Moors by Christian conquistadors. None of them would say much about the hired-hand Columbus sailing the ocean blue. The conflict of two civilizations and religions—Christianity and Islam—went better for the Christian side in the west than it was proceeding in the east.

Few figures in history have run the gamut of being judged on one hand as a brilliant, daring hero to on the other, a genocidal, warring maniac more than Christopher Columbus. Weeding through the fiction to get to some semblance of historical facts about the man is a yeoman's burden, but I'll be your huckleberry—after all, it is part of why you bought this book.

He most certainly was:

- A highly skilled navigator and mariner from Genoa, a Northern Italian city that long had a reputation as a hub of trade and even libertarian sentiment.
- A devout Catholic who viewed himself as an exponent of his salvific faith, so much so that he hoped that enough gold would be discovered during his discoveries that the Spanish crown would be financially equipped to launch a new crusade to regain Jerusalem.

- A man firmly convinced to the bitter end of his life that he had discovered the best route to Asia, particularly to the East Indies rather than the New World West.

He most certainly was not:

- What you've most recently been told about him, either in school or through modern treatments.
- A genocidal maniac, hell bent on wiping out the indigenous populations of the Americas.
- Someone who engaged in and promoted heinous measures against the Indians; in point of fact, multiple extant sources show him punishing Spaniards who were cruel to the Indians.

Most if not all of the current interpretation of Columbus relies upon the virulently anti-Catholic and ahistorical *la leyenda negra* or black legend which characterized all of Catholic Spain's exploits in the New World as malevolent and exploitative. English and Dutch Protestants and competitors with Spain and Portugal in Europe and beyond popularized these myths. They remain extremely popular and hard to defuse and deconstruct today.

Well, How 'Bout That?

Unlike other Italian city-states in the Renaissance period, Genoa's government was so minimalist that libertarians and near-agorists today cite it as an example of how less state intervention can lead to more prosperity. As such, Genoa's sailors faced little to no restriction or qualms about sailing for whomever offered the highest bids for their services. Cf. Matteo Salonia, **Genoa's Freedom: Entrepreneurship, Republicanism, and the Spanish Atlantic,** ***2018.***

That is not to say that subsequent Spanish and Portuguese colonization was positive or beneficial to the Native American populations. One has to remember a point already emphasized in this work but rarely touched upon in others; namely, the Iberian explorers and eventual colonizers of the New World were almost without exception *conquistadors* or direct descendants of *conquistadors.* They had no experience, no careers outside of how they and their ancestors had been employed. They had fought Moors for centuries and that experience of course impacted their dispositions and activities in the New

World. Whereas the Spanish and Portuguese had warred against Andalusian Muslims during the reconquista at home, they would continue the fight for Christianity against pagan animists in the Americas. Add in an admitted lust for gold and glory, and it is not too far off to describe the modus operandi of the conquistadors in the New World by the old mantra, a search for gold, God and glory—but few of them or the European settlers who accompanied them made any real distinctions between the three. Cortes and Pizarro conquered the Aztec and Inca respectively and admitted as much when they diagnosed themselves as having been diseased with gold fever. In order to extract as much wealth as possible from their new lands and settlements, large-scale farming and an *encomienda* system featured, sadly, tragically, forced labor by natives. Spaniards' abhorrent treatment of the Indians warranted reprobation, especially from Catholic missionaries who by and large sought voluntary conversion of the natives to Christianity, the most notable advocate for the Indians being the Dominican friar Bartolome de las Casas.

It is rather risible, when looking back on these episodes, that English and Dutch contemporaries claimed with a straight face that Spanish treatment of the Indians represented some sort of unique evil. Whereas many Spanish, Portuguese and later French settlers worked for integration (not a bad thing at the time) of natives into Catholicism and into the colonial, increasingly intercontinental economy, English and Dutch Protestants often saw Indians as inherent enemies and as utterly disposable.

2
The Colonial Era, Independence, and Constitutional Period, 1550-1789

ARRGH!-The English (Sort of) Arrive

By the time that the English became serious contenders in the New World, thanks to Spanish and Portuguese exploration and colonization, the Americas had been transformed from their pre-Columbian conditions. After 100 years of European settlement, from the crops grown and harvested, to the animals inhabiting the land, to the population make-up, the Americas represented a truly New World. This ecological and demographic revolution included a trans-Atlantic exchange that is sometimes called the Columbian Exchange. The 16th-18th centuries saw the integration of the Americas into an increasingly global economy wherein Europeans facilitated the transference of peoples, raw materials, finished goods and yes, diseases across the globe.

Students of Early American History often lose out on a more complete, comprehensive understanding of the period in large part because their teachers themselves know little of the complementary disciplines—economics, philosophy and theology—necessary to decode and explain the actions of people and nations of the time. Good thing your humble author here has extensive knowledge in all three.

Return to the centrality of the Protestant Reformation for a moment to understand the imperial rivalries that so characterized the age of exploration and expansion. What Martin Luther began in 1517 in Saxony and then John Calvin, Henry VIII of England and John Knox among others extended, was the fracturing of Europe along religious—and thus, political—lines. Think of Luther as a rock, a united Christian Europe as a windshield, and the others as cracks that develop after the initial hit and shock. After a rollicking, wild ride, England and Scotland (the two most important components of Great Britain—sorry Wales) turned firmly Protestant by the third quarter of the 16th century.

Given this religious division of Europe, old enmities intensified into what contemporaries including Elizabeth I of England and Philip II of Spain considered existential contests. Spain emerged as the power of Europe thanks in large part to the wealth it derived from its overseas conquests. Hold off on thinking that all was sunshine, lollipops and rainbows everywhere in Spain though.

All of that gold and silver as well as derivative wealth accumulated through colonial production and trade were both blessings and curses. There was an actual golden age, literally and figuratively. El Greco and Velaquez painted. Cervantes wrote *Don Quixote de la Mancha*. But, the importation of immense amounts of bullion, a fifth of

Well, How 'Bout That?

Native American populations were devastated by European diseases including smallpox, measles and mumps. However, the exchange of diseases was indeed a two-way street. Syphilis (the sexually transmitted disease from which Native Americans seem to have been immune) was spread throughout Western and Southern Europe throughout the 16th century. Europeans contracted syphilis at alarming rates thereafter as the disease afflicted the Old World.

which by law went to the Spanish crown, set off a price revolution in Europe, and also set off a ridiculous spending spree by the Spanish Hapsburg monarchs. After all, to protect the flow of precious metals and equally precious raw materials from the Americas, the monarchy spent like drunken sailors on drunken sailors. That is to say that the expense of an immense armada as well as the cost of expansion of the magnificent Escorial to house the kings weighed on the finances of the state so much so that—despite all of that bullion turned to coin—the Spanish monarchy declared bankruptcy 9 times (9 times!) between 1550 and 1670. All the while, the Anglican English and the Calvinist Dutch served as major irritants and enemies.

Just how did the English do that? In truth, until well into the 17th century, the English program against the Spanish did not include constructing large, extensive colonies that might threaten Spain's stranglehold in the New World. Oh, the English were interested in obtaining some share in the Atlantic trade—the English prized gold and silver as much as their rival Spaniards—but why go through all of that excruciating, risky, expensive and arduous work of settling and colonizing in order to steal or extract such treasure? Just steal it from the Spanish and Portuguese as they attempted to bring the bacon back home. Larceny on the high seas is piracy. And, Elizabeth I, the Protestant queen of England unofficially officially supported notorious bands of English pirates (more formally called "privateers") to gain Spanish loot.

Francis Drake succeeded in capturing Spanish ships in multiple oceans and then brought back significant portions of their loads back to England, though portions well short of the whole. Walter Raleigh was also a favorite of Elizabeth's among the sea dogs whom she openly commissioned to rob on the high seas; perhaps Raleigh was the favorite as court rumor would have it, Raleigh was just as good at getting English booty as he was Spanish. In other words, (and hysterical jokes are admittedly less humorous if one has to explain them), Raleigh most likely made Elizabeth's moniker "the Virgin Queen" a misnomer. Raleigh represented one of the few sea dogs who possessed a wider vision for English foreign policy than simple piracy: Raleigh established the Roanoke colony along the eastern seaboard of North America and named the greater area Virginia, even though a more accurate name might be, "Secret-Love-ia" or "Oh-Yeah-Land". Cue Barry White's greatest hits. He—Raleigh that is—maintained that the colony would operate as a launching point from which the English might go on to discover the secret golden city, El Dorado, of Spanish lore. The settlers should have planted crops, built lasting shelters, and constructed a port in place of searching for absent precious metals. It failed. A similar fate befell an English settlement established two years earlier at Newfoundland in modern-day Canada. If English piracy was to morph into imperialism, the English would have to alter their goals from God, glory and gold to God, glory and grain.

What Raleigh and others took from their initial forays of settling the New World, however, proved of great value to future undertakings. First, searching for gold off the Eastern seaboard was a fool's errand, and one that proved lethal in the end. Secondly, one or two entrepreneurial adventurers could not take on the entire financial burden of founding a new colony. The risk was too great. So, the ingenious English created joint-stock companies so as to diffuse the risk of shipwreck and other ruination by selling shares in such ventures to a multiplicity of investors. It was this group of innovators that ensured English colonization—especially along the Eastern seaboard—would proceed.

The English government remained, for the most part, disengaged from the independent settlement efforts. This is a surprise to many students of history today; the size, scope, and authority of today's states tend to preclude any thoughts that governments could not have been the primary catalysts of colony creation. Regardless, the English navy defeated the Spanish armada in an epic battle off the English coast in 1588; of course in this time of hyper-religious rivalry, Elizabeth I attributed this to a divine "Protestant wind" that doomed the Spanish. The effects of this event have, historically speaking, been way overblown, pun intended. It did not mean that England supplanted Spain as the dominant power in Europe and the Atlantic world. It did however further open the window of opportunity for England to secure a greater share of the economic benefices redounding to Spain. The Stuart kings who succeeded Elizabeth Tudor to the English throne cared very little for English colonial ventures, as they continued to benefit from ever-increasing privateering.

Jamestown was the first, sort of, quasi, somewhat, hard-to-even-call-it permanent English colony along the Eastern seaboard of North America. Established by the joint-stock company, the Virginia Company of London, what is really important, historically speaking, about Jamestown was not the mud huts with thatched roofs that served as abodes for the settlers, nor the fact that life in Jamestown, paradoxically, was dominated by the omnipresence of poverty and death thanks to disease, malnutrition and exposure, nor that conditions became so awful that the settlers tried to bail and return back to England in 1610, just three years or so after arriving. (They were forced back by an admiral under the employ of the Virginia Company of London's shareholders; his name: Lord De La Warr—notice= DELAWARE). No, the real importance of Jamestown was the royal charter, granted by namesake King James I for the establishment of the colony. That Jamestown Charter of 1603 guaranteed to the settlers of the colony the same rights, privileges and protections as Englishmen back home in Liverpool, London and Leeds. That is to say that settlers in the first (yes, somewhat) permanent colony along the Eastern seaboard believed themselves to be protected under the English crown and, given English history, granted negative rights in what the English government could not do to them. Hold on to that point. It is critical to understand developments later, say in 1689, 1736, 1763, and very notably in 1776.

★ ! ★ ! ★

Well, How 'Bout That?

Captain Henry Morgan (yes, that Captain Morgan) rose up the ranks of the British navy to become one of the most successful English pirates in history. Recent discoveries and works by historian John Donoghue indicate that Morgan probably survived for a period of time on Jamaica after being deserted there (this happened often), operated as a pirate without commission from English authorities, and served as a bane on Spanish settlements throughout the Caribbean. He died, by all accounts, of alcoholism most likely with a heavy dose of lead poisoning in 1688, one hundred years after the defeat of the Spanish Armada.

The MORE THAN 13, UN-Original Colonies

There is perhaps no greater, apocryphal descriptor in American history than the notion of the "13 Original Colonies". And, by the way, there is a lot of competition in this space, including but hardly limited to: the American Revolution, the Emancipation Proclamation, the Wars on Poverty, Drugs, Terror, and the Patriot Act. This notion of 13 original colonies is akin to the old joke among European historians regarding the Holy Roman Empire—it was neither holy, Roman nor an empire. In truth, especially in the context of the greater English then British Empire after the 1707 Union Act, there were many more than 13 colonies and thus the ones we think of as original were anything but.

English North American colonies were settled in rather organic, haphazard ways. Some were refuges for religious dissidents. Some were land grants to friends of the king. In the case of Maryland, named after the French Catholic queen of England (!), we had both. Another started as a penal colony. Yet others had more Germans in them than English. Despite the colonies having very different origins, populations, climates, cultures and economic activities, evidence from broadsides to brochures, diaries to newspapers indicate that almost without exception, the colonists believed that they possessed the same rights and protections under the rule of law as Englishmen back in Europe.

There were, of course, some colonies outside of Jamestown that merit close attention because of their unique histories but more so because of the impact that they had on the course of general American history all the way to today. The oddest among them were Plymouth and Massachusetts Bay. The effect and reverberation of Puritanism from this community continues to characterize and curse the country. Yes; you read that correctly. Curse.

I am not trying to be witty given that European peoples throughout the 16th and 17th centuries were unduly obsessed with curses, sorcery, the occult and witchcraft, epitomized by the Salem witch trials in 1692. From 1620 when the Pilgrims left Holland and ventured across the ocean to found Plymouth, through to the Puritans arriving to join them in Massachusetts, and beyond to today, the Pilgrim/Puritan spirit continues to reign in American formal culture. The "witches" were not the only ones victimized by it in the 17th century. The Pilgrims and Puritans formulated heinous and cruel punishments for anyone who happened to deviate from the accepted life of God's chosen community, that "city on a hill", as John Winthrop called it. Community leaders branded—literally branded—drunkards and those who fell asleep during sermons (I would have had at least one if not both brands on me in about 5 minutes). They engaged in public shaming, including cutting off Quakers' earlobes, and for those of you who thought, "Well, at least children were spared," officials seem to have even delighted in punishing insolent kids with a cleft stick, wherein the juvenile offender was forced to thrust his tongue through a stick split at the end while being painfully and publicly mocked. Quite the tolerant lot.

There were of course differences between the two groups. The Pilgrims were also known as Separatists, which was a more accurate and telling title. The Pilgrims were strict Calvinists; so strict, in fact, that they did not just wish to purify (like the Puritans) the Church of England. Cleanse it of what? Well, anything that smacked of Roman Catholicism, of course. Because the Anglican Church had failed to eradicate all of the stuff that—let's face it—makes Catholicism rather appealing to the senses and emotions: stained glass, statues, relics, incense, vestments, chalices, music, etc., Pilgrims wished to separate from it. Their community consisted only of visible saints who had proven themselves through their faith, to be redeemed. The Puritans, instead, wished to remain in the Church of England, if at the low-church fringes of it.

Well, How 'Bout That?

The Pilgrims left England and then Holland to practice their brand of Calvinism. This is true. What is not accurate is what is often taught about the Pilgrims in your typical school; namely, that the intolerance of the majority expressed toward this minority group motivated the Pilgrims to seek a new home. No. Pilgrims left to form Plymouth Bay precisely because Holland was too tolerant. There were too many non-Pilgrims living in the vicinity of this rogue, perfect community—including moderate Calvinists, Dutch-speakers (the nerve, given that they were in the Netherlands)—and dear God, a sprinkling of Catholics and an occasional Jew! Hence, it was the preference of William Bradford et al. for homogeneity in place of diversity that led to the formation of Plymouth.

Calvinism itself is a mess of a theology with a mess of strange assertions that had already been defined as heresies by the Christian communities of the past.[1] It is no wonder then that its most passionate adherents built exclusive, theocratic societies whose founding documents and "constitutions" like the Mayflower Compact read more like a passage from Scripture than any sort of secular arrangement.

All that being said, forget about Squanto and Thanksgiving and the supposed cooperation (more borne out of survival necessity) between Native Americans and the early settlers at Plymouth. Something much more important than thanksgiving occurred. While Pilgrims did not follow the previous failed English settlements of Newfoundland and Roanoke into oblivion by wantonly searching for gold, their fundamentalist impulse to live the most strictly Scriptural Christian life led them to err through practicing socialism. Their experience is an excellent example of the tragedy of the commons, i.e. what results when there exists no private property nor ethic of protecting it. Because the Pilgrims treated land (then the most important means of production) as owned in common, starvation resulted. Once their leader William Bradford instituted care of personal property and encouraged the free division of labor, the Pilgrims thrived.

---

1 For a longer analysis of Calvinism, cf. Gary Richied, *A Catholic School Teacher's Guide to Modern European History*, 2016.

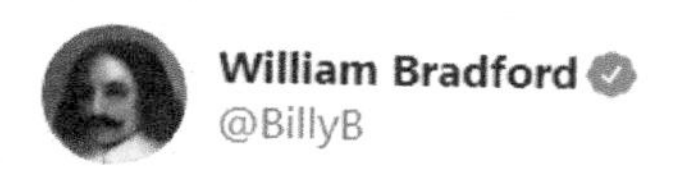

"By the spring, our food stores were used up and people grew weak and thin. Some swelled with hunger... So they began to think how... they might not still thus languish in misery."

1646 · Plymouth Bay Colony

Yay capitalism! The Pilgrims learned a universal, historical truth; namely, without free markets, price points and voluntary cooperation—poverty, deprivation and then death ensue.

The Puritans landed in the neighborhood of Plymouth in 1634 after some very un-Columbus-like mariners missed their desired destination of Jamestown in Virginia by a mere 600 miles! Their colony was as much a theocracy as that of the Pilgrims, if not more so. John Winthrop and a cadre of like-minded Puritan oligarchs ran Massachusetts and in so doing, established a society wherein the concept of the separation of church and state was so foreign as to be laughable. Beyond that, the very earliest notions of American liberty as understood by the Puritans speak to a loud statism, as the government was viewed as the conduit and authority on what constituted human freedom. This is altogether creepy.

"[C]oncerning liberty, I observe a great mistake in the country about that. There is a twofold liberty, natural (I mean as our nature is now corrupt) and civil or federal. The first is common to man with beasts and other creatures...

1645 · Massachustetts Bay Colony

Translation: Pace Rousseau, man is born free and evil and everywhere he is in chains until he submits his will to civil authorities which make him civilly free. All other freedoms when exercised represent expressions of broken human nature. They are repugnant to God. Only when one conforms his will and his behavior to that of the elite, civil authorities established by divine will, of course, will one truly be free in any sense of that term.

And you thought that American worship of the state started with Teddy Roosevelt, Woodrow Wilson and pals in the Progressive Era?!

Pilgrims and Puritans lived in this city on a hill for decades and eventually, the smaller Pilgrim community was subsumed into the much larger Puritan population. Congregationalist (read "Puritan") towns and churches came to dot the greater New England region, the most prominent among them were Boston with its appropriately named First Church. Hard work was such a prominent and admired virtue that it was viewed as a clear sign of one's redemption. Such a cultural attitude served the early settler communities well, as they engaged in farming, fishing, and some trade from relatively prosperous harbors in Puritan centers such as the aforementioned Boston, and yes, places like Portsmouth and Newport.

Well, How 'Bout That?

History clarifies literature. You cannot make sense of the classic American novel, Nathaniel Hawthorne's The Scarlet Letter, *without a sound understanding of its historical setting. It is natural to wonder why these 1630s Puritans are so damned judgmental and punitive toward Hester Pryne and others in the community who commit sins. It isn't just the fundamentalist Calvinism at work; it is fundamentalist Calvinism on steroids. Think about it: the Separatist community was in the process of being absorbed into the larger Puritan body. Pilgrims saw even Puritans as morally lax, so when sinful offenders went unpunished or punished in less than severe, often corporal ways, well, Puritans lost face. They were losing the battle to be seen as the most authentic, holiest community of the elect of God. Anne Hutchinson (a real figure in history) felt the brunt of not conforming to Puritanical demands due to her antinomianism, a theology that is actually more in keeping with Calvin's beliefs than Puritanism was at the time. She was banished from Massachusetts in 1637.*

In the end, the first truly successful, permanent English colonies consisted of settlers who were religious rejects from England, who had a deep-seated distrust of official church and old government authorities (outside of their own), possessed an insular culture and who, without any real oversight from the English government, built an economy free from outside say or help. That—all of that—is a volatile admixture that would become explosive should outsiders ever endanger the Puritans' way of life. Is there any shock then that the first troubles that led to the American War for Independence included a protest against a sugar tax, the hanging of tax collectors in effigy, a mob attacking of British troops, an arson of the royal governor's residence, and a dump-tea-into-the-Harbor rave for the ages—all in Boston? That was a rhetorical question by the way.

Other colonies established under ostensible but limited English control and oversight, in truth, did not look very English at all. Before New York became New York, it was populated by Dutch settlers who called their chief encampment New Amsterdam, thus we still have names for New York boroughs and locales like Harlem, Brooklyn and (unfortunately) New York families like the Roosevelts. Maryland was a refuge for English Catholics like Lord Baltimore, a royal friend whose Catholic community was later persecuted by English Protestants.

Pennsylvania was a royal land grant to William Penn meant to serve as a refuge for yet another dissident Protestant sect in Europe, the Quakers, but ended up having high numbers of Germans residing there. Cavalier Anglicans populated the Carolinas in the first waves, and then were soon outnumbered by emigrating Scots-Irish, an immigrant group that like the Pilgrims and Anabaptists before them tried to find new homes in Europe only to be unwanted at every turn. They preferred western, frontier districts to the coasts. This rendered the Scots-Irish independent, self-reliant, pugnacious, as well as prone to dance, drunkenness, and gambling. In other words, inherently interesting and eminently better than the Puritans of New England.

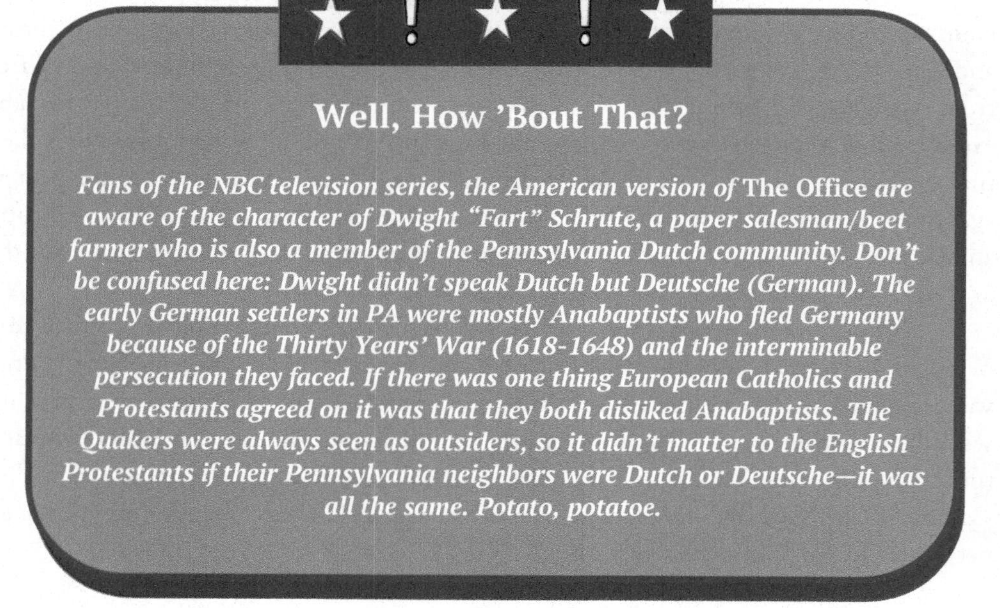

Well, How 'Bout That?

Fans of the NBC television series, the American version of The Office *are aware of the character of Dwight "Fart" Schrute, a paper salesman/beet farmer who is also a member of the Pennsylvania Dutch community. Don't be confused here: Dwight didn't speak Dutch but Deutsche (German). The early German settlers in PA were mostly Anabaptists who fled Germany because of the Thirty Years' War (1618-1648) and the interminable persecution they faced. If there was one thing European Catholics and Protestants agreed on it was that they both disliked Anabaptists. The Quakers were always seen as outsiders, so it didn't matter to the English Protestants if their Pennsylvania neighbors were Dutch or Deutsche—it was all the same. Potato, potatoe.*

The Northern and Mid-Atlantic colonies focused on the production of foodstuffs like wheat, rye, barley, and corn; the Chesapeake region cultivated tobacco and grains; the Southern-most settlers especially in the Tidewater, coastal region grew rice and eventually the cash crop of cotton.

Though they all settled along the eastern seaboard, the colonies were unique and different from one another. Colonists used the word "peculiar" to describe the various ways of life, customs, dispositions, and cultures of each. Further distinctions of climate, race, ethnicity, economic activities, and religious affiliations far outnumbered the qualities they shared. As the colonies developed over the course of the 17th then into the 18th centuries, there were, however, some outstanding commonalities. First, the American colonial populations grew very rapidly. Perhaps the most famous physician in England, Dr. Samuel Johnson, said it best when he declared, "The Americans multiply like rattlesnakes." A number of factors were in play here besides the fact that early Americans liked to have sex; even the Puritans engaged in a lot of it, even if they might have preferred to A) never talk about it, and B) remove any physical pleasure from the sex-equation. Compared to Europeans of the time, Americans enjoyed a considerably higher standard of living. This resulted in better nutrition and decreased infant/child mortality. Proof of this is found in the pure demographic data but also in anecdotal evidence. For instance, historian David McCullough in his book *1776* relates that when Hessian (German mercenary troops) arrived in the colonies to fight what the British at that stage figured was a limited colonial insurrection not unlike others that had routinely transpired in the empire, the Hessian troops were amazed at the very high standard of living that the average American appeared to enjoy. Undoubtedly, they looked around the abandoned colonial homes they were looting and muttered to one another, "*Was ist los?* What is wrong?".[2] They could not figure out why the Americans were rebelling if their wealth was so much higher than that of contemporary Europeans.

TEN-HUT!: Salutary Neglect and Life in the Northern and Southern Colonies

But rebel they eventually did. That rebellion was not years but rather decades in the making because of a trend and term well known to American historians: salutary neglect.

Relative to other parts of the English then British Empire, the planting and development of the Eastern seaboard colonies transpired with little to no interference or governance from back home. In other words, American colonists were left to their own devices to forge a living and develop institutions that would ensure their survival amid often hostile Indian tribes and even more hostile Catholic European powers enveloping them. So long as these afterthoughts of colonies contributed to the economic functioning and

[2] My one semester of college German is kicking in here.

prosperity of the English/British empire, the powers that were in London left them alone. Think of The Beatles song, "Let It Be"; Parliament and Crown essentially sang the refrain of "Let Them Be" from the early 17th century to the mid-18th century.

The effects of salutary neglect are evident in both the Northern and Southern regions/colonies. The New England and Northern settlers mostly engaged in agricultural work which produced foodstuff surpluses that matriculated to ports. From there, merchants transported much of that food to feed African slaves laboring in the really valuable colonies—the jewels in any of the European powers' American colonies—those in the Caribbean. Sorry to injure your patriotic, more so nationalistic U-S-A, U-S-A chanting sensibilities (it won't be the last time), but Brits cared little about New Hampshire or Connecticut: They cared a great deal about Bermuda and Barbados. With good reason. The Caribbean colonies were the money-makers because of the slave-sugar-rum economic engine located there. In point of fact, the French Caribbean colony of Guadeloupe, an island about 600 square miles in size, made more money for the French crown in the 18th century than all of French Canada and Louisiana. Sugar was white gold.

The Andros Affair reveals how pugnacious, voluntarist, and independent the colonies wished to remain in the face of even the slightest oversight by the powers-that-were in London. In 1643 (that's early) without the sanction of crown or Parliament, domestic merchants in New England ports banded together to form a trade association known as the New England Commonwealth. Rather than have these small communities compete for trade, Newport and Boston and Portsmouth merchants cooperated in enhancing commerce, forming militias to fight Indians, and selling their wares to the highest bidders. In essence, the New England Commonwealth evaded English mercantilism, a central feature of imperial activity—for 45 years! In 1684, new British King James II had other ideas in mind. A devotee of mercantilist policies, the New England Commonwealth was a notable digression and innovation. It is important to note here the semantics: The "commonwealth" was coordinated in a voluntary fashion for the common-wealth of the New England communities. By royal authority, that Commonwealth was disbanded and replaced by the Dominion of New England. Mark the word "dominion". Dominion means something that is lorded over, and the lord who the king appointed to police and regulate commerce in New England was Sir Edmund Andros.

Well, How 'Bout That?

Mercantilism, the economic system by which a European nation and state directed wealth to itself from its colonial holdings, proved utterly attractive to an 18th century Britain that eventually dominated the high seas. With the power of His Majesty's navy, the merchants of Dover, Glasgow, and Liverpool imported massive supplies of raw materials from the colonies to be then manipulated by the hands of peasants in cottages. In turn, when markets in England and Scotland had their fill of products, the colonies and indeed the rest of Europe, sat as hungry markets for British textiles, shoes, barrels, furniture, candles, and chandeliers. Though mercantilism required, by its nature, state intervention to ensure that foreign competition was eliminated, it produced wealth for the commercial class of Europe. Thus, mercantilism was the state's attempt to create a commercial and industrial monopoly—and it worked until high-minded, free-marketers like Edmund Burke, Adam Smith, Samuel Adams, and John Hancock came around and stole all the fun with all their "freedom and rights" talk... Finally, to understand the nature of mercantilism and the crazy love British authorities had for it, is to understand the primary cause of the American War for Independence.

@SirEdmundAndros is a faithful Anglican. The territory he will govern will be Puritan for the most part. What could go wrong?

1684 · England

3.2K Retweets **423** Quote Tweets **10.1K** Likes

Andros was like oil to water in New England. He was a faithful Anglican who spoke openly about wanting the Anglican Church to gain power there. Yikes. He headquartered right in the Puritan lion's den—Boston. Worst of all, Andros represented a danger to salutary neglect as it had been enjoyed in New England for decades. He restricted the operation of colonial courts. He curbed town meetings, taxed without the consent of colonial assemblies, and enforced the mercantilist Navigation Acts of 1651, laws that the New Englanders had gleefully ignored (nullified) for decades.

By 1689, the Bostonians had had enough. Political unrest at home for the king moved them to form a mob armed with musket and torch to oust Andros.

Say what one will about Andros, he did at least know when to get out of dodge with his scalp intact. In the dark of night, he fled Boston by ship to more hospitable environs in royalist, Anglican New York. According to dubious (and oddly typical American) propaganda at the time, Andros fled in women's clothing, so his scalp might have been intact but hardly his dignity.

And, Boston and greater New England returned to doing things their way; the hell-no-to-mercantilism way.

Notice the formula here: As early as the late 17th century, Massachusetts colonists resorted to protest and then ultimately violence when mercantilism was imposed upon them. It would not be the last time, and resistance of that sort would be the most popular export from Massachusetts to the other colonies.

Moving Southbound (pace Allman Brothers' Band), Virginia had its own version of anti-state violence in Bacon's Rebellion (1687) wherein a group of mostly indentured servants and poor frontier farmers burned down Jamestown hoping to get at Governor William Berkeley. Moreover, the Southern colonies faced the same existential problem as their neighbors to the North; namely, an abundance of land to be cultivated but too few laborers to do the cultivating. The problem seemed to have found a solution in indentured servitude, but the problem was more acute in the South, especially given the type of large-scale, cash crop farming conducive to the region. It should be noted here that slaves were imported to all of the colonies throughout this time. The reason for their comparative concentration in the Chesapeake and Tidewater regions of the South pertains to, again, perceived economic need. Recall those cereals produced in the Northern colonies, some of which went off to feed slaves in the Caribbean? Well, as more and more slaves were brought to work in sugar cane fields there, those cereals from the North just were not enough to feed them. Rice from the Tidewater did. Rice was produced in abundance in the Carolinas and what would become Georgia.

Soapbox

Puritans were always good merchants, ready to provide a good or service to those willing to pay—basic human decency and rights be damned, especially if they did not have to live with the repercussions of their actions. Who were those responsible for importing so many black slaves to the South? Well it wasn't just the African Company, an English joint-stock company. It was also a host of Northern, often New England families, including one whose name might be familiar: the Browne family. Drop the -e and you might reconsider attending such an Ivy League university.

Have you ever been to a rice paddy?! It's plain awful. Rice is grown in what amounts to a swamp. Just the bugs alone are enough to get you running for the hills, and the conditions of rice cultivation were no different back then. Slaves were imported to do a great deal of the work, albeit in a forced labor system much different from that of others in the English/British colonies.

Slave owners and even overseers developed the task system of slavery as a result, one in which slaves were given production quotas and should those quotas be met, slaves were free then to live independent lives, often in fringe, autonomous slave communities, frequently a sizeable distance from the plantation, and sometimes among Indians. Conversely, the cultivation of tobacco and sugar (due to the complicated processes involved) often featured the gang system in which slaves were closely (at least as closely as possible) observed at work in the fields. What is absolutely and undeniably true about slave life and experience, whether under the task or gang systems, is that despite the incredibly difficult circumstances of their lives, African slaves in the Americas exercised an incredible amount of agency, perseverance, creativity, and ironically freedom under the harshest of conditions. They shirked work. Slaves engaged in whole-scale sabotage, including often breaking farm equipment. Worse for the owner, they ran away, sometimes to distant slave refugee colonies. And, while doing all of that, slaves formulated the most distinct and attractive culture in American history. American language, art, music, dance, cuisine, design, fashion, religion and perhaps most importantly, that spirit of rebellion—none of it can be called American today without acknowledging the fundamental contributions of slave culture. Later, it was as much this culture as slavery itself that New England, Puritanical abolitionists wished to eradicate. Thank God that pertaining to the former—and to later American culture in general—they failed.

Well, How 'Bout That?

In Spanish Florida, the colonizers there formed Gracia Real de Santa Teresa de Mose *as a colonial slave refuge for slaves fleeing the British Carolinas. The slaves were granted freedom after a term of work and became* Maroons, *who were just about the toughest, most rugged, and thus, most impressive people in all of history. It is one thing for a people to go rogue and live off the land not far from their homes, but the Maroons distinguished themselves by their agorism in a totally foreign land. Escaped slaves joined their communities, and punishments to Maroons for harboring slaves were severe, ranging from leg amputation to castration. When necessary, the Maroons warred directly with white settlers, and enlisted Indians and foreign pirates to their cause. Just damn impressive.*

The institutions and frankly the very ways of life of Americans—from the creation of labor systems to their own legislative assemblies—formed with little to no involvement from British authorities. The American colonies were, simply put, very different entities—relative to one another and definitely distinctive to old Mother England. Incidents of Old England intrusion on the lives of the colonies, one a religious movement, the other dealing with the law and press, further prove just how unique these colonies were.

Zeal and Zenger: Americans Get Woke

While a German royal family took over ruling England from the Scottish Stuarts in 1689 (the actual English kings and queens apparently were not very good at it), and Parliament accrued more power and independence vis-a-vis these Hanoverian kings, the American colonies under their rule grew in size and economic output. More and more, from New Hampshire to the Carolinas, the Eastern seaboard colonies engaged in the Atlantic economy, becoming veritable bread baskets to the British Caribbean islands (which British mercantilists applauded) and to foreign colonies as well (which British mercantilists detested).

Americans and visitors alike noted a stark decline in religious fervor and participation in the early 18th century. Among the learned, inroads were made by initial Enlightenment thinkers in Europe who tended to be skeptical of organized religion, deeming it superstitious and unreasonable. The faithful remnant of preachers and ministers observed both in Britain and the Americas a sharp decline in service attendance across the Protestant denominations. Fearing that Christianity was losing its centrality in the hearts and minds of Brits everywhere, mainly Congregationalist, i.e. Puritan ministers engaged in a revival movement known as the Great Awakening.

Jonathan Edwards and George Whitefield were the apostles of this movement: Their success in stoking renewed religious zeal made them celebrities of the era. The message was not much different than that of the more traditional, established preachers in pulpits from Boston to Charles Town; namely, you are all going to hell. If you happen to live in any big city in the United States today, you have heard this message before, probably from a fundamentalist street preacher yelling it at you through a megaphone downtown. Accept Jesus Christ as your personal Lord and Savior, stop incurring His wrath, or else—you guessed it—you're going to hell. Before you dismiss this message as wholly unappealing, consider the audience and setting in which it was delivered in the 1730s and 1740s. Appreciate it in its historical context. Most of the people in the pews and then in the fields during revivals subscribed to a Calvinistic view of salvation. John Calvin emphasized the notion of predestination, thus at some point in time, God predetermined whether you were going to end up in heaven (yay!) or hell (damned!, literally). Thus, one's actions and behaviors on earth mean little to nothing. God could not be wrong in already choosing your destination; He's God. Therefore, people engage in no meaningful, cooperative act pertaining to their salvation.

So, then, why were Protestants of the era, across the board, so concerned about sin and personal behavior? Why were they so obsessed with punishing the sinner? Two reasons: first, perception. Second, their notion of unconditional love. When Edwards or Whitefield testified to God's justice coming to the wicked, or in the words of Edwards, that we are all sinners in the hands of an angry God, ready to be justly plunged into hell like a spider dangling precariously from a tenuous web which God can easily snip, they were not really talking to those in the congregation.

"There is no want of power in God to cast wicked men into hell at any moment." #StayWoke

Jul 8, 1741 · Enfield, CT

1.9K Retweets **108** Quote Tweets **12.3K** Likes

They were talking about the others; those not in the pews or in the fields. The drunkards. The fornicators. The adulterers. The dancers. Perhaps worst of all, the laggards, the lazy ones. Why? It is not as though the people in the pews had made some free, salvific choice not to offend God and not sin; rather, they were showing the symptoms of being saved. Put another way, the congregation was comforted by such fire and brimstone preaching because, oddly enough, it put them at ease seeing as they were listening to the word of God instead of carousing and enjoying themselves like those who were, and thus, showing the signs of damnation.

Beyond perception—which is enormously powerful in Protestant communities to this day ("Have you been saved?")—why did preachers encourage charitable acts at all? Whitefield captivated enormous crowds with his rallies, turning skeptics like Benjamin Franklin himself, into major contributors for funding an orphanage in Georgia. Charitable acts did indicate the symptoms of one who is elect or saved to be sure; however, the impetus to be self-sacrificial for some greater good also emerges from the Protestant notion—one distinct from Catholicism—that to do good shows one's true, unconditional and hence genuine love for God. Doing good works is not going to get you into heaven (cf. predestination), but that is all the better, because if without any pretense for reward or compensation, you still are moved to do good by one's neighbor and follow the precepts of Scripture, well that shows true, genuine love of God.

Combine all of that theological messaging with the novel and innovative methods of evangelization employed by the Great Awakening preachers, and what resulted was a veritable, transformative movement that swept the colonies. Note too: this is an era absent of radio, television, podcasts, movies, the internet, and most sports. So when Whitefield came to town, it was an event; better, it was *the* event. Franklin estimated that a revival preaching featuring Whitefield just outside of Philadelphia drew 30,000 people. Considering that the entire population of Philadelphia at the time was around 25,000 souls, the impact of the events is evident. The preachers of the Great Awakening engaged in theatrics. Their voices boomed, and their sermons were drama. Whitefield himself was a skilled thespian, having studied theatre in college. All of these new methods rankled the old guard establishment clergy. What truly unnerved them was Edwards and Whitefield's appeal and that such appeal spanned across the numerous denominations of Protestants in America. It did not particularly matter to the revivalists whether one was a Puritan or Anglican; Methodist or even an Anabaptist. It was crucial to them to reignite Protestant zeal for the faith.

The Great Awakening produced unique trends that are alive and well within American religion even today. It undermined old religious authorities in favor of charismatic, even populist preachers. It increased both the number of congregants in the churches, but unlike in Europe where national churches still held immense sway, the Great Awakening inspired an open competition among the various Protestant churches for said believers. To this day, Protestant congregations pull out all the stops to get asses in the pews; a new band, expanded foyer, high tech sound system, popular minister—you name it. Lutherans in Germany today don't wake up on Sunday morning and determine that they are going down to the Baptist church because they have a new guitarist there. American Protestants do this routinely. Thirdly, the Great Awakening affected how ministers (the most prestigious men in the colonies) were educated and formed in Christian "new light" centers at places like Harvard, Yale, and Dartmouth. Today, graduates of those institutions still preach with zeal in a God-less cathedral, but it is one of Progressivism rather than Protestantism. Their ministry and preaching became much more charismatic and evangelical in nature. Finally, the Great Awakening tended to unify American colonists across the denominational divide and refocused their worldviews on their commonality vis-a-vis the other; namely, the Catholicism of their existential enemies, the French and Spanish.

From colonial religion to the press. The John Peter Zenger case in New York, 1734-1735 represents just one of several *causes célèbres* pertaining to the establishment of a free press in the colonies. The facts of the case are as follows: Zenger was a German-born newspaper publisher who editorialized on supposed (likely) corruption involving the then royal governor of New York, William Cosby. Yes, the first famous, now infamous, Bill Cosby in American history. As a reward for his investigative reporting, Zenger was charged with the crime of seditious libel. In effect, Cosby argued before the magistrate that Zenger published information that was injurious to the government and to Cosby himself. And by the letter of the laws against sedition, Zenger was guilty.

Funny thing about sedition laws: The government gets to be both judge and plaintiff in such cases. That is to say that all the government has to prove, according to the law written by the government, is that the defendant wrote and disseminated something that harmed the ability of the state to function and govern. What a system. Zenger's lawyer knew, strictly speaking, that his client was guilty, so like every good lawyer, Andrew Hamilton (I have to stress here—NOT ALEXANDER) made the case about something else. That something else was the principle of freedom of the press.

Well, How 'Bout That?

Andrew Hamilton might have been the first but he was hardly the last American attorney to utilize the, "Hey, look over here jury" defense. It would be used to great acclaim to get O.J. Simpson exonerated in his 1995 murder trial. The Simpson defense team consisted of famous lawyers Johnny Cochrane, Barry Scheck, and Robert Kardashian—the patriarch of, well, you know who.

"By it we are charged with printing and publishing 'a certain false, malicious, seditious, and scandalous libel.' This word 'false' must have some meaning, or else how came it there?"

Aug 4, 1735 · New York, NY

1.1K Retweets **132** Quote Tweets **18.5K** Likes

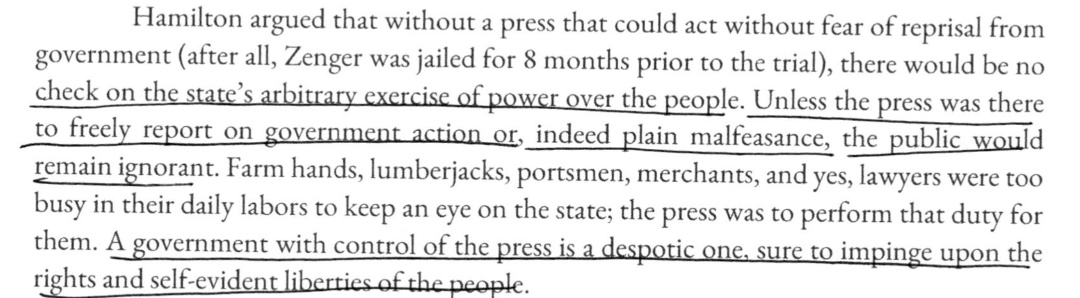

Hamilton argued that without a press that could act without fear of reprisal from government (after all, Zenger was jailed for 8 months prior to the trial), there would be no check on the state's arbitrary exercise of power over the people. Unless the press was there to freely report on government action or, indeed plain malfeasance, the public would remain ignorant. Farm hands, lumberjacks, portsmen, merchants, and yes, lawyers were too busy in their daily labors to keep an eye on the state; the press was to perform that duty for them. A government with control of the press is a despotic one, sure to impinge upon the rights and self-evident liberties of the people.

The jury took just ten minutes to deliberate and render a not guilty verdict.

The Zenger case and ones like it established in the American mindset the need for an independent press.

Besides zeal and Zenger, allow me to offer some final notes of import regarding Americans' way of life before tackling the big showdown with France in 1754. The vast majority of American colonists—beyond 90%—were engaged in agriculture. Others worked in various trades as sailors, trappers, glaziers, fishermen, blacksmiths, bakers, millers, cobblers and coopers. The most revered profession was Christian ministry. Doctors and lawyers were not all that highly regarded, as doctors tended to prescribe bleeding as a remedy for every serious ailment and lawyers bled their clients dry through exorbitant fees. Ba-Dum-Bum. When they were working and when they were not, Americans were drinking. In fact, they were generally sauced. By the mid-18th century, the average American male imbibed about three pints of rum a week. That is not to mention the other preferred local (craft) beers and ciders that distillers offered to an insatiable consumer base.

In attitude, they were tough-minded and fiercely protective of their ways of life. What made them dangerous was their growing affluence and thus influence in the British Empire and, worse, their passionate desire to expand westward. One such young Virginian's ambition to do so sparked a world war.

The Duel for North America: Britain Wins… and Loses

There would have been no War for American Independence without the French and Indian War, 1754-1763. Americans of bygone eras understood the historical importance of this war, one which represented a theatre in the larger imperial struggle of the Seven Years' War, 1756-1763. James Fennimore Cooper set his epic novel in it (*The Last of the Mohicans*, 1826), and the conflict was the culmination of a series of wars featuring European rivals in North America.

George Washington was a catalyst for the whole thing. In fact, one might argue that George Washington and Winston Churchill represent the only two people who own the ignominious and bizarre distinction of being responsible for starting not just one, but two world wars. Quite the bloody feathers in their respective caps.

After serving as an official negotiator of the British crown in 1753, the perpetually ambitious Washington went on an unofficial campaign to survey land and build fortresses in the French-occupied Ohio River Valley in 1754. This is where things got hairy very quickly. Washington and his merry band of Virginia militiamen had been tasked with determining the value of massive land claims made by Virginia planters. He was not tasked with engaging French troops and Indian scouts. He did anyway. Why? Because he was George Washington.

If placed in his shoes, few to none of us would do what Washington did. In hostile territory, far from home, upon encountering the French and their Indian allies outside of what is today Pittsburgh (then the location of the French Fort Duquesne) at the confluence of three major rivers—the Ohio, the Allegheny, and the Monongahela (God, I just love saying, MON-ON-GA-HELA...), Washington did not order his men to quietly slink back to comfortable Virginia. That would have been the prudent, sane move. No, he ordered the militiamen to fire upon the French detachment, then retreat. He and his men were eventually captured and shortly thereafter, released. This small incident, which left one French commander dead, ended up being a major spark to a much larger, global war.

Here's the thing about the evil that is imperialism: The world becomes much, much smaller. Of course, what is not meant here is that the globe literally shrinks. It becomes *politically* smaller. Think for a moment of that hideous, nightmare-inducing Disneyland/Disneyworld ride, "It's a Small World, After All". Remember that one? Parents with considerable masochistic streaks force their kids onto what amounts to be a series of coal cars on a track which leads all of the unfortunate parties involved into a dark tunnel wherein demonic, robotic characters start singing the eponymous Disney tune. At this stage of the ride, 90 percent of the kids are wailing in fear. As if that is not enough, the cars then move into the next stage of this burp of hell on earth (clearly a level of hell Dante forgot) ride wherein more and more characters emerge from the darkness singing in the most cacophonous, Tower of Babel ways, "It's a Small World" in a variety of languages! "*C'est un petit monde, néanmoins!*" et cetera. Genuinely horrifying. By the end of the ride, all of the children are crying, demanding that their parents explain to them why they put them through that, and the parents laugh with an altogether wanton sense of *Schadenfreude.*

With 18th century imperialism, the world became a scary place as a result of the adjacent and sometimes overlapping land claims and settlements of European powers. Any small engagement in the boonies of the empire (the Ohio River Valley, for instance) had the potential of igniting a gigantic conflict between European colonies, then European rivals themselves, then their respective allies in Europe itself. Such was the case for the Seven Years' War, and many a subsequent conflict to the present day.

As the map above indicates, the British colonies were enveloped by hostile, Catholic powers France and Spain. This is something of which the colonists were well aware. But, before one makes the mistake of characterizing the British colonies as underdogs in the fight, the British had major advantages in fighting in this theatre. First, the British navy was superior to that of the French. Secondly, the sheer population advantage: By 1754, there were approximately 1.5 million people living in the British colonies as opposed to about 60,000 French settlers in all of New France. That is right—only 60,000 from New Orleans to Montreal. The French compensated for their numerical inferiority by closely allying themselves with the Native Americans throughout their claims. This was borne of convenience but also necessity. French settlers formed a rather symbiotic relationship with the natives. The major industry and means of survival was fur trading, a practice that naturally required the expertise of Indians. Frenchmen and Indians who forged this way of life were called not "fur trappers" (lame to the French ear) but rather "*les coureurs de bois*"—"runners of the woods". Much better. The French cooperated with the Indians. The English tended to view them as obstacles and disposable. It would be these natives, armed with French muskets and guerrilla warfare techniques who rendered the French side full of formidable foes.

In this book, aside from a few exceptions, we are not going to go into terrible detail regarding military campaigns, troop movements, naval battles and the like. Sorry to all the war buffs out there: We think it's a little odd to be obsessed with war, but to each his own. So rather than waxing poetic about the epic battles of Wolfe and Montcalm on the Plains of Abraham along the St. Lawrence River, let us go ahead and address the historical significance of the war.

Britain and her allies won the Seven Years' War and the French and Indian War in North America. The resultant Treaty of Paris, 1763, granted nearly all of France's North American mainland holdings to Britain. Quebec. Louisiana. Excluding a couple of fishing islands off the coast of Canada, it was all under the Union Jack now.

People throughout the British Empire were exuberant, including North American colonists, including the king; although his excitement was tempered.

Others in Parliament like Prime Minister George Grenville worried as well, for while Britain became the dominant power in North America with its lands now extending to the Mississippi River, that victory came as a result of a catastrophically expensive war. For the time wars are conducted and even afterwards for the victors, any perceived prosperity created by war proves illusory, and that was certainly the case for Britain in the Seven Years' War. As the greatest economist in history, Ludwig von Mises remarked in 1919: "War prosperity is like the prosperity that an earthquake or a plague brings." It could not be any other way. In war, especially a world war like the Seven Years' War, immense production and resources are diverted away from providing for the needs, wants and preferences of normal civilian living and instead turned towards destruction. Moreover, Britain now had to administer and police all of that new territory. Anticipating clashes with expansionist American colonists and Native Americans in the region, Parliament created the Proclamation Line of 1763, forbidding any European American settlement west of the Appalachians. The Americans by and large just ignored it. Finally, the prodigious expense of such wars results in equally gigantic levels of debt.

Red Ink Leads to Red Coats

So, what is the big deal about national red ink, i.e. debt? Why was the British government so obsessed about finding a remedy for it? The best way to think about this is that national governments have credit ratings just as individuals do. Your credit rating depends on the amount of borrowing you have done, your record of paying it off, and your ability to pay it off. Good credit rating? That means it is easier (lower interest rates) for you to borrow. Bad credit rating? That signals risk to creditors and risk is expensive for the borrower (high interest rates). The war along with the cost of building and maintaining the largest and most formidable military in the world (especially the navy) far exceeded the gold reserves that rested in treasury coffers. Therefore, unlike any other institution on earth, governments can tax, and the British government paid for that war by forcefully confiscating British subjects' wealth through legal plunder. But even that was not enough. Crown and Parliament depended on loans from domestic and foreign investors to make up the deficit between their tax revenues and expenditures. Those monies needed to be paid back. Now, governments possess a variety of means by which to pay off debt. The first of which is to cut spending and thus use surplus revenue to pay off debt. Funny thing about especially modern governments: Cutting expenses and size is really not their thing. Another method is to find new lenders and take on more debt; though this hardly solves the problem in the long run. One more is to increase taxes. This ended up as the preferred course of the Brits in 1763. There is, however, another method, one that is preferred today by governments. It is sneaky. It is terribly unethical. But, it is very effective especially in the short term, and that is inflation. Coin, or worse, print more money. No one in 18th century Europe maintained that creating a paper or fiat currency would work; however, there were still some lingering believers in John Law's central Bank of France schemes wherein states manipulated the value of currencies in order to pay off debt or create huge market bubbles. With inflation, a government issues devalued or denuded coins into the market, uses said coins to pay off creditors, forces everyone to use that currency, and in so doing robs people of the value of the money they have saved while prices rise and often skyrocket. What a system! The British opted to avoid the inflationary route because inflation tends to crush an economy as it blocks the flow of credit to worthy enterprises and ruins accurate value/price discovery. In short, inflation blocks investment and economic growth because all lenders get freaked out about getting their actual principal and interest back when repayment takes place.

The Brits, in essence, left the pound sterling alone and as such looked to the colonies to submit some of their pounds sterling to the British government. It should be noted that this was an altogether reasonable position taken by King George III and Parliament. The British military had just fought a war for the protection of the colonies; a war to which there was little contribution by the colonists themselves. It was thought that the colonists should therefore bear some of the burden. Essentially, the British were asking for some money, you know, for the effort.

Soapbox

For more on this topic, read some very accessible and important economics. Books I would recommend would be* Economics in One Lesson *by Henry Hazlitt,* Basic Economics *by Thomas Sowell, and if you want to have some fun for you and the kids,* The Tuttle Twins Series *by Connor Boyack.

And, here is the crux of the problem: British taxation and regulation policy seemed more than reasonable from the British perspective. However, the British were dealing with colonists who were quite unreasonable. To be fair, their historical position was not that they could not be taxed, nor that British laws did not apply to them. However, colonists did maintain that should taxation and regulation be directed their way, it should go through their elected colonial assemblies and legislatures—unlike in virtually any other part of the British Empire. Colonists preferred the local to the distant. They had extended British civilization in a hostile, frontier environment without any real assistance or interference from British authorities up to that point. And, now that the threat of the French and their Indian allies was no longer present, Americans wondered aloud when normalcy—salutary neglect—would return.

Sadly for the Americans, the French and Indian War put the nail in the coffin of salutary neglect. One can understand the psychological reasons for why salutary neglect could not continue to typify the relationship between the colonies and the motherland. The British saved up (okay, borrowed and spent a lot) to buy, keep and then upgrade a shiny new imperial car. The empire was the pride of Britannia, and those colonies which had once been just breadbaskets for the Caribbean had by the mid-18th century become economically prosperous in their own right. They were not about to keep the car in the garage and pay it no mind. The British wanted to play with them, and take a spin at direct governance over them.

Here's a table of the subsequent and most significant laws that the British passed in the decade after the French and Indian War:

LAW	EXPLANATION	REACTION
Proclamation Line of 1763	-precluded American colonist settlement west of the Appalachian Mountains so as to avoid conflict with Indians	*-colonists protested; what was the point of the war if "victory" meant surrendering Ohio et al. to the French and Indians?!*
Navigation Acts (1763)	-strengthened and reinforced the old, mercantilist Navigation Acts of 1651; forced Americans to trade only with British merchants	*-colonists protested; who were the men in Parliament to tell Americans what and with whom Americans could do business?*
Sugar Act (1763)	-placed a tariff (import tax) on the purchase of refined sugar and molasses from merchants other than the British	*-colonists protested and subverted the law; problems: this was a direct tax to gain revenue and (as future events in American history would suggest) it is not a great idea to mess with their ability to drink rum.*
Quartering Act (1765)	-allowed royal governors to set aside already vacant buildings for the housing (quartering) of British military personnel	*-colonists protested; why again were so many British troops remaining in the colonies? War was over, enough already*

Stamp Act (1765)	-enforced the purchase of stamps supplied by the British government to be affixed to any paper materials and documents: wills, newspapers, licenses, even playing cards. Violators were tried in admiralty (military) courts.	*-colonists protested, rioted – tarred and feathered tax officials, even engaged in arson – formed the Stamp Act Congress which urged the boycott of British goods; most odious law, why were the British directly taxing the colonists? Their arbitrary taxation was without limits. The power to tax is the power to destroy.*
Declaratory Act (1766)	-declared (appropriate, right?) that the British king and Parliament represented the official and only sovereign government over the colonies	*-colonists protested because even though the British government had bent to their wish of repealing the Stamp Act, what was the role of colonial legislatures? Apparently, none.*
Townshend Acts (1767)	-the brain-child of "Champagne" Charles Townshend, it created export taxes on British goods ranging from paint, glass, paper, to (of course) tea.	*-colonists protested and then largely ignored the laws, bought cheaper goods from foreign merchants; why were the British raising prices on goods that Americans themselves could not manufacture per mercantilism?*
Coercive Acts (1774)	-the punitive reaction to the Boston Tea Party and the breakdown of British authority in Massachusetts, included the: • Boston Port Act= closed Boston Harbor • Massachusetts Government Act= closed the colonial legislature • New Quartering Act And later, • Quebec Act= extended the province of Quebec into the interior of N. America; granted French Catholics religious freedom	*-colonists protested and organized in the form of Committees of Correspondence, then Continental Congresses which initiated an intra-imperial trade war.* *-tensions grew to such a fever pitch in Boston that a detachment of British troops were fired upon by Massachusetts militiamen in April 1775.* *"The shot heard 'round the world"*

The overall story of colonial history from 1763 to 1775 then is the story of the unforeseen and incredible erosion of the immense pride, patriotism, goodwill and allegiance American colonists felt toward Britain in the aftermath of the French and Indian War; an erosion that culminated in open and armed rebellion with the intent of wresting sovereignty from Crown and Parliament in favor of self-determination.

It is unfortunate that the vast majority of Americans today, when asked what the causes of the American Revolution were, will either grunt in ignorance while shrugging their shoulders or trot out that tired and ahistorical canard of "no taxation without representation". The conflict, in reality, was at its core an economic dispute. Why you likely did not hear that from your high school or even college history teachers is that they are bad historians and even worse economists. They fear economics like the plague because they fear what they do not understand.

The American Revolution all boils down to the dogged conviction of British officials who espoused and defended mercantilism as the only economic system by which wealth could be generated by the empire and the impossibility, the irreconcilability of said mercantilism with the tradition of autonomy enjoyed by the colonists.

Examine the major events and players interlaced with the passage of the above laws. Desperate to defray the debt, King George III and Parliament attempted to enforce regulatory mercantilism and mercantilist taxes. The Navigation, Sugar and Stamp Acts met fierce colonial resistance not because said laws lacked American, democratic approval but because they impinged upon the business and economic activities of Americans. The laws hit them in the pocketbooks so the response was to hit the British in the wallet. In other words, American colonists were ardent capitalists; they were fierce defenders of the free market. The raw materials they produced, they believed, ought to be sold to the highest bidder rather than unnaturally monopolized by British merchants. In turn, colonists maintained that freedom included the ability to purchase manufactured goods, from rum to robes, from those who made such things most effectively and efficiently. Whether they be from Edinburgh, Marseilles, Seville, Lisbon, Amsterdam or Mars— price and quality were to be the determinant factors.

Not all of the complaints about the British obsession with mercantilism originated in the colonies. Vocal and erudite champions for liberty railed against the inane measures as well. The most notable among them were Edmund Burke and Adam Smith—yes, that *The Wealth of Nations* author Adam Smith.

Adam Smith
@Adam$mith

"To prohibit a great people, however, from making all they can of every part of their own produce, or from employing their stock and industry in the way that they judge most advantageous to themselves, is a manifest violation of the most sacred rights of mankind."

1776 · London, England

3.7K Retweets **2.4K** Quote Tweets **24K** Likes

Note the year there: 1776 marked the year of publication for Smith's magnum opus, but to be sure, Smith articulated his support for free markets and thus the colonists in the years leading up to that, and of course, the beginning of the American Revolution itself. From the perspective of Burke, Smith, and the Americans, prosperity came through trade, i.e. voluntary exchange that rewarded the advanced division of labor operative in the British Empire and Atlantic world as a whole. Mercantilists obsessed about gold and silver reserves and keeping the productive energies of the Empire within purely British hands; the Smiths of the world argued that doing so would stifle innovation, employment, production, work, and prosperity for individuals and the Empire as a whole.

The able Doctor, or America Swallowing the Bitter Draught.

One more point of emphasis on the twist above from Smith: His assertion was particularly poignant considering that anyone who cannot "make all they can of every part of their own produce, or from employing their stock and industry in the way that they judge most advantageous to themselves," is, by definition, a slave. What makes a slave a slave is that not even his body and certainly not the fruits of his labor are his own. They are appropriated by someone else. So when Franklin, Washington, Hancock, Revere, Henry, Jefferson and the Adams's (Sam and John) used language decrying the Sugar or Stamp Acts and such language sounds grandiose and hyperbolic, suggesting that the British were engaged in a program of enslavement of the Americans, it was on this point of economic restriction—not some platitude about political representation—that they rebelled.

In all of their various iterations, from the Navigation Acts to the Townshend Acts, the British mercantilist taxes and regulatory policies were greeted with protest and subterfuge by leading voices and significant numbers of ordinary Americans. The British responded—often led, ironically, by the efforts of King George III to act as a mediator between the colonies and Parliament—by repealing the taxes and regulations. The problem with this toxic historical formula was that the central problem remained paramount and unresolved; namely, how were the British to pay down the debt if the colonies did not cooperate?

In response to that insolence, especially when the Townshend Acts reeled in considerably less revenue than the 40 million pounds sterling their namesake anticipated, the Parliament deployed two army regiments to Boston to, for all intents and purposes, put teeth and muskets behind what the Declaratory Act had already asserted—the British government was the sole sovereign over the colonies. British military presence and policing stoked ancient and contemporary enmities and the Boston Massacre of 1770 resulted. The historical record of the incident is varied and some witness accounts are contradictory, but Paul Revere's propagandic rendering of "the Massacre" defies reality. Propaganda so often hits its mark; the British as "butchers" from Butchers' Hall indeed.

The truth of the matter was that aggressive and violent Bostonians lobbed snowballs, bricks and bottles at the unwanted guests and cornered a contingent of British troops. In the utter confusion, said troops fired on the crowd—as the later legal proceeding would assert—largely moved by self-defense. Following the Massacre, the resistance organized and mobilized. Funded by John Hancock (the richest merchant in the colonies) and guided by Samuel Adams to whom no one less than George Washington would later affix the title of "father of the American Revolution", colonial Committees of Correspondence demanded the restoration of the fundamental liberties Americans had been guaranteed way back in the Jamestown Charter, 1603.

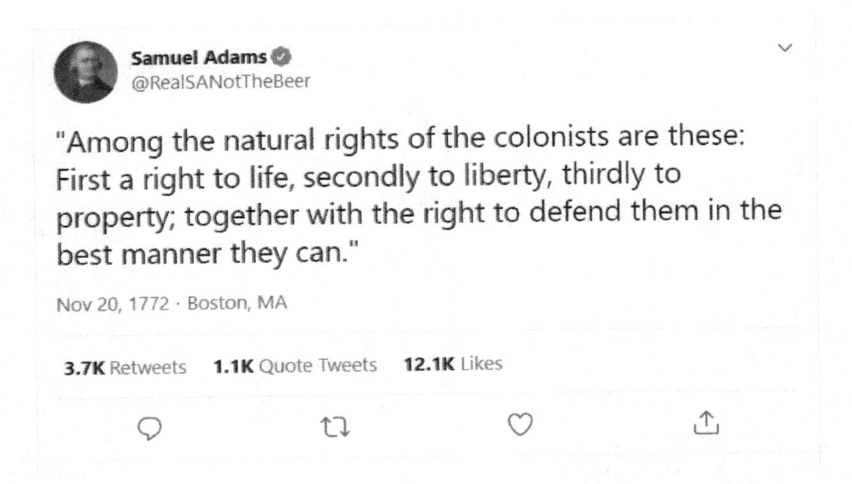

The Committees also frustrated the implementation of British laws and even created a large espionage network beyond Massachusetts. Less than three years later, again in Boston which had felt the brunt of British mercantilism more than any other colonial city, Bostonians led by Adams, disguised as Indians, boarded ships harbored there and dumped cask after cask of discounted British East Indian tea into the waters.

The Boston Tea Party was not some out-of-control, wild rager. It was planned. Intentional. A padlock that the colonists broke on board one of the ships was replaced. A colonist who attempted to abscond with some of the discounted tea was stripped of his clothes and sent home naked. Again, there is something weird about the colonial obsession with clothes and nakedness. Anyway, the message was sent.

So what was the message behind this tea terrorism? Why was the Boston Tea Party—not the Stamp Act Congress, not the burning of Thomas Hutchinson's home, not the Massacre—seen as such a turning point on the road to revolution? The Tea Party was the epitome of gesture politics. And the gesture was a gigantic middle finger to Britain.

Ponder the circumstances for a moment: In late 1772, the British government happened upon a surplus of tea from the British East India company. In order to extend an olive branch to the colonists, the government ordered the cheap tea to be sent to the colonies. It was a conciliatory gesture meant to smooth things over. Even with a minimal tax surcharge placed on the tea, it would be cheaper than the price of tea in most colonial ports.

All the American rabble-rousers focused on, however, was that tax. Instead of seeing the tea as a gift, they viewed it as a Trojan horse: Should Americans pay for that tea and the attendant tax, they would be admitting to Britain's arbitrary right to tax them whenever and however. So, in dumping the tea into Boston Harbor (probably turning it brown for some period of time), the colonists declared to the British that they could take their tea and go f-ck themselves.

The message was received loud and clear back in London. Parliament moved to punish the colonies for the Tea Party in a way that resembles a scorned mother attempting to discipline her insolent children. Take the Freudian family psychology out of the matter and note, too, how myopic and confused British foreign policy was at the time, like a mother who punishes all of her children when only one or two were the problem kids. The response in the form of the Coercive Acts universalized what had been, even as late as 1774, a problem with Boston and Massachusetts. In other words, what the new Quartering Act and later Quebec Act achieved in very short order was something Adams and his Committees of Correspondence had been trying to attain for years, mainly stoking pan-colonial suspicion of and resistance to the British throughout the colonies.

★ ! ★ ! ★

Well, How 'Bout That?

The Quebec Act drove the colonists crazy. Alexander Hamilton called it a "perfidious extension of popery into the interior of the continent." Do not confuse 'popery' with 'potpourri'. To Hamilton, 'popery'—a pejorative for Catholicism—was the opposite. It left a stench. The Quebec Act, on the surface, was an act promoting diversity in the British Empire. It granted French Catholics the freedom to worship and assemble, and it extended Quebec into the Mississippi River Valley which was inhabited by a lot of French Indian allies. Americans like Hamilton did not like diversity, despite what the popular musical might have you believe. Now, there was an alternative motive behind the Quebec Act. British imperialists do what British imperialists do. In other words, anticipating unrest and possible rebellion in their largely English colonies, the British allied themselves with the French and the Indians in Canada and Louisiana. Playing colonial populations off of one another would become a treasured and repeated modus operandi of British imperialists well into the 20th century.

A cadre of colonial legislators and leaders from 12 of the 13 colonies felt compelled to meet in Philadelphia in 1774 to coordinate and negotiate a resolution with British authorities. The First Continental Congress, at least initially, took a very conciliatory and conservative tone—few of the delegates advocated for aggressive resistance against Britain and none of them spoke of something as illusory and distant as independence. The Adams' cousins turned the tide. Key to their rhetoric was the notion that resistance to British despotism did *not* make them revolutionaries. Colonial leaders detested the idea of revolution. They were instead, according to John and Samuel, resisting British policy so as to preserve their 'ancient chartered rights'. They were then, in that 18th century sense, conservatives, not radicals when they approved the following measures: 1. A Declaration of Rights, 2. The Association which was an organized boycott of British goods and exportation of colonial raw materials, and 3. A promise to meet again in May 1775 should their grievances not be redressed.

An intra-imperial trade war resumed and threatened the viability of the whole mercantilist system. Merchants could not get finished British goods to American markets and could not extract from America raw materials to fuel the mills and cottage industries at home; and that made for a lot of angry merchants. This time, however, despite American intractability, British authorities refused to back down. As part of the crackdown, on April 19, 1775, a detachment of British troops from Boston marched out to achieve two aims: 1. Secure a stash of Massachusetts militia weapons, and 2. Arrest John Hancock and Samuel Adams, the two men considered (rightly) by the British to be the main rabble-rousers. They succeeded at neither task. First at Lexington and then at Concord, the same armed Massachusetts militiamen fired on the king's troops and that constituted a treasonous act whose penalty was death. It was the catalyst for war. It was what later American writer Ralph Waldo Emerson declared in his 1837 "Concord Poem", "the shot heard round the world."

The American, and British, and French, and Indian and World War for American Independence

The war was on—sort of. As the Second Continental Congress convened in May 1775, hostilities between colonial militias and British forces had been limited to Massachusetts and upstate New York at Forts Crown Point and Ticonderoga. The truly "continental" nature of the Congress rendered it, even by this point, conservative and conciliatory. Massachusetts and some Green Mountain boys with Ethan Allen had crossed the Rubicon, but that did not of necessity entail that the die was cast for the other colonies, most of whom shared neither New England's economic concerns, religious affiliation, nor rebellious disposition. Still, as a sort of insurance policy, this self-appointed colonial government drafted George Washington as the general over a Continental army force of about 1200 men. What this army was to do other than get drubbed by the British was anyone's guess, but it did go to the field eventually in and around New York City. In the meantime, the Continental Congress held onto the hope that some sort of compromise could be reached with British officials so as to avoid outright war. In July 1775, the Congress offered the "Olive Branch Petition" only to have it arrive in London after King George III declared all of the colonies to be in rebellion and in turn shipped Hessian (German mercenary) troops to fight. Some more Sigmund Freud here—just for a moment if you will indulge me. Colonial reaction to the importation of Hessian troops resembled that of a sibling who rejects the inclusion of some member outside the family to resolve a dispute and mete out punishment. It's one thing for siblings or children and parents to fight, but to involve a foreigner who has little knowledge or care for the future well-being of the relations involved, well that was considered beyond the pale. That bit of family psychology did not, however, inhibit the most rebellious colonists from embracing the rhetoric of Englishman Thomas Paine—mainly because Paine expressed the frustration of the more radical wing of rebels so well.

In Paine's *Common Sense*, colonial angst against British rule was honed and directed to the hope of independence resulting in a more prosperous and free America. The Americans, according to Paine, were the hunted and the only means by which the Americans could continue to realize the liberties guaranteed in those ancient charters was to sever the political ties that bound them to Britain. For good measure, Paine advocated for a republic to emerge in the wake of independence, an outcome that appeared so extremely remote and yet Paine spoke of it like a college basketball coach of an underdog team going up against Duke: *When* we win, rather than *if*.

Quixotic optimism was, perhaps, most needed in the first two years of the conflict, 1775-1776. By the summer of 1776, Massachusetts men lost at the Battle of Bunker (Breed's) Hill on the outskirts of Boston, the British had burned Falmouth (modern-day Portland, Maine) in Massachusetts, and the British had successfully repulsed an ill-advised American invasion into Canada. The British did evacuate Boston for the much more hospitable environs of New York in March 1776. When British general William Howe encountered the Continental Army in New York, he and his redcoats dealt Washington a string of stinging defeats in the Battles of Long Island and Fort Washington. Washington did what he was best at as a field commander; namely, he retreated. It would be only with a huge French army and attendant navy at Yorktown in 1781(!) that Washington would secure a major victory against British forces.

Well, How 'Bout That?

Canada, like Russia, is mostly a vast forested wasteland. It's very cold and (though they will try again later the next century) American forces failed to secure British fortresses along the St. Lawrence River so as to preclude a British invasion, staged at Quebec and Montreal. In fact, the goal of British foreign policy in Quebec was so successful that the Quebecois—to the Americans' dismay—fought to expel the Puritanically-inclined American Protestants in favor of their more amenable-to-Catholicism Anglican Protestant overlords. To this day, a street sign in old Quebec City reads: **Les Américains étaient arrêté ici.= The Americans were stopped here.** ***Still a thing of pride in Quebec to stop anything American, except tourist dollars of course. Winter Carnival is fun but you will freeze your ass off.***

Best to address this now, especially if you are under the misapprehension that the American Continental Army or colonial militias alone won the War for American Independence. The French did, coupled with incredible blunders by the British military. So, if you hate all things French—from berets to crepes, and you insist on calling burger side dishes "freedom fries"—this historical fact will surely upset you. I would apologize, but in the interest of authenticity, I cannot because I don't care. Plus, I am kind of a Francophile, so I love the language, food, culture, and I have a general air of contempt for everyone who does not like France. The odds of an American victory were extremely low in 1775. Britain possessed a workforce three times that of the colonies, she wielded a standing army of 50,000 men, and she had access to the resources of the world's largest and most diverse empire at the time, with control of the high seas. Early campaigns in the war demonstrated the discrepancies. Thus, success in the war depended in no small way on the ability of Benjamin Franklin, dispatched to Paris and Versailles, to woo King Louis XVI to jump into the war.

Prior to the fall of 1777, this was an exercise in futility. The American colonial leaders had signed a formal Declaration of Independence in July 1776 only to within a year be forced to flee the de facto capital of Philadelphia when General Howe occupied it in September 1777. Franklin seemingly had no more cards to play with the king. The war appeared over. And yet, Benjamin Franklin, being the genius that he was, rhetorically snatched victory from the jaws of defeat.

Well, How 'Bout That?

If any doubt remains about the conservative nature of the delegates at the Second Continental Congress, including Thomas Jefferson himself, do read the actual text of the Declaration of Independence. It is notable not for its revolutionary nature but rather for the painstaking efforts undertaken by the delegates to **avoid being labeled revolutionaries at all.** *Jefferson adroitly argues that government exists for the Lockean purpose of defending God-given individual liberties. To the extent that king and Parliament did not do so rendered them posers rather than legitimate sovereigns over the American colonies. Jefferson then enumerated the various crimes of the British "government". It is a thoroughly natural law argument. Birds fly. Bees buzz. Tigers eat antelope. Governments protect individual liberties. When a state fails to do so and yet retains imaginary sovereign powers over people, it is the "Right of the People to alter or to abolish it, and to institute new Government, laying its foundation on such principles and organizing its powers in such form, as to them shall seem most likely to effect their Safety and Happiness." Oh and one more thing: When Jefferson concluded the document with the words "with a firm reliance on the protection of Divine Providence, we mutually pledge to each other our Lives, our Fortunes, and our sacred Honor" he and the other signatories recognized that, should they fail, that Declaration was to be more death warrant than political theory gold.*

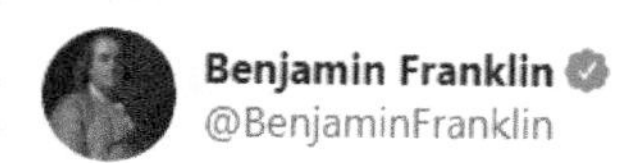

Benjamin Franklin
@BenjaminFranklin

It is not so much that Gen. Howe has occupied Philadelphia but that 'Philadelphia occupies Howe.'

September 1777 · Paris, France

1.1K Retweets **312** Quote Tweets **28.5K** Likes

This was masterful diplomacy. Play upon the nationalistic desire for revenge against Britain for the Seven Years' War. Downplay the fact that the main British army had delivered an ostensible knock-out punch to the American rebels. Guard and profess unbridled optimism that the tide would turn, that one of these engagements would be at least some sort of victory.

Franklin was more prescient and right than he could have forecasted or known. That fall of 1777 was the turning point, the hinge upon which the entire conflict swung. As it turns out, occupying Philadelphia was not part of the British war plan. General William Howe was a general who did not like war—talk about a duck not quacking. No, this does not mean that he possessed an elevated humanitarian streak and was secretly a dove. He did not like the fighting, being in between British infantry battalions. He preferred to be in between the sheets—with the wife of one of his senior officers. Howe enjoyed the creature comforts of his rank and wished to avoid fighting in the cold of a colonial winter. According to the British war plan, Howe was to have rendez-voused with General John Burgoyne and his British-Canadian army in upstate New York. Howe instead ventured with relative ease to Philadelphia where he and his paramour and army quartered for the winter. Better there than out in the plains of Valley Forge where the Continental Army encamped, freezing and starving to death and desertion.

Well, How 'Bout That?

About Valley Forge: Washington famously said that the winter of 1777-1778 constituted the times that try men's souls, but along with the relative resiliency of the Americans there (at least those who stayed) Valley Forge should be remembered for something else. Two highly valued American aides-de-camps, John Marshall of Virginia and Alexander Hamilton of New York by way of Nevis in the Caribbean, made salient observations at Valley Forge that proved foundational to their politics and to the future of America. They noted that the men of the Continental Army had no care about, much less allegiance to the notion of "American" independence. Delaware men were encamped together and fought for Delaware. Virginians, New Yorkers, Pennsylvanians the same. Massachusettans or whatever you call people from Massachusetts concerned themselves with defending their Commonwealth and no one else's. In other words, it was on those frigid plains that Marshall and Hamilton became ardent nationalists (misnomer= Federalists) insisting later that a strong central authority was needed to bind the states into a nation-state.

While Howe was warm in bed, Burgoyne and his army trudged down the Hudson River Valley expecting to meet up with Howe and his men, thus effectively cutting off New York and New England from the rest of the colonies. It was a sound war plan and—should it have been actually carried out—it would have meant the end of the colonial insurrection. But, rather than meeting Howe and red coats, Burgoyne encountered a patriot army under the command of General Horatio Gates at Saratoga. It was Saratoga that was most important; not Yorktown, not Cowpens, not Breed's Hill or any other battle within war. At Saratoga in 1777, the American patriots scored their first major pitched battlefield victory against a sizable British army. However, as important as the pure strategic victory component, Saratoga was a diplomatic lodestar. Franklin finally had his bargaining chip. At his urging, King Louis XVI saw his opportunity, and France entered the war just months later.

With the initial British war plan crushed by Howe and Saratoga, the British devised a new grand scheme that focused on an amphibious landing in the South. Under new commander Lord Charles Cornwallis, the British were to subdue the Carolinas and then move up into the Middle Colonies, gaining loyalist support along the way. Instead, the Americans engaged the British in an exhausting hit-duck-run war of attrition which lured Cornwallis's men further into the interior of the country and away from reinforcements and supplies provided by the British navy on the coast. Finally, by 1781, the British were exhausted in the Americas. Back home, war weariness escalated, and who could blame the British tax payer for that. For generations within the 18th century, the burden of creating and maintaining that huge empire fell on them and depleted their wallets. At Yorktown in Virginia, Cornwallis's army was surrounded by American and French forces on land and at sea. This time, Washington did not retreat, nor did the Comte de Rochambeau or another expatriate of France, a trusted confidant of Washington, the then 23-year-old Marquis de Lafayette. The Treaty of Paris, which concluded the war, was signed almost 2 years later, but after Yorktown, the war was for all intents and purposes over. The miracle had come to pass. So otherworldly was the illusion-turned-reality, of an American win in the American War for Independence, that a legend grew that the British martial bands played the tune "The World Turn'd Upside Down" as they left the field. Probably apocryphal but fitting nonetheless because it underscores just how improbable it all was, from the British, the global—and to a certain degree—even American perspective.

Soapbox

The American "Revolution" was not a revolution in any major sense of that term. Sure, Colonial Insurrection for Independence does not have the same ring as "American Revolution", but the former is a much more accurate moniker than the latter. As previously stated, the Americans argued and fought for the return of things old, even traditional: salutary neglect, local rule, ancient chartered rights. Revolutionaries fight for things new. So in relative terms, the American "Revolution" especially if you push Thomas Paine to the side as an anomaly, was as dissimilar to the French, Industrial, Russian, Chinese, Cuban—name your favorite revolution—as day is to night. I mean, the French Revolution was so sweeping that it changed religion, language, fashion, class, education, the calendar and the system of measurement. Maximilien Robespierre procured a prostitute dressed as the Goddess of Reason to dance on the altar at Notre-Dame Cathedral in Paris in 1793. That's a revolution! *I can guarantee you that no ladies of the night ever danced on the altar of Old North Church in Boston during the War for American Independence.*

Ding-Dong, Daddy's Dead—State/Sibling Rivalries and Unrest, 1783-1787

The American colonies fought a war of colonial independence together. They, together, recognized an existential threat to their traditional rights and liberties, and together, achieved autonomy. And, in 1783, that was the extent of the colonies' commonalities.

After all, only about one-third of the colonial population could be described as patriots, meaning those who supported the independence movement. Another third were indifferent about the outcome; the rest were outright royalists. As was the case with General Benedict Arnold during the war, these categories were not static. Beyond differing allegiances and dispositions, one must recognize that those assembled at the Second Continental Congress understood that their unity and cohesion depended upon their recognition of a common enemy in Crown and Parliament. Once eliminated, what stood were 13 independent former British colonies, all with their own special interests and few of them ascribed to what might be called a national vision.

This was not a nation. The term in the formal title of the Declaration of Independence—namely, "united" as in the "united States of America"—was lowercased for a reason. If there is one aspect of this American movement for independence that typifies revolutions, it was in the aftermath of the fighting. Once the common enemy was dispatched, the thirteen sovereign entities—the new American states—took to fighting with one another—and for the half-decade after the Treaty of Paris, looked to make King George III as prescient as he was pompous regarding the future of America.

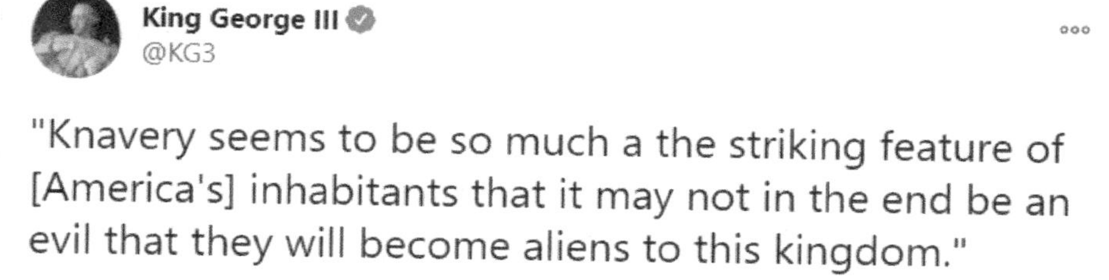

September 1783 · London

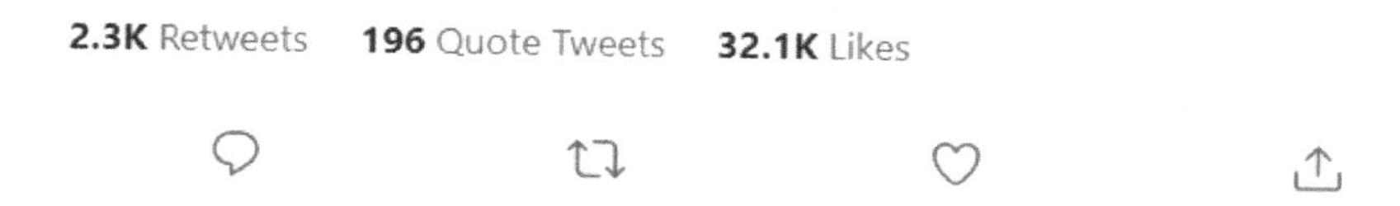

The new states squabbled over boundaries, new territory to the West, currency, and which English football team to cheer for. Okay, that last one was just made up, but these disputes were nothing to easily dismiss. Pennsylvania and Connecticut almost declared war upon one another a year after independence over occidental land claims. Occidental= fancy word for "western".

This is not to say that the colonists, their chosen representatives and even self-appointed leaders desired anything more as a political union than the very loose confederation of states agreed upon during the Revolution, the Articles of Confederation. All thirteen had contributed something to the fight, and now they fiercely guarded their returned autonomy. In truth, this is where your run-of-the-mill U.S. History text and equally unsatisfying conventional U.S. History class review all of the perceived and supposed ills of the Articles of Confederation. To pass a bill that affected all of the states, a supermajority of 9 out of 13 states was needed. To amend the Articles, unanimity was required. As such, naturally speaking, little got done on the federal level—and that was just the way most citizens of the respective states wanted it. Truth is, per natural law—that Aristotelian concept the founders all purported to support and uphold—the Articles of Confederation did exactly what they intended. The document frustrated and restrained government. Yes— there was actually a time when the people were able to restrict the powers wielded by their governments.

Debt represented the fundamental problem impeding American progress postbellum. Ironic, is it not, since it was concern about sovereign debt back in 1763 that drove British authorities to clamp down on the colonies, producing the very laws that created the climate for rebellion? Some states, like Massachusetts, were awash in red ink while others, like Virginia which had not been engaged in the war for as long as the New England states had, debt was a lesser concern. The Congress under the Articles of Confederation could not afford to operate itself much less pay off its own debts, including back pay to veterans in the Continental Army.

So, the American states and national government faced the same economic realities as their British overseers after the Seven Years' War, just without all of the resources the British had at their disposal. Their remedies were unoriginal. Heightened taxation was an option, but a terribly unattractive one as the tax base (ordinary citizens) was struggling financially and those same citizens—especially in Massachusetts—had not reacted kindly to previous taxes. Pronounced understatement. In point of fact, the standard of living of the ordinary American was *lower* in 1783 than it had been in 1776. The misery index (if it had been invented and measured at the time) was much *higher*. The governments' financial solutions were two-fold: first, if taxing most of one's own citizens proved so unpopular, well then, tax other states' goods coming into your state, i.e. tariffs. Second, inflate the currency that your state used, whether it was the Spanish dollar or British pound sterling. This was done by issuing paper, fiat promissory notes backed by little to no actual gold or silver reserves.

The combination of the two—tariffs and inflation—grounded the American economies to a near halt. Trade wars erupted and commerce disappeared as various states placed tariffs on everything from eggs to pig iron. Furthermore, the various, constantly devalued currencies increased the costs of commodities and goods, both in the production and consumption phases. Thus, Americans were progressively impoverished by decreasing incomes and concurrent, often sharp rises in prices. That is the thing about tariffs and inflation: In the short term and in a short-sighted way, they look as though they are solutions to vexing economic problems. However, *pace* the great Frédéric Bastiat and Henry Hazlitt (read them; they're foundational), economics requires examining both the seen and unseen.

"In the department of economy, an act, a habit, an institution, a law, gives birth not only to an effect but to a series of effects. Of these effects, the first only is immediate; it manifests itself simultaneously with its cause — it is seen...

1850 · Paris, France

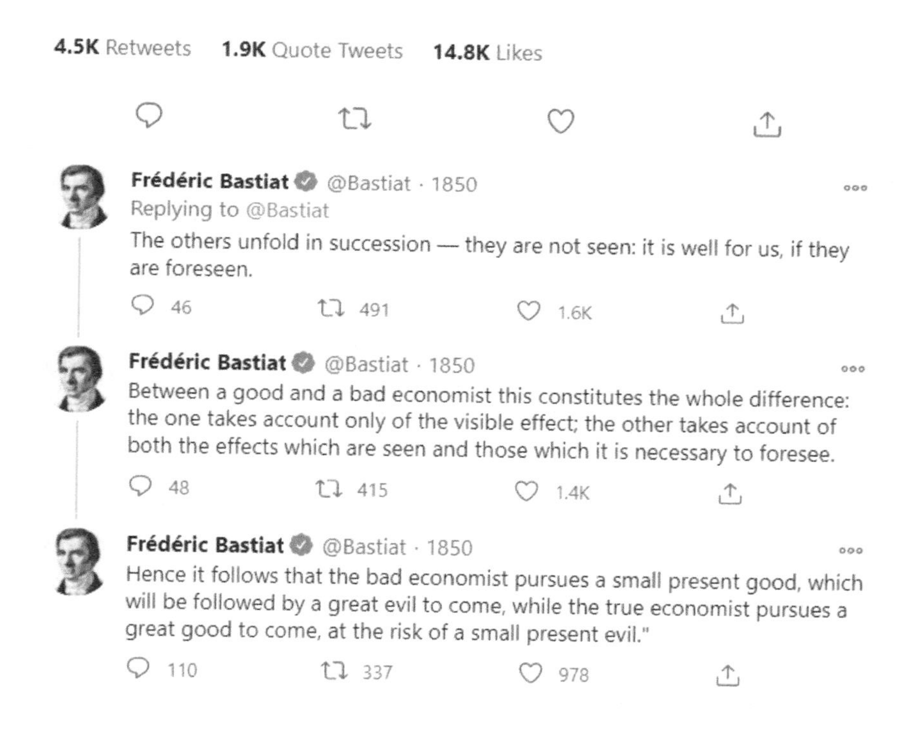

Tariffs resemble a magic wand: you're not, in a direct and obligatory way, taxing your own people. Good. You're raising revenue only when they purchase outside, i.e. foreign goods, and you're incentivizing domestic production. How so? Say that a dozen eggs cost 1 Massachusetts Spanish dollar—as weird as that sounds. If the Massachusetts legislature passed a 15 percent tariff on Connecticut eggs, then the price of buying Connecticut eggs would be 1.15 MSD (Massachusetts Spanish dollars) after the tax is assessed. Hence, people in Massachusetts are incentivized to purchase eggs from Massachusetts chickens and their owners. Great! All that money stays in Massachusetts and none leaks to the benefit of dirty, inferior Connecticut citizens. (Sorry people from Connecticut—no insult intended—this is for dramatic effect.) Here are the problems, though. The Massachusetts egg producers are then incentivized to raise their prices to a level just below the artificial price increase created by the tariff. Even if they increase it to something like 1.10 per dozen eggs, the general price of eggs increases well beyond the market level price. In addition, because tariffs naturally pick winners and losers, tariffs are protectionist; they award, in this case, Massachusetts egg producers (all due deference to the hens) and punish everyone else, not just Connecticut eggers but everyone in Massachusetts who purchases eggs—not only the guy who likes a couple over easy for breakfast, but also restaurants, eggnog makers, and other producers who use eggs and any by-products of eggs. (Do eggs have by-products? Not sure. Can the shell be used for anything?) Just one more thing too: One might retort to all this (like every protectionist) that the higher price of eggs would increase incentive and profit for more Massachusettans producing more eggs. Would not that competition create an immense market for domestic egg producers and with it attendant competition? The answer in short—or more so, "in long"—is no. While there might be more competition in the egg market, that means that valuable resources from other productive areas would be diverted to egg production wherein there was never a natural market force demanding more eggs. This is what classical liberal economists, like the aforementioned Adam Smith, and later Austrian school economists called "malinvestment". In essence, no one benefits long-term from government manipulation of prices in the economy.

Had enough econ for now? That's understandable, but understanding the nature of the blob that is tariffs, their operations and effects is absolutely essential to understanding the rest of American history.

Gary Richied
@garyrichied

If you really want to understand American history, study and understand the tariff. No joke. It is like the inescapable blob.

2021 · Twitter for American History

3 Retweets **11** Likes

Gary Richied
@garyrichied

BTW, there are two more constants in American history:
1. Limiting Americans' consumption of alcohol=not a good idea.

2. If you're president of the United States, avoid theatres, train stations, and open air rides through major metropolitan areas.

2021 · Twitter for American History

2 Retweets **1** Quote Tweets **14** Likes

Just three short years after the Treaty of Paris granted the American states formal independence, the turmoil that ensued from economic depression created an environment ripe for rebellion. In Massachusetts, 1786, a farmer and war vet, Daniel Shays, led a rebellion that has all too often been characterized as a debt revolt. Sure, the rank and file in Shays's army that marched on Springfield with aims for Boston was comprised of poor homesteaders from the central and western part of the state who were justly enraged. Many of them had fought in the war, and upon returning from campaign after the months or years that their fields remained fallow, they then faced mounting bills and ultimately foreclosure on their lands. Because of the debt crisis, they remained unpaid from their service in the war. However, Shays and his closest followers were not destitute farmers; they were among the wealthy within the state. Shays's Rebellion was as much a tax revolt as it was a movement pushing for debt relief/cancellation. Shaysites rejected not only the onerous level of taxation but challenged the power of the legislature to tax them at all. Eventually, Shays and his men were repelled by the state militia, Shays was arrested, and the rebellion petered out. But, that was only after Shaysites shut down many courts in the western part of the state, freed those in debtors' prison, and forced the Massachusetts legislature to cancel debts and print even more money. The legacy of Shays' Rebellion (like several other similar rebellions that occurred in other states at the time) provided a foreboding message of how unwieldy and prone to mob rule the state governments seemed to be. The question was then: What would be a better model for reestablishing order, more centralized or local state power?

Soapbox

More economics—you don't say?! Well, it is necessary here. Why did Shaysites push for even more money to be printed, naturally exacerbating inflation? Simple answer here: debtors love inflation. If I borrowed $100 from you at an annual interest rate of 5%, at the end of the 12 months, I would owe you—you guessed it—$105. However, if there is a simultaneous rate of inflation (devaluation of the currency) of 10%, the $105 dollars you receive in return is really only worth $95. What a deal to the borrower; what a steal from the creditor.

For Alexander Hamilton, the answer was always the former. Recall, though Hamilton called New York home, he was not born there so unlike most of his compatriots, he had no real loyalty to his state, per se. He attributed the post-independence unrest to the turmoil that naturally resulted when a strong central authority was absent and thus unable to direct the economic energies of society toward their proper ends. As state after state passed tariffs against one another and even threatened one another with war in some instances, Hamilton was tearing hairs out of his wig, indignant due to the lack of coordination and cooperation among the states. Hamilton had always had a grand national vision for the United States which he saw only able to be realized should the loose confederation crafted by the Articles be scrapped and replaced with some more centralized and authoritative government, like that of Britain.

Yes, Hamilton liked pretty much everything British: tea, crumpets, and strong central government. He also admired how diversified the British economy was. It had an agricultural sector to be sure, but it had become the world's superpower on the strength of its industrial output which produced attendant and vibrant commercial and financial markets. In other words, what Hamilton wanted for the United States was to avoid what I call the "Detroit-ification" of the American economy. He did not want the national economy to be a one-trick economic pony of producing agricultural goods.

Now, take that vision for the future of the United States and turn it on its head, and one has Thomas Jefferson's take. Their rivalry began long before their famous spat over the Bank of the United States. Jefferson envisioned an America of yeoman, self-sufficient farmers who could live independent from the morally corruptive influences of cities, especially cities with ports. Hamilton was an Anglophile; Jefferson, a Francophile. Hamilton detested the Articles of Confederation; Jefferson called them the greatest governmental system known to man. Hamilton was the yin to Jefferson's yang—except I would not call them harmonious opposites.

Back to Shays's Rebellion: Hamilton used the rebellion (he seemed to love capitalizing on rebellions—stay tuned for that later) to serve as an excuse to orchestrate the scrapping of the Articles of Confederation in favor of some new constitution. He seized victory from the jaws of defeat, when in convention at Annapolis in late 1786 he got the delegates to agree on—well, nothing, except to meet again in Philadelphia the next year. In 1787, Hamilton got his wish; nearly all of the American states sent representatives (Rhode Island held out) and George Washington came out to lend his prestige to the Constitutional Convention.

The Conspiracy of the Constitution

The Constitutional Convention of 1787 was, by definition, a conspiracy of the highest order. Without approval of the people or the respective state legislatures, luminaries from 12 of the 13 states gathered in Philadelphia to secretly create a revised governmental order for the federated union. Thus, the Constitutional Convention was unconstitutional. The Articles of Confederation, forged during the war, allowed for no special convention to be called that would scrap the Articles in its entirety and create a new national government. But, that is exactly what those assembled in that hot, dank Philadelphia summer did. This was a coup. Sure, the plan was to be sent back to the states for ratification, but this was still an illegal coup.

The audacity of these guys! But, their actions were still in keeping with their sense of natural law. Remember: birds fly, bees buzz, the great minds of any time and place ought to make government. Franklin, Washington, Jay, Hamilton, Adams and Madison—among others—labored to craft a new order that they hoped would solve long unresolved questions pertaining to the nature of the state. Could a government be created that was at once responsive to the majority will but yet did not deform into mobocracy? Could a balance be struck between local power and national authority? Based on Enlightenment conclusions, how was this new government going to be crafted with the particular nature of the culture, history and even geography of the American states in mind? Could such a government, responsive to the majority will, also establish dedicated protections for the minority?

Soapbox

Perhaps the greatest (certainly most entertaining) history of the United States written in recent times is Thaddeus Russell's A Renegade History of the United States. *In this work, Russell expounds upon how—from "America's" earliest days—a formal culture and a popular culture emerged within the country, and that the formal, elite culture has often been at war with the popular or mass culture, and vise versa. This was as true in the early republic as it is apparent today. The Constitution's main composers did little to hide their disregard of and contempt for the masses and simply assumed that they had the right to speak on behalf of all of the states and of all of the people. Russell's thesis is that—though the masses and renegades among them have little written about them in history texts—the renegades are truly the ones who have driven and formed American culture and history. In exercising agency, often against the formal culture and the powers that be, saloon keepers, bordello madams, anarchists, gangsters, rogue preachers, and drug dealers are the real forces in American history. Compelling and rich (pace Ron Burgundy).*

This is not a political science book, so an examination, line by line of the Constitution of 1787 is not in order here. However, what follows is a bullet point list of the most crucial elements and developments of the Constitution essential to understand given the unfolding of American history as it is analyzed in this text. Get ready: some of these will shock (maybe, awe) you because, by and large, you were taught a bunch of tacky cliches about the Constitution, many of which are of decidedly ancillary significance or utter unimportance.

Here's the meat:

- The Preamble of the Constitution—taken by itself—is ridiculous. First, the "We the People" thing and then the immensely broad powers granted to the new government: One might argue that these powers are later and explicitly limited by the rest of the text (cf. Article I, Section VIII), but who really reads into the Constitution that far anymore anyway?

Well, How 'Bout That?

Admittedly, the original text was changed from "We the people of the States [then named]" but that is still presumptuous in the extreme. The states had not yet ratified and their people certainly had had no say on the whole thing. Furthermore, the original preamble stated nothing about establish[ing] Justice, insur[ing] domestic Tranquility, provid[ing] for the common defence, promot[ing] the general Welfare, and secur[ing] the Blessings of Liberty to ourselves and our Posterity"[!] Gouverneur Morris penned the new draft which presumes that government both can or should be doing all of that.

- Article I is dedicated to the legislative branch. In terms of primacy and scope, the new Congress of the United States was to be the most powerful branch of government. So much for that dumb and ahistorical idea of "co-equal branches". In point of fact, Article III which is dedicated to the creation of a federal court system, is so tiny and in no way even established a "judicial branch".
- By design, regarding terms, election and specific powers, the House of Representatives was to give voice to the majority will, while the Senate was to rein in the populist passions of the House. The House was to think short-term for immediate remedies; the Senate was to play the long game.
- Article I, Section VIII is the most important part of the whole damn thing. Just so happens, it is also the part that (if read) is also the most misunderstood. The section lists the delegated or enumerated powers of the federal legislature. The Congress can tax (Hamilton happy), regulate interstate commerce (Hamilton happier), borrow money (Hamilton elated), declare war, build forts, etc. There are 17 clauses that state rather specific powers. The 18th is the big one—the necessary and proper clause. It reads: "To make all Laws which shall be necessary and proper for carrying into Execution the foregoing Powers, and all other Powers vested by this Constitution in the Government of the United States, or in any Department

or Officer thereof." At first, it sounds as though the Congress can do anything. No! The Congress can only enact laws that are based explicitly on the 17 enumerated powers or that are "necessary and proper" for executing the 17 enumerated powers! Proof of this lies in the following: What would be the purpose of carefully listing specific delegated powers if, in the end, the 18th clause granted the Congress *carte blanche*?!

- Does this mean that the Federal Congress has overstepped its bounds in absurd ways, by making laws on what you can consume, who you can marry, what you can sell, what you can buy, who is to educate you, how you are to obtain health care, how you can run your business, if/when you are to run your business, how they can steal from you beyond mere taxation, and 150,000,000 other things? Well, yes. Duh.
- Your standard American Government class will address, *ad nauseum*, the numerous checks and balances and compromises in the document. But, it will invariably omit the most important, pseudo-equilibrium and compromise; namely, that the original Constitution created a decidedly *federal* structure. The states were to retain most of their sovereign powers. Proof of this lies in the various sections of the Constitution. Look closely again at Article II. There is the aforementioned Section VIII which lists the powers *granted to* the Congress; Section IX lists the powers *denied to* Congress; Section X lists all of 3 clauses with powers *denied to* the states. See what's missing in that pattern? There is no section in the Constitution that *granted powers to* the states! Why? Because the states already possessed them and would retain them! In fact, the states were the parents to the child, i.e. the national government created by the Constitution. The states were both the creators of and partners to the compact.
- The Executive Branch is, in essence, one person—the president of the United States. His powers are pretty limited, that is, in the Constitution. He was to execute laws, veto, approve, or ignore bills, negotiate treaties, appoint officers of the national government, and be the civilian general of the military generals. In other words, the vast majority of the framers of the Constitution envisioned presidents more like John Tyler and Calvin Coolidge than Abraham Lincoln and Barack Obama.
- Article III creates a federal courts system. That's about it. It does not empower the federal judges who would make up the court system to judge the constitutionality of laws, both federal and state. This is a later invention of John Marshall, Hamilton's nationalist buddy.
- There is real genius in the Constitution. And, most of that genius came from the mind of James Madison of Virginia. He provided the core political philosophy supporting the whole thing. For Madison, the diversity or multiplicity of local, state, regional, professional, ethnic, and religious concerns—what we might call

"special interests" today—would be the salvation by which no one interest would be able to gain enough control of the government so as to use the levers of power to abuse the minority.

- The Federalist Papers, authored by Madison, Hamilton and John Jay, are eloquent arguments in defense of the Constitution. However, if one really wants insights into the debate over the strengths and deficits inherent with the Constitution, it is necessary to read the ratification arguments and documents from the various states. It is here that true brilliance lies.

Soapbox

The best way to describe and summarize Madison's core Constitutional insight here is through addressing what I call, 'the ice cream effect'. A few decades ago, before new major ice cream chains took over, the dominant retailer was Baskin Robbins/31 Flavors Ice Cream. Despite offering a considerable variety (at least 31 flavors of ice cream guaranteed) the most popular flavors remained chocolate and vanilla. So, if chocolate and vanilla were so dominant, why have 31 flavors? Why not have just 2, to the exclusion of the 29 others. Here's the thing: chocolate and vanilla were indeed the most popular flavors, but they never came to dominate sales. In other words, the derivatives of chocolate and vanilla still constituted a majority of sales despite the popularity of the two most popular flavors. The mere presence of the other 29, in fact, meant that neither chocolate or vanilla so controlled the market. So it is within even a two-party system that might form in a republic. The diversity—or better, multiplicity—of factions (flavors) ensures that no one party gains so much state power so as to trample upon the minority flavors.

The ratification debates reveal the deep apprehensions many prominent Americans had regarding this new Constitution. They objected on the basis of consent, on how too much power was being surrendered by the states, and on the absence of a bill of rights to guarantee state sovereignty and individual freedoms.

Brutus
@maybeRobertYates

"In a republic of such vast extent as the United-States, the legislature cannot attend to the various concerns and wants of its different parts...

Oct 18, 1787 · New York, NY

1.6K Retweets **191** Quote Tweets **2.8K** Likes

Brutus @maybeRobertYates · Oct 18, 1787
Replying to @maybeRobertYates
It cannot be sufficiently numerous to be acquainted with the local condition and wants of the different districts, and if it could, it is impossible it should have sufficient time to attend to and provide for all the variety of cases of this nature, that would be continually arising.

14 456 1.5K

Brutus @maybeRobertYates · Oct 18, 1787
In so extensive a republic, the great officers of government would soon become above the controul of the people, and abuse their power to the purpose of aggrandizing themselves, and oppressing them."

3 85 453

Patrick Henry
@PattyHenry

"Let Mr. Madison tell me when did liberty ever exist when the sword and the purse were given up from the people? Unless a miracle shall interpose, no nation ever did, nor ever can retain its liberty after the loss of the sword and the purse."

Jun 14, 1788 · Richmond, VA

8.2K Retweets **509** Quote Tweets **24.6K** Likes

These anti-Federalists suffered not from a lack of political and rhetorical brilliance, but rather poor marketing, for though among them were great American minds Robert Yates, Patrick Henry, George Clinton, Samuel Adams, George Mason, and St. George Tucker, they allowed themselves to be branded with a negative prefix (anti-) when, in truth, they were the true, the real federalists! Marketing 101 stresses that a key to salesmanship is avoidance of the negative and accentuation of the positive. You do not want to be branded anti or old. Think of all of the products the average shopper encounters in, for example, the detergent aisle at the supermarket. The companies flash key words like "new" and "improved". None of the products feature "not" and "old". You might retort that Coca-Cola Classic is a success; however, "classic" is not old, and you were probably not around to taste "New Coke" in the 1980s—it was abysmal. Even good marketing could not save that product.

In the end, the Federalists (read "nationalists") won out based on assurances that the new Constitution was not going to diminish state power but rather protect it within the structure of a rather loose confederation. The previous anarchy and rivalry did nothing to preserve the rule of law nor state sovereignty, and thus per Hamilton, the new union would do so in a cooperative structure. It should be stressed that the Constitution barely won out. In Massachusetts, the vote to ratify prevailed by a mere 19 votes out of 355; much more narrowly in New York where 3 votes carried the day. Virginia ratified by an equally slim proportional margin. Other horse-trading was necessary: fiscally solvent states objected to the new national government taking on the debt, on par, from the previous regime as well as the debt of *all* of the states. Hence, in a famous Jefferson/Hamilton compromise, the new federal district and seat of national government was to be located in the South, spanning the Potomac River. There was also a promise from a reluctant James Madison, one meant to satisfy the still adamant anti-Federalists, of the inception of a bill of individual rights and liberties.

"Congress shall make no law respecting an establishment of religion, or prohibiting the free exercise thereof; or abridging the freedom of speech, or of the press; or the right of the people peaceably to assemble, and to petition the government for a redress of grievances."

Sep 25, 1789 · New York, NY

24.4K Retweets **3K** Quote Tweets **89.3K** Likes

By December 15, 1791, the necessary three-fourths of the states ratified the first ten amendments to the document. Thus, the 1787 Constitution with the attached Bill of Rights became the law of the land.

3

The Early Republic and Federal Period: National Power vs. States' Rights, 1789-1865

Hamilton's Republic

What *was* the new Constitution then? It was theory on parchment. If ever there was an episode in human history to prove the point that principles, paper and ink do not rule men—but rather, that men rule other men—it is this one. The new Constitutional order had been created, but for it to become reality, it had to be implemented. It had to be put into practice. And, while George Washington, James Madison, John Adams and Thomas Jefferson played roles in establishing the new republican arrangement, the Constitution was vivified by Alexander Hamilton. This government was his baby.

Placed in the proper historical context, the most glaring and central of the compromises that comprised the Constitution was the accommodation between what Alexander Hamilton wanted and that for which most every other framer pined. From an aristocratic Senate to ensuring that the document provided a chance for him to be elected president (cf. Article II, Section I, clause 5), the Constitution itself has his fingerprints all over it, and he had already proven himself willing to lie so as to attain its passage and implementation.

As the first and unanimously chosen president, George Washington appointed Hamilton as Secretary of the Treasury, and it was from this loft that Hamilton would execute his economic plan for the country; a scheme that aimed to create prosperity and to adhere the states to one another and the national government. He always was a schemer; a masterful political chess player of whom even his enemies recognized his genius. This man who had once been a Caribbean orphan only to take over a shipping enterprise as a teenager, now held such immense power in the United States executive cabinet of 1788 that he often referred to the Washington regime as "my administration". No one could rightly correct him either, including the president himself.

Hamilton's plan called for resuscitating the United States' credit score. This was to be accomplished by assuming the debt on par and through payment of previously thought-to-be worthless bonds. Few missed that this necessarily involved a massive transfer of wealth from the ignorant poor to wealthy swindlers/speculators who had bought up the notes at heavily discounted prices. Next, that debt would be serviced by a series of taxes (yes, indeed, tariffs), and most notably a federal tax on whiskey. This move was designed to result in rebellion as the burden of the tax would fall on poor western frontier farmers who

Soapbox

So as to allay fears of those on the proverbial fence at the 1788 New York ratification convention, Hamilton obfuscated his own preferences and designs regarding the Constitution, especially when objections rose about the dissolution of states' powers and sovereignties. He declared: "The states can never lose their powers, till the whole people of America are robbed of their liberties. These must go together, they must support each other, or meet one common fate. On the gentleman's principle, we may safely trust the state governments, tho' we have no means of resisting them: but we cannot confide in the national government, tho' we have an effectual, constitutional guard against every encroachment. This is the essence of their argument, and it is false and fallacious beyond conception." Feigned concern about states' rights and hyperbolic attack. He repeated his "assertion" that states need not fear encroachments from the new national government in his entries as "Publius" in the Federalist Papers. For all the dog and pony show though, his actions during the early republican period reveal Hamilton's decided preference for centralized, national power over that of the states to the point at which it is rather clear that Hamilton would have liked to do away with those silly state lines altogether.

grew corn instead of wheat and—with no operative roads to transport their yield—distilled their corn into the very much in-demand and easily transportable whiskey. This was Hamilton being the master chess player. It is also important to state that this "sin tax" also won favor with Puritanical Easterners. Drinking is bad, don't you know? Finally, Hamilton called for a national bank to be created to direct the flow of credit to interests Hamilton determined worthwhile and to, in part, finance the federal government's more expensive initiatives, from infrastructure to war. Remarkable then, that the diminution of American freedom was conceived well before the end of salutary neglect and, indeed in 1757, at Nevis with embryo Alexander Hamilton. To be sure, Hamilton detested democracy—with good reason—but he was not nearly as suspicious of government as even most of his fellow Federalists. So long as elites like himself controlled the levers of the state and of credit, government could facilitate the linear ascendency of society.

Hamilton obtained really all he had designed and desired. Secretary of State Thomas Jefferson railed against the formation of the national bank of the United States, seeing that no such power was granted to the Congress by the Constitution. Furthermore, Jefferson and other still vociferous anti-Federalists protested the very nature and operation of centralized banks. Historically, they were engines of speculative bubbles and favored the rich and already well-heeled.

To understand these objections requires an understanding of centralized banks. Banks, by their nature, are financial institutions. They take in deposits from creditors with excess capital who opt for a time period not to use their funds to consume but rather save. Bankers then redistribute those funds, or notes backed by funds, to those who they deem creditworthy. Bankers are risk-managers. Should they deem the creditworthiness of a loan applicant to be high, then those with said good credit score will get more capital at a lower interest rate. The riskier or greater time duration it takes other loan applicants to pay back the funds, those applicants receive higher interest loans. For Jefferson and company, who would be receiving the easy credit to fund their enterprises, whether they be to expand their inn and tavern, or build new ships to add to their shipping fleet, or buy more slaves to add to their plantation? Well, it would be the already affluent and those who had significant connections to the central bankers and politicians who voted for it. Joe and Jane Doe American farmhands who might desperately need credit would have the doors of such a monstrosity/engine of inequality slammed in their faces. All the more egregious from those in the Jeffersonian Republican camp was the fact that the credit base and funding for this bank would come from tariff revenues acquired from injured agrarian instead of urban and manufacturing sectors. What a scam.

With Washington's support, the Congress legislated the creation of the Bank of the United States, granting it a 20-year charter in 1791.

In the same year, as expected, a rebellion against the whiskey tax began in western Pennsylvania while frontiersmen in other states like Kentucky simply ignored the law. Hamilton reacted in the most expected of ways:

"[This] persevering and violent opposition to the Law [requires] vigorous & decisive measures on the part of the Government. My present clear conviction, if competent evidence can be obtained, [is] to exert the full force of the Law against the Offenders."

Sep 1, 1792 · New York, NY

4.3K Retweets **775** Quote Tweets **23.8K** Likes

He urged Washington to march a federal army of well over 10,000 men into Pennsylvania to crush the rebellion, despite the fact that the state's governor, Thomas Mifflin, had objected to such an invasion of his sovereign state. As he always did as President, Washington himself did Hamilton's bidding. He headed a federal army that invaded the state of Pennsylvania to suppress the rebellion of poor western farmers in 1794. In so doing, he established the national government's right to invade a state. Now, where was that in the supposedly federal Constitution of 1787?

Hamilton's administration achieved much more than creating a national bank and establishing the right of invasion for the central government. His pro-British itch was scratched as Washington proclaimed neutrality (without Congressional debate or law) in the French Revolutionary wars raging between London and Paris. When Washington dispatched John Jay of New York to negotiate a treaty with the British that, you know, would actually make the British do what they had promised in the Treaty of Paris back in 1783, such as abandon old British forts in American territory in the West, Jay returned with such a lop-sided, pro-British treaty that the French believed it to be a de facto American-British alliance.

What developed during the Washington presidency then was a two-party system of the establishment Federalists and the anti-establishment Jeffersonian Republicans. They were strident factions, divided on everything from domestic and foreign policy to the proper interpretation of the Constitution itself. Funny then, that in his Farewell Address, the President would lament the creation of tribal political factions:

His action or more so acquiescence to Hamilton in all things caused the divide!

Washington was much more eloquent and prescient when he advised future administrations to stay out of foreign intrigues and conflicts:

"Tis our true to steer clear of permanent alliances with any portion of the foreign world."

Sep 19, 1796 · Philadelphia, PA

7.1K Retweets **3.9K** Quote Tweets **17.8K** Likes

His advice would be heeded for about 18 months.

Adams and Jefferson—Drama Queens

One has to have a little sympathy for John Adams, right? He had to follow the act of the "father of the country" and hero-general of the American Revolution. That's a tough role to play. Beyond that, his chief political rival served under him as Vice-President, the most powerful figure in his party campaigned against him, and he inherited a rather discombobulated foreign policy from the great Washington. Thus, the years of the Adams and then Jefferson administrations—often held up as paragons of strong, altruistic leadership in the early republic— were filled with drama, affairs, intrigue, a famous duel, and an emerging dynasty. Fun.

After Adams won a narrow victory over Jefferson in the 1796 election, he attempted to define and assert American sovereignty vis-à-vis the Atlantic and European powers; all this despite being terribly unpopular in the country outside of New England and despite possessing little to no political mandate to do so. However, Adams persisted in resolving the unofficial or quasi-war with France that had emerged as a result of the lop-sided Jay Treaty of 1794. The United States had benefited from France and Britain at war. American merchants happily traded grains, sugar, rice, cotton, lumber and other raw materials with the belligerents. In order to hit the British economy, French ships engaged in seizing American vessels on their way to British ports and looting them of their cargo to the tune of over 300 American merchant ships in the first half of 1797.

Soap opera number 1 of the era: the XYZ Affair. So as to avoid outright war with France, Adams dispatched John Marshall (yes, that crazy Nationalist/Federalist John Marshall before he did any of his real damage to the republic) to France to negotiate an end to the dispute. Once ashore, Marshall was allegedly intercepted by three French spies: We don't know their names, so of course they became X, Y, and Z. The spies demanded 32 million gold florins in loans from the United States and a bribe of $250,000 just to get access to the wily, political chameleon, French foreign minister at the time, Lord Talleyrand. No guarantees. Marshall responded by impolitely declining and shook his shoes of French soil to return to New York empty- handed. Upon his arrival, he was heralded as a staunch defender of American liberties and integrity in newspapers and bulletins throughout the North. Marshall was making a name for himself while most of the rest of the country could not have cared less.

Soapbox

You have to give it to American historians: We do come up with fantastic, intriguing sounding names for episodes in American history, and the XYZ Affair is just one of them. How about the Corrupt Bargain of 1824? Or, the Teapot Dome Scandal and Zoot Suit Riots? Damn good stuff.

Meanwhile in New York, the Federalist Congress and John Adams readied the country for war with France. They created the Navy Department and re-established the Marine Corps. For the better part of the next two years, those American forces fought the French mostly in and around the Caribbean. By 1800, an odd and murderous Corsican had gained power in France; he detested wasting resources on far off colonies, and signed the Convention of 1800 to end the conflict. Though he would work late to put down a slave revolt in St. Dominique (Haiti), Napoleon had bigger (British) fish to fry in 1800.

John Adams considered avoiding war with France to be his greatest life achievement, which is weird because the guy was, after all, a founding father, prominent lawyer, and delegate to the First and Second Continental Congresses. Still, he insisted:

When I die, put "Here lies John Adams, who took upon himself the responsibility of peace with France in the year 1800" on my grave.

1800 · Washington, D.C.

Far more important than the XYZ Affair and the skirmishes with France was what transpired on American soil because of the war. In order to consolidate support in the effort against France, the Federalist Congress passed the Alien and Sedition Acts in 1798. They aimed to, respectively, grant the president control over naturalization and deportation of subversives in wartime and shield the national government from criticism during this "national crisis". One poor bloke in Boston, clearly not a fan of Adams aka. "His Rotundity" nor his rhetoric during a speech by the president, declared that he hoped Adams would get hit with a cannonball in his ass. That guy got fined and jailed!

Now, it is easy to object to the obvious assault on the first amendment that the Sedition Act entailed. Furthermore, the law closely resembled the old British statute under which John Peter Zenger and others were prosecuted earlier in the century. But beyond the dubious legal justification and historical blindness of the law, opponents of it focused on how it constituted an assault not on the first amendment, but on the tenth amendment. In other words, James Madison and Thomas Jefferson denounced the Alien and Sedition Acts because they struck at the supposed and fundamental *federalism* of the republic.

Both Virginians penned resolutions that struck at the laws: Madison's would be promulgated by Virginia; Jefferson's by the state of Kentucky. Together, they would form what should rightly be called the Principles of 1798, and to dismiss or misunderstand the arguments contained therein is to lose a serious appreciation for American history, certainly prior to 1860, but beyond as well.

The question was not that government had no authority to curtail free speech—after all, legal punishment for libel and slander had been long established powers granted to the state—but rather what *level* of government could exercise such powers. The Alien and Sedition Acts confirmed Jefferson's long held suspicion that those in power in the national government could not but help themselves from usurping power away from the states. Both acts and their implementation converted Madison from a decided federalist to a defender of states' rights, albeit an inconsistent defender throughout the rest of his life and political career.

The key takeaway here is that, from Madison and Jefferson's perspective, if the individual and sovereign states within the Union did not exercise their proper authorities in resisting the implementation of what they saw as a clear violation of the compact that was the Constitution, then the rest of American history would proceed as a certain and unabated series of violations of states' rights by the national government. The Constitution's foundational compromise was to be respected: the Constitution existed as a compact, a voluntary cooperative union, formed with the explicit understanding that should one party to the compact break the terms of the agreement, then the contract was no longer binding. From this, Madison and Jefferson, the state legislatures of Virginia and Kentucky, and many ordinary Americans asserted the right of any state to nullify or suspend the enforcement of a national law that the state deemed as unconstitutional. Without the power to nullify, the states would be left in the position of being unnaturally subservient to the entity they created (the national government) and/or a collection of battered wives in a bad marriage; perhaps Mormon before Mormonism. That is to say that without recourse to nullification, Hamilton and other High Federalists (if only they were figuratively so, ala. Bob Marley), would have been granted their inmost desires and wishes; namely, the dissolution of the states altogether.

Jefferson and Madison established this intellectual and legal bulwark against the central government's intrusions upon the states as Vice-President and as former Speaker of the House of Representatives, respectively. Much is made in ordinary U.S. History textbooks that no other states joined Virginia and Kentucky in said resistance. However, other states did send supportive delegate observers to the Virginia and Kentucky legislatures. Plus, in terms of authority, does it get any better than the primary authors of the Declaration of Independence and Constitution itself? The identity of the Resolutions' authors was shrouded by pseudonyms, with prudence, because in arguing for state's rights, Virginia and Kentucky incurred the wrath—which tended to be boundless—of Alexander Hamilton who wrote just a month into 1799 that the new federal army ought, "to act upon the laws and put Virginia to the Test of resistance". Nothing spells unity and cooperation like ordering the federal army to invade a sovereign state. No telling what Hamilton might have proposed as punishment to the authors. Charges of insurrection or treason?

The Federalists miscalculated the gains to be achieved by the passage and enforcement of the Alien and Sedition Acts. Hostilities with France subsided over the course of the next two years. The acts and the Adams administration's decidedly pro-British foreign policy proved wildly unpopular outside of New England and ensured a Jeffersonian Republican wave election in 1800. Consequently, both houses of Congress fell under the control of the Democratic-Republicans, and Jefferson himself won the White House after a brief controversy with Aaron Burr.

Soapbox

Aaron Burr was not the wild yahoo that he is often characterized as in normie American history courses. He was an accomplished entrepreneur, founder of the Bank of Manhattan (today, Chase Manhattan), and brilliant political tactician. Without Burr's electioneering in New York, a second Adams term was inevitable in 1800. Sure, he did lead irrational, bungled, and failed secessionist movements in the North and then frontier, but in my estimation, Burr has been vilified by modern American historians because most of them are thorough-going Hamiltonian nationalists, and Burr killed their guy in 1804.

In the waning days of his presidential term in 1801, John Adams ensured that the emergent conflict between state's rights and national power would continue for decades. It would not be the American electorate who willed the fight to go on, but rather judicial appointments by a lame duck president. Adams and his fellow Federalists rushed through and confirmed federal justices who would for *decades* forward protect nationalism against popular, representative support of states' rights and, ironically, federalism. The Federalist Party was all but dead in the executive and legislative branches in Washington, but the Federalists would hold on to the judiciary with a rigor mortis-like grip in the person of Chief Justice of the Supreme Court, John Marshall. Marshall went on to reign over the federal judiciary like a dictator over the course of the next 35 years. His rulings in *Marbury v. Madison, McCulloch v. Maryland, Cohens v. Virginia* and numerous other cases established the power of judicial review of federal and state (!) laws, and always augmented the scope and power of the central government. Those memories from Valley Forge remained. Marshall was a master politico, deftly increasing national authority and doing so in such a way as to preclude executive, legislative or state resistance. To be sure, none of the enormous power he claimed for the judiciary can be found in the Constitution itself, but for Marshall, the Constitution had to be a living, breathing document or the nation would cease to have life at all.

He did more to ensure the Civil War than any man not named Abraham Lincoln.

Dr. Jefferson and Mr. Jefferson

Thomas Jefferson operated a dual presidency. What I mean here is that federal policy for the next eight years took odd, often antithetical turns depending on which Jefferson prevailed. Was it Jefferson the idealistic scholar who remained principled, acting in keeping with his pre-presidential positions of local power, strict interpretation of the

Constitution, and small government? Or, was it Jefferson the political actor who was willing to suspend ideological consistency to further his own ambitions and that of his fellow Democratic-Republicans? This Jefferson was much more willing to utilize the national power recently gained by him and his party. This is why historians quip today that contemporaries like John Randolph and St. George Tucker—bred from the old anti-federalists—were better Jeffersons than the man himself.

To illustrate: Jefferson for years had railed against the Alien and Sedition Acts, the Bank of the United States and what he deemed as the decidedly interventionist foreign policies of the Adams administration. And yet, it was only with the Alien and Sedition Acts (they sunsetted in 1801) that Jefferson acted in an oppositional and decisive manner, pardoning all those who had been fined or imprisoned as a result. He did not engage in any effort to disband or defund the Bank. After a passive and bungled attempt to impeach Justice Samuel Chase, Jefferson did not move to remove any of the partisan midnight judges, nor did he mount any real resistance to the federal government's power grab endorsed and enshrined by them. His first term began with a war against Barbary pirate states and ended with an ignominious and interventionist embargo to halt hostilities with Britain and France. All it did was suffocate the American economy and enrage New England merchants. Even when it was apparent that to acquire Louisiana from Napoleon in 1803 Jefferson would have to operate at the margins of the Constitution, Jefferson would admit to friends in letters that the Louisiana Purchase was a deal too good to pass up or for that matter, endanger Constitutional grounds. So, he went ahead and purchased Louisiana, only gaining Congress's approval *post hoc*. So much for the principled, originalist, small government Jefferson. Once in the seat of power, the position and the opportunity proved too alluring for him not to expand executive control.

Ploughed and Venerating It

While Jefferson's presidency was schizophrenic, there was a concurrent, widespread social and cultural movement afoot with a more focused outlook. With over 90 percent of the country employed in agriculture, most Americans viewed farm life as virtuous while city living bred vice. Fathers emphasized passing on agrarian competency to their sons. Jefferson himself had devoted a lot of time and energy to banning primogeniture (the practice of all the inheritance going to the first-born son) statutes in Virginia. This was to prevent the displacement of younger sons to the western frontiers to find their fortunes, or worse, to cities. Long had Americans celebrated the republican virtue of farm life; to that end, various fraternal organizations formed, including the Philadelphia Society for Promoting Agriculture which continued such work for decades forward.

One of the vices prominent in the cities was drunkenness. Elites like famous American doctor Benjamin Rush advocated for temperance and abstinence laws, lest the masses have too much fun. Dancing might ensue. Prostitutes lurked, wooing otherwise "honest men". The truth is though, both in the cities and out in the country, Americans were plowed as much as their fields. Consumption of hard alcohol was constant and heavy, with rum and whiskey being the drinks of choice. These were supplemented with various ales, meads and ciders. It is estimated that the average American consumed six gallons of pure alcohol a year. Consumption rates were much higher on the frontier.

Why did Americans drink so much? The quick answer: Life was hard. Labor fell on the backs of laborers—black, white, red and every race in between—before the advancement of the American industrial revolution had machines produce more and bear more of the burden of labor. Alcohol was an escape. It was also used as an anesthesia in the absence of alternatives.

In essence then, a rather clear social and cultural divide continued to develop, one that was apparent in the immediate years after independence and had only widened since. It was a divide between the monied, powerful establishment types which included New England merchants, Eastern bankers, and Southern plantation owners. More and more everyday Americans allied against this establishment that had, for all intents and purposes, formed a new, American aristocracy in place of the British; they were the Scots-Irish frontiersman, the Baltimore dock worker, the ubiquitous farmhand—whether he was white or black, free or slave. Historian Thaddeus Russell refers to these classes of the elite and the excluded as those of American *formal* versus *popular* culture, respectively. As Marxist as this analysis might sound, i.e. bourgeoisie vs. proletariat, we must admit of a couple of things within American history: 1) Marx did not get everything wrong—he rightly assessed the historical problem, but, 2) Marx misidentified the culprit that divided people and thus proscribed a heinous, envious and ultimately murderous cure. As is revealed time and time again in American history, the chasm between those belonging to the formal and those of the popular classes worsens thanks to the government, the state, which benefits from the constant division and strife. Such division allows the state to issue unrelenting defenses for its *raisons d'etre* and actions; namely to referee the class, race, gender, generation, you-name-it struggle and to moderate the "excesses of capitalism". It is both arsonist and then firefighter, but the infernos rage in perpetuity.

'Right or Wrong: Our Country' in War and Panic

Jefferson left the man who would succeed him as president, James Madison, a mess of a foreign policy epitomized by the counter-productive Embargo Act, a law which entangled foreign affairs with the economy in such a way as to damage both spheres beyond the otherwise inherent connections. Exports dropped off a ledge. The act stymied American trade. To be sure, Madison proved himself ineffective in mending relations with Europe as chief foreign policy officer in Jefferson's cabinet as Secretary of State.

In 1809, Jeffersonians again came to dominate Congress, despite growing frustration in New England with national interference in free trade from the self-professed party of restricted government. The Jeffersonians in both the executive and legislative branches crossed their fingers that the goal of the Embargo Act could still be attained; namely, that by blocking commerce with the warring powers of Britain and France, both powers would concede that impressing American sailors and looting American merchant vessel hulls accomplished little toward ending Napoleon or strengthening the French Empire. Ponder that for a moment though: Americans were right in their enmity of Britain and France at the time. Imagine you're the widowed mother of some Nantucket 18-year-old who, out of sheer need, signs on to be a sailor for some Massachusetts shipping outfit. When back in port after long sojourns, he hands much of his pay over to his mother—it's her only means of support. Then, suddenly, she receives word that her boy's ship was seized in the Caribbean by the British Navy who claimed that deserters from His Majesty's flotilla were on board, and then that her son was forced (impressed) into the limey navy himself, destined to fight against imperial French forces and their Little Corporal-turned-maniacal-emperor! You would be more than incensed too. To the government, that is a fundamental attack on American sovereignty; to the widow, that is her son!

Congress lifted trade barriers with Britain and France in 1810 with the passage of Macon's Bill No.2. But, this is where the law should have ended. Instead, the law guaranteed that whichever power agreed not to impress or harass American sailors and shipping first would essentially be granted favored nation trade status while the embargo continued against the other belligerent. As misfortune might have it, this scheme fit in nicely with Napoleon's own program to strangle the British economy through his Continental System, so France was the first to answer the call. Of course, the British viewed this as nothing short of a Franco-American alliance.

From the perspective of pro-British Federalists and even more moderate Democratic-Republicans, this was disastrous. However, these two groups were few in number. Young, brash, Jeffersonian Republicans dominated the body, men who wanted to outdo their fathers and grandfathers—and if that meant actual war with the British, then so be it. After all, not only had the British impressed American sailors, but they were also active in arming Indians in the West in order to frustrate American settlement and control of the Great Lakes and the Mississippi itself. This stoked the already bellicose sentiment in the House, especially. Felix Grundy of Tennessee and his brother, Undy, constantly railed against interminable British "insults".

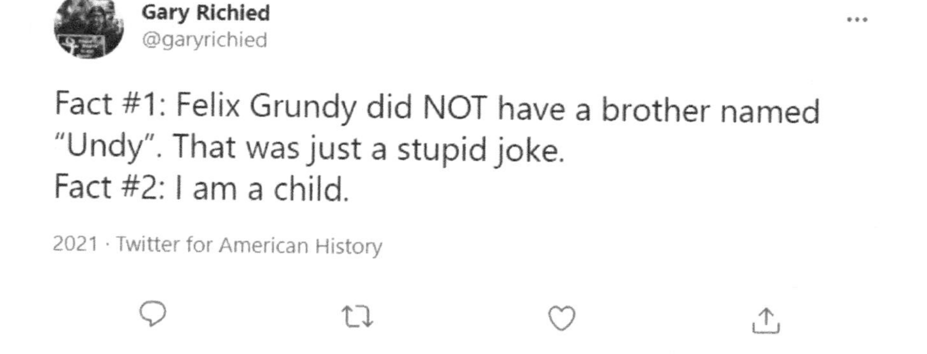

Eventual giants in American politics John Calhoun of South Carolina and Henry Clay of Kentucky began their careers as hawks against the British at this time.

Soon enough (and at a convenient time since the British were more than ever occupied by the French in Europe), Mr. Madison asked Congress for a declaration of war against Britain.

He got it. It was the first time in American history under the Constitution that the Congress had declared outright war, and the Americans got to work right away to, yet again, invade Canada. It was as abysmal a failure as the first invasion of Canada during the War for American Independence. The Americans fared better against the British in the Great Lakes where actual naval battles transpired. However back in Europe, by 1814, Napoleon had limped back to Paris after his own disastrous invasion of a vast, winter wasteland (Russia), and the British turned more attention, men, and resources to the American campaign. British forces occupied Washington, and proceeded to dine in the White House before burning it and other capitol buildings. The decisive battle of the war took place in the fall of 1814 around Baltimore, the city the British referred to as a "den of pirates" with good reason. American forces repulsed a land and sea invasion of Maryland at Fort McHenry at which a reluctant Baltimore lawyer penned a poem in honor of his native land. Francis Scott Key wrote "In Defence of Ft. McHenry" on board a British frigate. The song was later set to the music of an English drinking song, and boom: you get the "Star-Spangled Banner".

For all the song and dance about the Battle of Ft. McHenry, the most famous battle of the war transpired *after* the treaty to end it was officially signed. At New Orleans, a rag-tag force of American vets, creoles, freed slaves and Indians (maybe angels?) under the command of Andrew Jackson thwarted a British assault. Jackson became a national hero, and on the way home to decommission his army, he stopped off to invade Spanish Florida, hang a few Seminole leaders and thus ensure American annexation after the Adams-Onis Treaty in 1819.

Well, How 'Bout That?

French Ursuline Nuns prayed for the intercession of Mary, Our Lady of Prompt Succor to aid the underdog Americans. Jackson attributed his miraculous victory to the nuns' prayers. To this day in New Orleans, on January 8, a Mass of Thanksgiving is offered and special hymns sung to commemorate the occasion.

In all, the War of 1812 is not remarkable because it is some second American war for independence. That's hyperbole; it does not need that moniker to take its rightful place as a war of import in American history. Three developments emanating from the war would have long-reaching significance. First, incensed and disenfranchised New Englanders gathered at Hartford, Connecticut for a convention that aimed to limit—by nullification or even secession—the national government's war-making and regulatory powers. In point of fact, it was here, in 1814, in New England—not South Carolina, not in the South more generally—that serious men seriously entertained voiding unconstitutional laws at the state level and breaking away from the union should Washington pursue their enforcement. Delegates from the convention arrived in Washington to demand Constitutional amendments. Tensions were high. What resolved the issue? The end of the war and attendant rise in nationalistic sentiment deflated these passions. It was impossible to get much of a hearing from officials when everyone seemed to be celebrating Jackson's miracle at New Orleans. Second, the aforementioned uptick in nationalism. The United States had drawn the world's foremost superpower into a 1-0-1 record in two wars in the span of 30 or so years. Not too shabby. It appeared to many in the shadow of Alexander Hamilton that the United States was blessed by God and destined for greatness—so long as the Union remained united. Joseph Story saw the "triumph" in the war as evidence of such, and Commodore Stephen Decatur declared:

A more nationalistic expression, I do not know. Think of it for a moment: "Our Country! (not confederation) we hope she is always right, moral, upstanding, but even if she isn't, she's always our country!" It is not a great leap then to see in Decatur's statement the seed of America as an ever expansive empire; that is, in the West and then overseas, once the country was powerful enough to secure one by the end of that century. Moreover, it's not a stretch to see a rationalization for American economic dominance and unending wars in places like the Middle East today. As long as American intentions are good, well no matter how destructive the ends, the nation must be reverenced. The god of American intentionality has served to absolve many national transgressions while peoples abroad take on the punishment.

Thirdly, the War of 1812 produced economic conditions through which a deep panic took hold in 1819. The Panic of 1819 was the first in a string of economic downturns in the 19th century—biting recessions that continue to our own days (the Crisis of 2008 is an example)—but ones which have been coincidentally renamed following the creation of the Fed. How convenient. The institution created by the government to ensure an end to panics apparently achieved its end—no more deep recessions post-1913! How wonderful! Close the font of dripping sarcasm...

Tariffs, as previously argued, are inescapable in any sound study of American history. Panics are equally unavoidable and even more so, essential to truly understanding the course of American history. It is advantageous, therefore, to do something of a deep dive into the anatomy of the Panic of 1819 because such will ground our knowledge of future iterations.

The Panic of 1819 did not occur due to some irredeemable and inherent flaw in the operation of free markets. Socialist ideologues wish such were the case; however, as is so often true, reality indicates the opposite. Per Murray Rothbard, the great economist and historian whose detailed treatment of the Panic stands unchallenged since he penned it in 1962 (!), the conditions that brought on the Panic in 1819 formed due to the War of 1812. As anyone in attendance at the Hartford Convention could tell you, the War and previous embargo choked off mercantile activity. This is why New Englanders were so incensed. One unintended consequence and short-lived benefit of the cessation of foreign exchange was an uptick in the amount of domestic manufacturing in the years leading to 1819. Americans could not obtain the goods once purchased with ease and low cost from Great Britain, so industry increased so as to compensate. What this artificial increase in demand for textiles, Wedgewood cups, paint, tea, iron, and rum increased, in turn, was demand for commensurate easy credit. In addition, the War of 1812—as is the case for all wars to obviously varying degrees—was inordinately expensive. The Madison administration borrowed heavily to finance it, so banks obliged. Prices rose thanks to all of this credit injected into the market. What also increased was the number of corporations, interests, and entrepreneurial ventures that, under normal economic circumstances, would not have thrived or survived. That's the often unseen damage caused by war: War leads to a misallocation of resources and credit which create an ostensible albeit temporary boom that concludes with a sustained bust.

Soapbox

Now, before a bunch of neo-conservatives perish from apoplectic shock, I am not claiming that all panics and depressions arise from wars. Neo-conservatives already have thousands of talking points to defend the murder and slaughter of innocent people throughout the globe—why pile on one more problem with war for them to address? Their logic is burdened and strained enough. What I am asserting, however, is that government intervention in the otherwise naturally emergent economy does create conditions that so skew real price discovery that crashes result. Keynesians turn a blind eye to these realities as well, that is why they make convenient, gross bedfellows for the neo-cons. For further explanation on this, examine the Austrian business cycle theory, explicated by Mises and Frederick Hayek.

Bad investment created by easy credit naturally causes recessions. Think of it like a cocaine high. At first, there is a rush of ecstasy and energy (from what I'm told), but every subsequent use creates less pleasure as dependency on the drug increases. Eventually, sustained use only worsens the inevitable withdrawal which takes the form of tightened credit, business failures, and mass unemployment.

The Monroe Administration and Federal Congress responded correctly to the crisis—by doing nothing. You read that correctly—doing nothing. In other words, 19th-century politicians recognized what modern statesmen absolutely fail to first, entertain, and then second, comprehend; namely, economic crises created by state interventions cannot be remedied with more of the original toxin. The national government's reticence to cure the perceived evil of economic panics ended up being the balm of the economy in 1819, 1837, 1857, 1873, and 1893. In all of those cases, markets were allowed to bottom out so as to allow non-viable enterprises and firms to fail and to permit natural price discovery to transpire which in turn served to resurrect sound economic investment and growth. In short, this is why these "panics" did not become "depressions" of any great length. Things changed in the proceeding century.

Speaking of the Monroe Administration, the Monroe Doctrine represented the culmination of all of the previously mentioned nationalist fervor generated by the War of 1812. Brain-child not of Monroe but rather his Secretary of State, John Quincy Adams, the Monroe Doctrine was not law. It did not pass Congress. It was more of a foreign policy pronouncement to which the rest of the world paid little heed. In analogous terms, in the first half of the 19th century, the United States resembled a kind of gangly, awkward early adolescent whose faux-confidence far exceeded his actual strength. Recollect high school, for a moment. You might have noticed such characters who projected an air of superiority, especially when among other freshmen. Upperclassmen pay them little attention, but that just makes the overly cocky freshmen more envious of their elders' status.

So too with the United States on the world stage with France, Britain, Russia and even Prussia at the time. The Doctrine stipulated that the United States would not permit any further European colonial incursions or land claims in the Americas. Often lost in any typical discussion of the Monroe Doctrine are its two most significant features. First, it pronounced the United States as the paternalistic guardian of the burgeoning American republics gaining their independence at the time, largely from Spain. And second, the justification for this guardianship and guidance was to preserve democracy in the New World. Ugh. What insufferable arrogance based on no history of effectiveness in doing so! Beyond that, since the inception of the Monroe Doctrine, almost every venture of the U.S. military to this day gains the imprimatur that U.S. forces were sent to kill people in order to "preserve democracy", "self-determination", and other made-up nonsense. Quite the cover.

It should not be lost on the reader either that at the very point of the announcement of the Monroe Doctrine, Europe had lost its taste for the traditional imperialism of the past—at least in the New World. France was busy in Algeria. Spain's empire was crumbling. Britain was focused on Africa and India before its own prime minister would declare within the century that their colonies represented a "millstone 'round our necks." The United States did not, therefore, have to confront European powers over infractions against the Monroe Doctrine. The first major test of it would come in 1861 when France invaded Mexico and installed an Austrian emperor there. Yes, you read that correctly. At the time, however, the Lincoln administration had its hands tied recolonizing the American South, so enforcing the Monroe Doctrine was an impossibility—it would be resurrected as a defense of American interventionism later and when abundantly convenient.

Feelin' Alright and Utopias Everywhere

The Era of Good Feeling, c. 1815-1824, is one of those periods in American history with a pithy name that is nonetheless quite misleading. The title came from a contemporary newspaper editor who characterized the era as such due to the apparent lack of political—more so partisan—division. Jeffersonian Republicans reigned supreme. The Virginia Dynasty of Jefferson and Madison continued its dominance over the executive branch in the person of James Monroe. The Federalists were essentially dead in the Congress.

Uniformity in Washington did not mean that all was sunshine, lollipops and rainbows everywhere (*pace* "Cloudy With a Chance of Meatballs") in the country. The Panic of 1819 occurred. Furthermore, the Era of Good Feeling featured Marshall Court decisions that usurped proper powers from the states and other branches of the federal government. There was considerable division among factions in the dominant party. For example, Henry Clay of Kentucky consistently advanced bills so as to make his American System a reality. Clay's American System required federal expenditure, enabled by higher tariffs, to be allocated to the construction of roads, bridges, levees, canals, and other infrastructure to unite western frontier districts of the country with the more developed East. He found opponents to this plan among principled Republicans who saw no such powers in the Constitution, including James Madison himself who, in 1817, on his last day as president, vetoed the famous American System Bonus Bill.

Missouri applied for statehood in 1819, and the famous compromise to usher it into the union stood as a preview of the power struggle between North and South. Just like the eventual "Civil" War, admitting Missouri as a slave state within the union had little to nothing to do with any ethical objections about the extension of slavery, much less slavery per se. In point of fact, it was all about how Missouri's representatives and dual Senators would tend to vote along North/South regional lines, which geographically speaking, the then territory straddled. Today, ill-informed historians deride the compromise crafted by Clay that allowed Missouri to enter the union as a slave state while introducing Maine as a free state. The measure maintained a representative balance in the Senate. Still, this seems to be kicking the can down the proverbial road on the slavery issue. But, the historical record indicates otherwise regarding the effectiveness of the compromise. It accomplished its goal by design. Under the Missouri Compromise, the United States remained a constitutional, united confederation without severe bouts of disintegration (at least over slavery) for the next 34 years. The deal also outlawed slavery in the extensive territories left from the old Louisiana Purchase north of the 36-degree 30-minute parallel. And, one cannot foist blame upon the crafters of the compromise in 1820 as they could not have foreseen the Mexican War, the Kansas and Nebraska Act, nor the Dred Scott decision that, together, would vitiate the carefully constructed balance. In other words, Constitutional, political compromise was not the cause of the ultimate divide.

Aside from issues surrounding representation and expansion westward, America modernized in earnest in the first half of the 19th century, fueled in large part by increased innovation and industrialization. View some of the transformative advancements that radically altered American life and labor from 1793-1850 in the table below:

YEAR	INVENTION	INVENTOR	AREA
1793	**cotton gin**	Eli Whitney	*agriculture, textiles*
1807	**steamship**	Robert Fulton	*transportation*
1821	**canal (Erie)**	Benjamin Wright	*transportation*
1829	**locomotive**	Robert Stephenson	*transportation*
1831	**tunnels, suspension bridge**	I.K. Brunel	*transportation*

1831	**reaper**	Cyrus McCormick	*agriculture, industry*
1837	**light steel plow**	John Deere	*agriculture, industry*
1844	**telegraph**	Samuel F.B. Morse	*communication, transportation, markets*
1846	**sewing machine**	Elias Howe and Isaac Singer	*textile, industry*

It should be emphasized that the political economy of the time was extraordinarily liberal and laissez-faire. The near absence of government regulation and meddling in business affairs permitted entrepreneurial activity to occur. That is to say that consumer need was met with innovative and efficient production because entrepreneurs were both incentivized by profit and unhindered in their determinations about investments in capital goods. Furthermore, in the absence of an unhinged, fiat system in which the dollar today acts like *Monopoly* money compared to other countries' *Wits and Wagers* (or name your own preferred board game) money, credit was extended to worthy upstarts and enterprises. The risk that was taken on was either rewarded with generous returns or significant losses. The government was not there to provide substantial support for certain firms nor there to bail out banks that took on too much risk.

One aspect, or more so logical derivative, of the law of diminishing return is the blessing/curse dynamic of the sale of industrial, durable goods. From textiles, to wagon wheels, to saddles, much of the prosperity generated at this time was attributable to the manufacturing of products that did not wear out upon first or second use. As such, American manufacturers confronted a problem that manufacturers in Britain had faced since proto industrialization. Once a durable good is sold, there is a commensurate drop in the unit market demand for that product. In other words, should I sell a saddle to a rider in need, I am happy (yay, I made a sale) but sad in that there is now less demand for my saddles. There are economic solutions to this problem, some more valuable than others. A first possibility is lowering the quality of my saddles. This would mean making my Richied saddle less durable than I otherwise might. Problem here, however, in this move toward planned obsolescence, in the operation of the free market—I will eventually lose market share and thus viability to a competitor who does make the best, longest-lasting saddles. And I'll be damned if I'm going to close my doors because I got whipped by Westerman Saddles Inc. The best solution is therefore not to corner the local market, reduce the quality of my saddles, nor call for protectionism from the government, but rather to expand the market for my saddles. This means shipping them far away from Birmingham or Boston or Burlington. In this vibrant, free market, rapidly industrializing era, transportation innovations responded to this need for freighting in kind. Whereas in 1816, it cost an average of 1.3 cents per ton to transport downstream on the Ohio and Mississippi Rivers and 5.8 cents upstream, thanks to the steamboat, by 1830, that cost was reduced to .34 cents per ton. Any way you look at it, any direction you might wish to go, that benefited producers as well as consumers. Business, production and exchange is the proper, prosperous way to make the world smaller after all.

The prosperity generated in the era created conditions in which many moved from concentrating on economic and sustenance concerns toward social considerations. American social justice movements are always religious in character—note here: I do not assert that they are always *Christian* in nature. Modern social movements find their foundation in the secular progressive (read always—impositional) faiths of imperialism, statism, and corporatism. However, the 1820s featured the Second Great Awakening, popularized by the fiery preaching of Charles Finney. Finney's Presbyterian preaching differed little from the messaging of his First Great Awakening predecessors, Edwards, Whitefield, et al. This time, though, Finney and his generation of fire and brimstone zealots channeled religious fervor into social action that emphasized the idea that reformers could hasten the coming of the kingdom of God by preserving the country from "Papism", directing the mentally ill from prisons into asylums, vilifying alcoholic consumption, and condemning slave systems. In other words, this version of Awakening allowed for a greater humanism; the idea being that the learned and elite could transform human communities and conquer pervasive, perceived injustices.

Well, How 'Bout That?

Reform fanaticism took interesting forms. Men like Finney and Lyman Beecher (father of Harriet Beecher Stowe, a fanatic in her own right) so railed against Catholic "popery" that he unapologetically inspired a mob to burn down an Ursuline convent in Massachusetts 1834. Dorothea Dix labored to create an asylum system in the country, apart from jails. Early feminists like Elizabeth Cady Stanton and Julia Ward Howe were fervent tee-totallers who advocated for laws banning the consumption of alcohol outright. And finally, abolitionism focused its energies not so much on ending slavery for the benefit of the slave, but rather because they deplored as "ungodly" all of the attendant, decadent features that appeared, to them, as inherent in slave societies. Gambling, licentiousness, miscegeny, dancing, drinking, and carousing. Plantation life was repugnant. Theirs was an anti-liberty rather than liberating movement.

The Second Great Awakening, too, represented a fundamentalist response to increasingly popular, Enlightened quasi-Christian movements. Both Mormonism and Unitarianism denied basic and almost universally accepted doctrines—in the case of the latter, the Trinitarian God, thus, Unitarianism. Traditional churches responded with the one-two punch of revivals and charitable, reform activity. The fervor and fever of the reform movement era were not lost on one of the more famous Unitarians of the time:

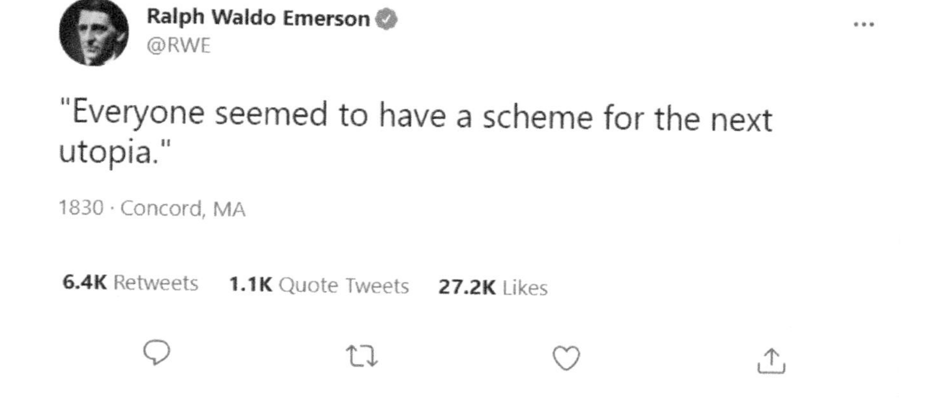

And speaking of utopias, some among the elites saw civilization as either too difficult or altogether impossible to redeem. They wished to transcend it. Among them: the aforementioned Emerson, Henry David Thoreau went out to Walden Pond, and Nathaniel Hawthorne lived at the utopian community of Brook Farm in 1841. It must be said, however, that Hawthorne did not venture out to Brook Farm because he agreed with its communal living experiment—he did it to save money so as to propose to his future wife, Sophie. One is allowed to speculate that he had the alternative motive of engaging in research on human nature and upstart settlements while there, observations that were sure to work their way into his future stories and novels.

The Jackson Five

The Era of Good Feeling ended with a thud in 1824. The very moniker came as a result of uniparty control of Washington and most state capitals, and that univocal melody went dissonant with the Corrupt Bargain of 1824.

John Quincy Adams secured the presidency in that year as a Massachusetts Democratic-Republican, running on his name recognition and his record as Monroe's Secretary of State. His challenger was none other than Old Hickory, the hero-general at New Orleans in 1815, Andrew Jackson. In the election, several viable candidates ran, including Henry Clay only to have Andrew Jackson win the most popular and electoral votes. However, the presence of these several candidates in the race meant that Jackson did not secure the *majority* of the electoral votes needed to secure victory. Per the Constitution, the election got thrown to the House of Representatives wherein Henry Clay deployed his considerable power and got John Quincy Adams to be president. A quid pro quo (this for that) was almost certainly at play (not that Clay really needed such a sweetener in the deal—he despised Jackson): Clay would become Adams's Secretary of State. Fingers crossed—history would continue to prove this as a stepping-stone office to the presidency. Jackson supporters cried foul. And, John Quincy Adams, despite having a sterling resume to be president, would prove to be one of the worst—and that is a rather dubious distinction given the incredibly low bar set by the other 45.

The Corrupt Bargain of 1824 set up conditions by which Andrew Jackson would become a transformative figure in five ways.

1. The notion that the powers that were in Washington conspired to keep Jackson out of the White House further solidified his repudiation as the champion of the little man as opposed to the establishment at the time.
2. While out of office, Jackson positioned himself as a defender of state and local power in opposition to the pervasive trend in the East; namely toward nationalism. Jackson spoke in dulcet tones of federalism. This aspect of Jackson was just one of the multitude of things Clay despised about Jackson.

"Nothing has ever heretofore occurred to create in my mind such awful apprehensions of the permanency of our liberty...

Nov 20, 1828 · Washington, D.C.

756 Retweets **102** Quote Tweets **3.1K** Likes

Henry Clay @GreatCompromiser · Nov 20, 1828
Replying to @GreatCompromiser
[The Jackson victory was a] 'calamity.'"

13 402 1.9K

3. Being seemingly shut out of national politics, and for that matter, significant state politics as well, ordinary Americans of ordinary means and no connections to the elite, came to believe that they could and ought to affect change through national elections. Thus, the sentiment and effects of Jacksonian democracy. States opened the vote ever wider to more men. For the first time in American history, in presidential elections, the popular vote was tallied and mattered.
4. John Quincy Adams's presidency proved to be as ineffective as it was unpopular. His opposition—albeit principled and Constitutional—to removing Indians from their ancestral lands angered many land-hungry whites. In addition, Adams, as a man of science and letters, supported such initiatives as the construction of an astronomical observatory in Washington. Imagine frontiers men's reactions to finding out that the tariff penalties they were paying to the national government went to fund something for the entertainment of Washington socialites. This did not augur well for Adams.
5. A Jackson presidency was not only a foregone conclusion by 1828 but that term in office was destined to be as antagonistic to Jackson's enemies as it was to be populist in nature. It was Jackson, more than any other president up to that point in American history, who was able to formulate and promote the very dangerous notion that the president was a direct and empowered representative of all of the American people. That is to say that Jackson metamorphosed into a central power nationalist when it most suited him—the cloak of federalism is dispatched so easily once one is at the helm.

The 1829 inauguration signaled things to come. After the formalities, a very informal rager broke out at the White House as crowds pushed into the executive mansion to get some spiked orange punch and see their man, the "Gin'ral". Jackson in fact had to carefully extricate himself from the proceedings as revelers celebrated the triumph of real American democracy while Clay and his cadre looked on aghast. There would be first four and then four more years of this, after all.

Inordinate ink has been spilled in the tomes of the accepted, banal histories of the United States on Jackson's Indian policies, but if you were to inquire with a contemporary (aside, of course, if you were a Cherokee or Creek Indian) American, this would have been one of the least controversial aspects of the era. There was broad agreement that the Indians could and should be forcibly removed from their ancestral lands so as to make more American *Lebensraum* by eminent domain. The Indian Removal Act, signed into federal law in 1830, called for the deployment of the federal army to orchestrate the confiscation. It was more segregationist than racist, per se. It was criminal. It was an abject denial of contract and civil rights. It was murderous. It required the relocation of tens of thousands of Native Americans, mainly from the South and Midwest, to designated Indian Territory in the West. And when John Marshall attempted to block the enforcement of the Act in the *Worcester v. Georgia* decision, Jackson did what Marshall had always feared: He simply ignored the Court's ruling and did it anyway. How's that for judicial review?!

Too few pages have been allotted to the other really big and subsequent issues of Jackson's day; namely, tariff policy, nullification, killing the Bank and the Panic of 1837.

Regarding the first two: one of the reasons for Clay's enmity of everything Jackson was Old Hickory's professed and consistent federalism. Jackson spoke eloquently and often in favor of localized government. But, as with his predecessor Jefferson, there were Jacksonians who were much better Jacksonians than the man himself, so on this score, Clay's apprehension was misplaced.

When South Carolina took steps to nullify federal tariff laws passed in 1828 and 1832 (the South Carolinians referred to these bills collectively as the 'Tariff of Abominations'), Jackson acted with all of the vehemence of a scorned lover against his once loyal Southern belle. His own Vice-President, John Calhoun, penned the *South Carolina Exposition and Protest* in defense of his native state. It was a reiteration of the classic principles of 1798 advanced by Madison and Jefferson in defiance of the old Alien and Sedition Acts. In short, nowhere did the Constitution empower the Congress to create and impose laws so clearly for the specific benefit of one group and so clearly to the specific detriment of another. In other words, nuts and bolts, Western and Southern farmers were getting screwed by high protective tariffs while New England and Mid-Atlantic manufacturers benefited greatly thanks to the laws, as described in previous pages of this volume. In both spirit and letter, then, the national government was not abiding by the general welfare clause within the Union compact, so the state legislature of South Carolina was well within its rights to suspend the execution of the unconstitutional law. Calhoun elaborated upon the doctrine of concurrent majority; namely that majorities in the major

(Union) and minor (state) parties to the compact needed to agree for a law to be justly applied. Otherwise, there is no such thing as federalism.

Well, How 'Bout That?

The Tariff of 1828 increased duties to the height of 38% on some imported goods. The Tariff of 1832 was supposed to be a compromise bill, but it ended up reducing so few tariffs to such a minimal extent that it was greeted by Southerners in and outside of South Carolina with unmitigated contempt.

At this point in the analysis, the imaginative almost invariably crow: "Well, if a state could just nullify a federal law at will, then there is no Union and then the states are all dominant sovereigns!" They might continue, "This is just a step to secession, which of course is an inherent evil. After all, we droned on every day in our state-funded juvenile prisons (public schools) that the nation is 'one' and 'indivisible', so there can be no other way." The vapidness usually concludes with something through their fatal modernist conceit they never think the Calhouns of the world—past and present—thought of: "Well, nullification and secession are not mentioned in the Constitution, so there—no state has the power to exercise either, Mr. Strict-Constructionist-You!"

A sound knowledge of history and a 101-class in American political science arms one with all she needs to swat down these arguments like the dumb cicadas with a tennis racquet. As Calhoun and other great political minds at the time like Virginia's Abel Upshur asserted, states could not, willy-nilly, nullify federal laws with which the particular state disagreed or even deemed unjust. The law had to be deemed clearly unconstitutional; a breaking of the contract. Calhoun was not a secessionist. He saw secession as the last of last resorts. But even in the scenario in which a singular state nullified a law, several outcomes would surely play out, all of them preferable to the national government invading said state and applying coercive violence.

Effect A: A state (let's use Vermont since I want nothing more than Vermont to secede...) calls a convention to draw up articles of nullification. Those articles are approved by the state legislature. The federal law then does not apply to the state. All of the other states in the Union deem the law constitutional and shrug their collective sovereign shoulders that some law won't be executed in Vermont. Big deal. Union and peace saved.

Soapbox

I live in the Midwest. Cicadas are a scourge. Cicadas are the dumbest of God's animal creation, somehow the species most disaffected by the fall from Eden, and as such invite all of the righteous human wrath with which they should be treated. As a libertarian, I do not advocate for anything more than a quick death, either by tennis racquet or other means.

Effect B: Vermont declares a law unconstitutional and nullifies it. The other states in the Union cry foul and argue otherwise. Vermont sees the errors of its ways and rescinds its objection to the law. Union and peace saved.

Effect C: Vermont nullifies a law. The other states in the Union cry foul and argue otherwise. Vermont's legislature sticks to its position and refuses to concede. At this point, the other states in the Union could get an amendment passed—in either of the two ways proscribed in Article V—to make it clear that the subject of the law (and even Vermont's specific objection to it) is now constitutional, at which point nullification itself is null and void, and Vermont can then determine whether to remain in the Union or not. Vermont stays—ok, the law is enforced and Vermonters cannot scream "unconstitutional!" Vermont goes, and the legislature therein petitions to become the province of Baja Canada. So be it. No one will be happier than the rest of us. Again: The Union (improved by subtraction) and peace, saved.

Lastly, the whole "nullification and secession aren't mentioned in the Constitution" argument: Well, neither is judicial review. And, dear Lord in heaven, do go and read the 10th Amendment. If the powers of nullification and secession are not delegated to the national government in the Constitution, those powers redound to the states. Not convinced? Read the ratifying convention documents and decrees back in the late 1780s, and you'll discover that state after state affirmed the right of secession should the national government (as it inevitably would) not honor the inherent federal nature of the Constitution. South Carolina was right to support nullification and (scandal) secession; this time over tariffs; later over representation.

These arguments fell on deaf, Jacksonian ears. Andrew Jackson never took well to open defiance, whether it was from Clay, Calhoun, or a bunch of "nullies" as he called the predominant South Carolinians. He threatened to march a federal army down to South Carolina and hang every last one of them from a tree. Compromise precluded such a move with no one other than Clay pushing through the Tariff of 1833 (which progressively

Soapbox

The only sound, rational, and tenable objection to these arguments that I have discovered is that of anarchist Lysander Spooner who said all of these mechanizations are absurd because the Constitution itself is of no authority because it did not originally gain just consent. To the great Spooner, I tip my cap—or should I say my "an-cap"?

drew down tariffs over time) and the Force Bill (which sanctioned Jackson to do his will to the nullies should they persist). But, the incident is thoroughly instructive. South Carolina, like New England and New York so many times in the past, asserted its legal and reasoned right to nullify laws it deemed as brazenly unconstitutional.

With the nullies nullified—at least for a time—Jackson turned his attention toward killing his beast of burden—the Bank of the United States. The Second Bank of the United States was the institutional manifestation of everything Jackson detested: ensconced wealth, aristocratic privilege, largesse attributable not to hard work but to cronyism and connections. The Bank's director, Nicholas Biddle, was in many ways the bizarro-Jackson with whom it seemed the hardscrabble general and man-of-action was destined to combat. It controlled lines of credit through its monetary and financial policies, all of which from Jackson's vantage point kept the rich, rich and the poor, poor. Jackson much preferred the so-called wildcat banks which issued credit, capital that was so needed by the farmers and adventurers of the ever-expanding West. He would concede to funding state banks as a sort of compromise, but the very existence of an American national bank that operated in ways imperceptibly different from the Bank of England—well, this was just anathema. He fixed on killing it in any way he could.

After Jackson trounced Clay in the election of 1832, in September 1833, Jackson defunded the Bank of the United States. A bank without money is like a tree without sunlight: It cannot live for long. This opening salvo in what became known as the "Bank War" pitted Biddle and Congress against the president in a bitter struggle for supremacy. This was, after all, a Congressionally created institution whose functioning independent of state control was affirmed by old John Marshall, and here was Jackson, taking a hickory stick to it all and then lighting it on fire. Even critics of the bank balked at the notion that the president could unilaterally kill the bank, but kill it he did. In response, Daniel Webster, Clay, and Calhoun formed the Whig Party, which in its name speaks of the party's *raison d'être*; namely, to oppose "King Andrew".

Eventually, the Whigs formed their own party platform which, to the surprise of no one, had Clay's American System at its heart.

Whether king, tyrant or just plain executive, by the end of his second term, Jackson had left his mark on the country. He remained so popular that he was able to handpick his successor, Martin van Buren of New York. Van Buren enjoyed Jackson's imprimatur and benefited from being from the most populous state in the Union as a Democrat. He would be assured of populist support from the West and South and carry

Well, How 'Bout That?

The founders of the Whig Party—Webster from Massachusetts by way of New Hampshire, Calhoun from South Carolina, and Clay from Kentucky—themselves represented the initial strength of the party but ultimately, also, its demise. The Whig Party was a truly American party with leadership from the North, South and West, respectively. So long as its leadership could unite in opposition to Jackson, Van Buren, or any of those newly calling themselves the "Democrats", Whigs had popular and electoral success. However, the future possibility (probability/inevitability) of regional squabbles would tear the party apart. Whigs also stood athwart of the more expansionist policies of the Democrats in an age of intense sentiment favoring Manifest Destiny. Thus, no Whigs today.

New York, which he did despite a strong challenge from Ohioan and famous general William Henry Harrison. Unfortunately for Van Buren, he also inherited a mess of a monetary problem in 1837.

Prior to vacating the White House and after killing the Bank of the United States, Jackson issued an executive order requiring that the purchase of federal land be executed not in paper promissory notes issued by independent banks but rather in gold or silver, that is specie. Jackson issued the Specie Circular as it was called in order to address concerns that all of the easy money was creating a speculative land bubble, especially in the lands forcefully vacated by the Indians and those out in the West. He was right to be concerned about this easy credit causing the problem of overvaluation. In just a few short years, old Indian trading posts and distant ports with odd Indian names rose up as boom towns all over the West. One of the most improbable was a place that the Sauk, Fox and Algonquin tribes referred to as the "place of stinky onion", a real swampy wasteland, "Chigagou"—the early French, now American frontiersmen simply called it Chicago. Just a few years after its eventual first major, William B. Ogden arrived in the swamp and advised his family to immediately sell their holdings there (he would obviously change his mind), plots of land had risen in value at an exponential rate. In 1836, a plot in what is now the heart of downtown Chicago sold for an average and then ungodly sum of $5000.

Due to the ensuing Panic of 1837, at the end of that accursed year, the same stretch of real estate was going for $50. The speculative bubble had burst.

Did Jackson's moves, including the defunding of the Bank of the United States and the Specie Circular, cause this biting recession? As is often the case, the most accurate answer in history is nuanced—yes and no. Yes, in that by killing the Bank, Jackson opted for financing state-run banks which in turn localized easy credit and did nothing to stem the tide of inflation. Inflation actually increased by 11% between the end of the bank in 1833 to the beginning of the Panic in 1837. *Yes*, in that by demanding specie, hard money for land purchases, the acquisition of land slowed as banks recognized how little in specie they actually possessed and therefore were willing to loan out. *No*, in that the Bank of the United States caused much of the inflation that occurred in the years prior to Jackson's attack on it, and no because banks ought to keep more than 14% of their note values in reserve. In short, as in most every panic and depression, the government had incentivised reckless speculation and ill-informed investment and then attempted to back away from the monetary cliff. It is true that British investors sold off their American holdings and a crash in cotton prices transpired at the same time, but these symptoms of an overall weak economy would have been mere inconveniences rather than factors contributing to a long business recession should banks have had real reserves to extend to viable instead of bubble businesses.

Some in Washington pined for rescinding the Specie Circular while residents in localities like Ogden's Chicago, incorporated in the spring of 1837 (bad timing to say the least) pushed debt forgiveness laws. Ogden objected, understanding that if Chicago did not honor her debts, no further credit from the East and beyond would be coming her way—and God bless him for that—Chicago could have become a St. Louis or a Toledo as a result. Van Buren recoiled as well. He sided with Jackson in arguing that the Circular needed time to work and the free market needed to reset prices so as to render them more commensurate with the actual values of land, wheat, freight, cotton, tobacco, you name it. Over the next several years, prices did recover, but as with all price revolutions, the rich swooped up cheap land and consolidated more wealth. They bought low and held high. Remember this dynamic. Progressives in 1913 sure did.

Our Clear Fate

Manifest Destiny sure is a weird term. It's not as though other countries lacked a feeling that somehow the uniquely superlative aspects of British or Spanish or French or Russian civilization merited for them a call, maybe even a divine ordinance, to spread and dominate. Americans, from the days of the Puritans onward, appear entranced by the notion of growth. Indeed, what separates American Manifest Destiny from those other, Old World impulses is American "democracy" itself. Manifest Destiny possessed the seal of spreading (at least perceived) notions of self-government whereas the European counterparts lacked such supposedly altruistic, democratic aspirations.

To be sure, the notion of Manifest Destiny was all wrapped up in the reform movement impulses of the American 19th century. Historians such as Anders Stephanson rightly find the same unfettered devotion, the same relentless zeal, and similar emotive displays employed by the devotees to American expansion as Mormons, abolitionists, tea-totallers, and suffragettes. This dream of expanding from Atlantic to Pacific and thus pacifying savage and sullen peoples was indeed a religion. Andrew Jackson himself gave expression to it:

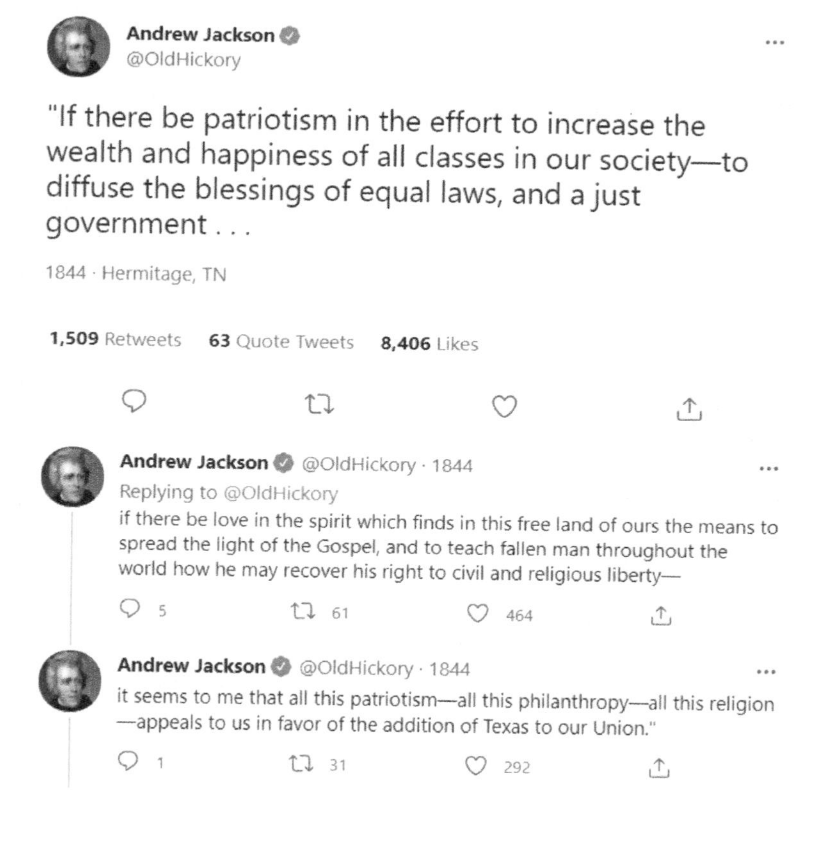

Notice the setup and then dramatic conclusion? This type of rhetoric was commonplace. Appeal to Americans' senses of patriotism. Assert that the United States is the lone force for good and civilization in the world. Stipulate that inaction regarding expansion is tantamount to sin or at the very least, milquetoast faith. Equate Manifest Destiny with evangelical Christianity. Conclude as only a patriot and Christian American could: Texas (or wherever is next) must be annexed for it is God's will.

Speaking of the psychology of it all for a moment: After such grandiose claims of American exceptionalism, the preachers of Manifest Destiny relished the process but also needed proof, confirmation if you will, of American superiority. All aspects of American civilization—religion, government, military, culture, spirit, language—were *required* to expand and dominate, otherwise, just how great was this city on a hill? Aspiration begot necessity.

In a turn of immense historical irony given what was to transpire in Mexican-American relations for the following century and four score years, in 1836, white American alien settlers in Mexican Tejas won Texan independence from Mexico after a provincial, civil war. Austin, Crockett, Houston and a bunch of fellow white Texans found themselves rulers of their own destinies, well that is, excluding Crockett who perished at the famous Battle of the Alamo. The resulting Lone Star Republic wasted little time in appealing to Washington for entrance into the Union. However, certain powers that were got cold feet and rightly so. The Van Buren administration balked. And in 1840, William Henry Harrison and his successor, Vice-President John Tyler, remained non-committal on Texas until the very end of his presidency. It was in the waning days of Tyler serving out the dead Harrison's term that Washington officially moved to annex Texas. It would be finalized under the next president, the ultimate Manifest Destiny Democrat, James K. Polk in December 1845.

The problem with Texas was a political one. In past years, as territories applied for statehood, in order to keep the regional balance in the Senate alive, a Northern state would enter coupled with a Southern allied state or vice versa. Indiana (1816) then Mississippi (1817). Illinois (1818) and Alabama (1819). Maine (1820) and Missouri (1821) thanks to the famous eponymous compromise. Finally, Arkansas (1836) and Michigan (1837). Florida entered in 1845, and Texan statehood meant another two Senators who would caucus with fellow Southerners.

Southerners began fearing more and more the growing industrialization and wealth of the Northern states. Their dominance in the House of Representatives was a foregone conclusion, especially with the successive waves of mostly German and Irish immigrants flowing into Northern cities and towns. Increasingly, therefore, Southerners looked to the Senate and saw in its Constitutional design a bulwark for the minority, one that might serve to shield the agrarian, Southern way of life from tariff onslaughts, impositions on slavery, and federal regulation.

The question of slavery, of course, loomed, but certainly the dynamics of the issue far exceeded those that almost all Americans have been taught, at least those who have attended public schools north of Lexington, Kentucky. It is as though their teachers look at history as if they were watching an old WWF wrestling match. So binary! There's the good guy. There's the bad guy. The bad guy is so heinous and deplorable that everyone is on board with the good guy kicking his ass. Good American historians contend with the bad in a cage match today. I wish we could say our side was winning; instead, Doris Kearns Goodwin, Eric Foner et al. have combined to form formidable tag teams, like Andre the Giant and Hulk Hogan (from my day) teaming up. Scary.

The Odd Couple: North and South in the Antebellum, 1831-1860

St. Augustine wrote in the 4th century that at the center of human weakness and vice was the *libido dominandi*, or the lust to dominate, to lord over creation, and especially to lord over other people. This was evident in slavery itself. Furthermore, the patristic sensibilities of Southern plantation slave owners spoke to this lust; lust being an operative word here since there were numerous incidents reported of mulatto children who looked suspiciously like the white *pater familias* of numerous Southern families. Less obvious but even more virulent was the Puritanical, Northern lust to impose Northern values and civilization on the South. At the very least, however, the North willed that if American civilization was to be defined as it spread, it was going to be in the form of Northern mores, values, and economics. The South could stay on board, so long as it played a subordinate role and financed a good portion of it.

Despite the presence of numerous anti-slavery organizations and undertakings throughout the country, including the South, abolitionist rhetoric and action ramped up in the 1830s. Abolitionism took the form of a reform movement, with all of the zealous and religious underpinnings of the era. In New England pulpits and through such avenues as William Lloyd Garrison's *The Liberator* publication, abolitionists railed against the pervasive evil of slavery. Slavery not only crushed the slave; it was the primary means by which other evils entered souls, white and black alike. It caused licentiousness, excessive drinking, gambling, and laziness, of all things. The institution tainted everything and everyone it touched. Ironically, Garrison said little about the historic largess built up from New Englanders of the past who won their prominence and fortunes importing slaves to the South. Convenient omission. Nor did he spill much ink in noting that Northern mills and factories appeared to benefit from the cheap raw materials cultivated in the South by slave and free hands alike. He failed to mention the national tariff policies that were designed to reallocate wealth from the South to the North. It is worth commenting here too that abolition of slavery required the immediate end of the institution by national governmental fiat. Abolitionists like Garrison were so uninterested in gradual, organic, federal, or compensated emancipation that contributors to *The Liberator* often decried such efforts as immoral half-measures. Famously, Garrison himself publicly burned the Constitution and advocated for the secession of the New England states from the rest of the Union.

Southerners regarded all of this as just typical, radical Yankee moralizing, that is until, in the same year that the first issue of Garrison's newspaper hit the press, Nat Turner, a Virginia slave who claimed that he had received divine instruction to kill as many white people as possible, led a bloody slave uprising. Women and children were not spared, nor were some free blacks. In the end, at least 55 people were killed by the rebels. Many more rebels—including Turner himself—were killed by the state militia and subsequent other anti-slave rebellion hysterias that reached from Virginia to North Carolina, and as far south as Alabama. Civil liberties for free blacks were restricted. Southern legislatures passed laws requiring local postmasters to censor abolitionist materials making their way southward. Even the national Congress intervened in 1836 with the passage of the Post Office Act which authorized postmasters to follow the local edicts. The Turner Rebellion served as justification for increases in the funding and number of local and state militia in the South, increases that would not be matched until another attempted slave revolt in Virginia would transpire in 1858, this time led by a white abolitionist from Ohio by way of Connecticut. John Brown's grandfather died fighting for American independence in 1776. His earlier ancestors had arrived on the Mayflower. He possessed the perfect bloodline for revolution and religious fanaticism.

Between those fateful years of 1831 and 1858, Southerners continued to devote much of their money to the purchase of slaves even though a relatively small minority of whites had the wherewithal to purchase such human capital. What fascinates me, and the subject on which it seems that too little has been written, was the triumph of patristic, plantation, and slave-owning families in 1) advancing the notion that ownership of slaves spoke to one's elevated social status, 2) persuading poor to middle-class whites that racial slavery was inherent to Southern life and culture, and 3) convincing them that protecting the institution of slavery (despite the clear labor/economic disadvantage to said whites) was essential to every Southerners' well-being. In other words, where was the class struggle? Where was Marxism when it was perhaps most needed, at least in its historic epistemology?

To understand and appreciate these factors is to appreciate and understand the true nature of the regional dispute that devolved ultimately into outright American war by 1861, thanks to the failure of the national state to keep up what might be the bare minimum requirement justifying its existence; namely, keeping Americans from each others' throats.

The truth is, it is doubtful that there is anything like what one might call the American Civil War (and the Constitutional crisis that preceded it) in 1861 without the American foreign war against Mexico in 1846. It screwed up everything.

And, many now famous names predicted as much. John Quincy Adams, Henry David Thoreau, Ulysses S. Grant, and an upstart representative from Illinois named Abraham Lincoln opposed it. Within the sizable anti-war camp, however, there were disparate reasons for campaigning against war with Mexico. Some feared that any land gained from Mexico would permit a wave of Southern, slave-holding allied states into the Union, and thus threaten the Northern stranglehold on Washington. Some saw the possibility as an illegitimate, imperial war of aggression—which it certainly was, thanks to a cooked up Tex-Mex border dispute—under the overly ambitious James K. Polk. Others like David Wilmot who authored the famous yet failed Wilmot Amendment, argued that with the admission of new territories and eventual states south of the Missouri Compromise 36 degree 30 minute parallel, free white labor would be shut out of Western lands by expansive slave labor. Interestingly enough, no notable people spoke of Mexico's legitimate, sovereign claims to *Mexican* territory, nor did they address the negation of the will of Mexican inhabitants to remain within Mexico. So much for self determination.

Despite the opposition leading up to the conflict, James K. Polk got his declaration of war on May 13, 1846. Funny, in a sick way, that American presidents (who almost without exception, are criminals) tend only to keep campaign promises dealing with aggression and war. They sure do love talking tough and then sending off other men to die in their causes. Polk campaigned hard on the idea of Manifest Destiny. If that meant war with Britain over Oregon, well that translated to "54° 40′ or fight!" If that meant war with Mexico over lands as distant and mysterious as the deserts of Nuevo Mexico, then let us go to war too.

Several other factors contributed to this odd, ante-shock of a conflict. The Mexican government itself lacked a clear mandate with the Mexican people themselves, in part because of its notorious corruption and disorganization. The various Mexican regimes refused to see the entirety of Texas as anything but a breakaway state that would eventually be brought back into the right fold. But, it was Polk's rabid expansionism coupled with convenience that won the day. And why Mexico and not war with Britain?

So, from 1846-1848, American boys and men waged war under the banner of a federal republic against Mexican boys and men who sought to defend the lands of another federal republic. They fought and died in exotic locales like El Brazito, Veracruz and Mexico City itself under the command of notorious generals like John C. Frémont, Zachary Taylor, and Winfield Scott. They marched through deserts and dense jungles. Disease itself ravaged the American ranks of Michigan and New Hampshire boys who never dreamed of being south of the border. Fighting was intense throughout; the outcome of the war was never a foregone conclusion. But, despite numerical superiority on the battlefield, Mexican forces often succumbed to the deployment of advanced artillery by their counterparts. It was in Mexico that Thomas J. Jackson learned more than just fluent Spanish; he along with other West Point grads like Lee and Grant gained lethal battlefield experience and proven tactics they were sure to deploy to disastrous effect in the future.

In the end, of the nearly 105,000 American men deployed to fight in the Mexican War, almost 14,000 died in it. Thus, by rate of casualty, the Mexican War is the bloodiest war in American history. That is a 13% death rate! Imagine a modern war with that high of a death rate! Public outrage would be so intense as to ensure a quick end to the conflict.

Instead, the war dragged on for almost two years. Mexican capitulation came then at a great loss of blood and treasure. The Polk Administration and Congress ended up as the lone beneficiary. The United States gained the Mexican Cession through the Treaty of Guadalupe-Hidalgo; thus Mexico lost about ¼ of its original territory.

The aggression and ambition of the United States directed toward Mexico moved a later president of Mexico to a perceptive insight:

In this, it must be emphasized that the United States plays the demon here. Time and time again, the United States has taken advantage of instability in Mexico to promote direct American intervention in the country. In the Mexican-American War, it was land that was procured. Later, interventions in Mexico will take the form of preludes to further imperial ambitions and a means to extract wealth from the country; all at the cost of Mexico. The United States is not a good neighbor.

After the war, the territory of the United States expanded like at no other time since the Louisiana Purchase. Alto (Upper) California and Nuevo Mexico de Santa Fe (including the current states of Utah, Nevada, Colorado, and most of New Mexico and Arizona) became U.S. territories. The looming question then was: Just how smoothly or peaceably would the new territories enter the Union as states? Would compromise win the day, or would the achievement of at least one aspect of Manifest Destiny, namely, the country reaching from Atlantic to Pacific, end up being more curse than blessing? History illustrates the former to be true, despite the numerous and authentic attempts by powerful names of the past—Webster, Clay, Calhoun among them—to lean upon compromise to serve as an adhesive to the Union. The regional divide between North and South proved to be insurmountable. It intensified the power struggle over the reins of national power to such an extent that one side felt so shut out of power that it opted to leave the Union. The other would force it to stay.

Causas Bello Americano

What follows is an analysis of the causes of the American Civil War that beats the pants off of anything that you have probably read before, that is unless your name happens to be Thomas Woods, Brion McClanahan, Mark Thornton or Thomas DiLorenzo. Dear readers: you will be shocked at how much you are nodding your heads and shouting affirmations over the next several pages. Keep it down so as to not upset your neighbors. For you less open-minded and irredeemably indoctrinated out there, well, heads exploding can be of equal volume. Take necessary precautions.

The Civil War came about because of hyper-partisanship which caused the de-evolution of the Whig Party, one whose ultimate dissolution exacerbated regional strife. A good barometer on this point can be seen in the electoral vote distribution of the electoral cycles leading up to the conflict. The first year that the Whigs were a viable national party was 1836. From 1836 onward to 1852, the Whigs operated as the alternative to the more popular Democrats. Like their founder, Henry Clay, they were leery of organic westward expansion, especially of the kind that might defray from their legislative representation in Congress. Per Clay's American System, the Whigs focused on keeping tariff levels high so as to finance internal improvements, i.e. infrastructure projects within the already extant United States. All of this was to benefit Northern industry. While consciously suspicious of actual federalism, Whigs prudently suppressed their unpopular nationalist leanings, at the very least, they held their tongues when appealing to the public. They were a mixed bag and motley crew as a result. The Whig Party's greatest strength rested, not in their charismatic leaders, and certainly not in a unified platform, but rather their status as an interregional party. Whigs came from the North, South and West. As time passed, however, that strength turned into a weakness as Northern interests demanded more protectionism, more subsidies, more national expenditure, more monopolization of the Western labor market for (ostensibly) white laborers, and yes, less land open to slavery. The result was that by 1856, the Whig Party's interregional character tore it apart and emerging from the rubble was the new Republican Party which made no bones about making the national government beholden to Northern, corporate/industrial interests. It was explicit in their founding and their continual platform.

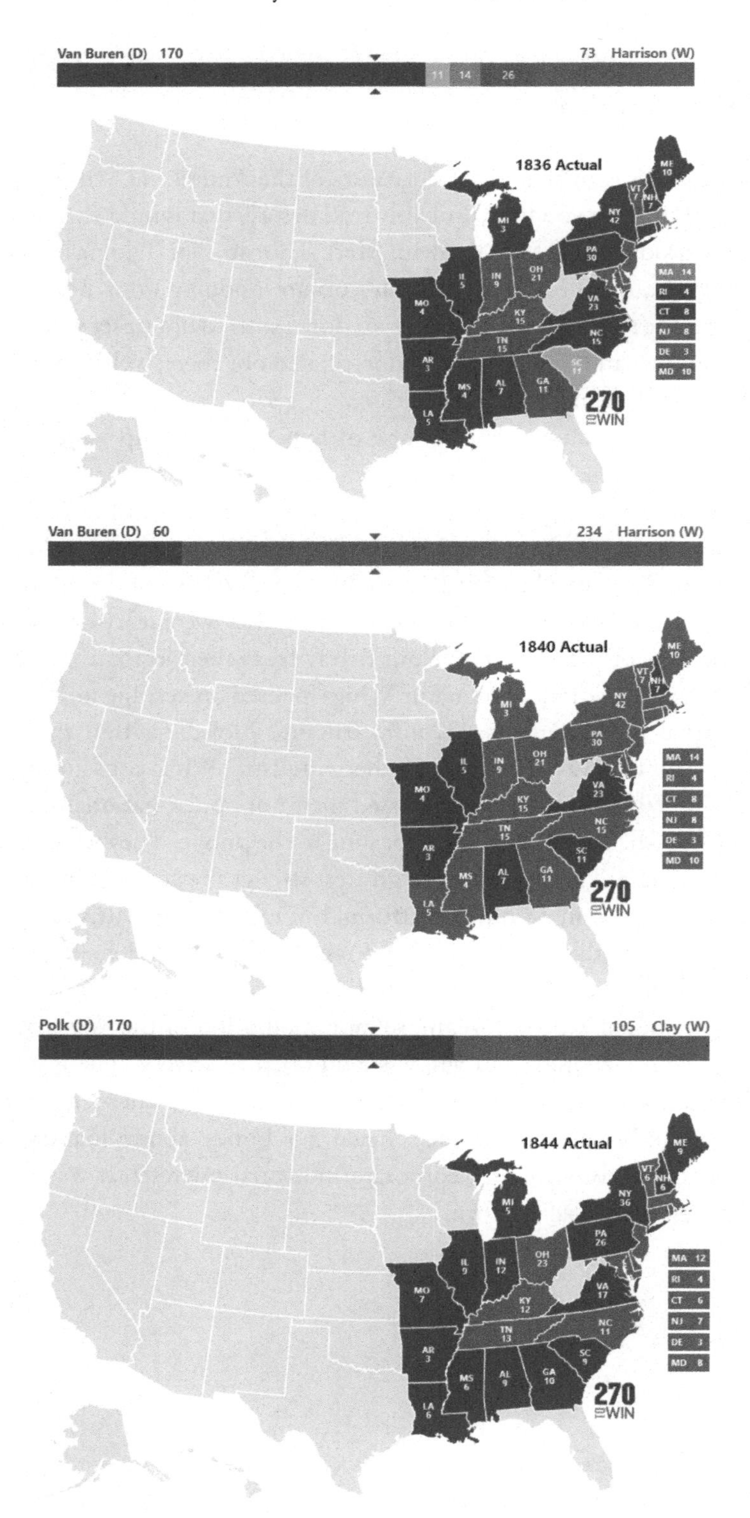
Van Buren (D) 170
73 Harrison (W)
11
14
26
1836 Actual
ME 10
VT 7
NH 7
NY 42
MI 3
PA 30
OH 21
IN 9
IL 5
MO 4
KY 15
VA 23
NC 15
TN 15
AR 3
SC 11
GA 11
AL 7
MS 4
LA 5
MA 14
RI 4
CT 8
NJ 8
DE 3
MD 10
270 TO WIN
Van Buren (D) 60
234 Harrison (W)
1840 Actual
ME 10
VT 7
NH 7
NY 42
MI 3
PA 30
OH 21
IN 9
IL 5
MO 4
KY 15
VA 23
NC 15
TN 15
AR 3
SC 11
GA 11
AL 7
MS 4
LA 5
MA 14
RI 4
CT 8
NJ 8
DE 3
MD 10
270 TO WIN
Polk (D) 170
105 Clay (W)
1844 Actual
ME 9
VT 6
NH 6
NY 36
MI 5
PA 26
OH 23
IN 12
IL 9
MO 7
KY 12
VA 17
NC 11
TN 13
AR 3
SC 9
GA 10
AL 9
MS 6
LA 6
MA 12
RI 4
CT 6
NJ 7
DE 3
MD 8
270 TO WIN

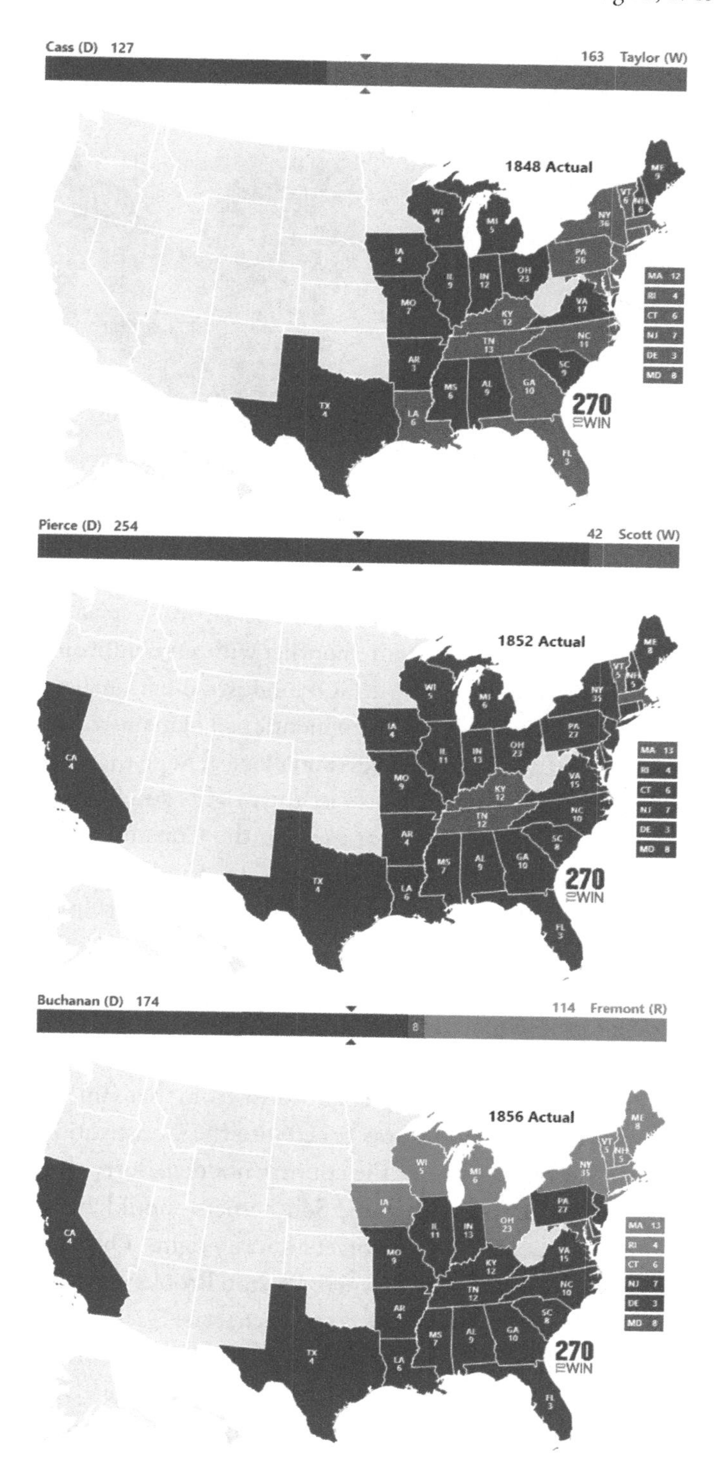
Cass (D) 127
163 Taylor (W)
1848 Actual
270 to WIN
Pierce (D) 254
42 Scott (W)
1852 Actual
270 to WIN
Buchanan (D) 174
8
114 Fremont (R)
1856 Actual
270 to WIN

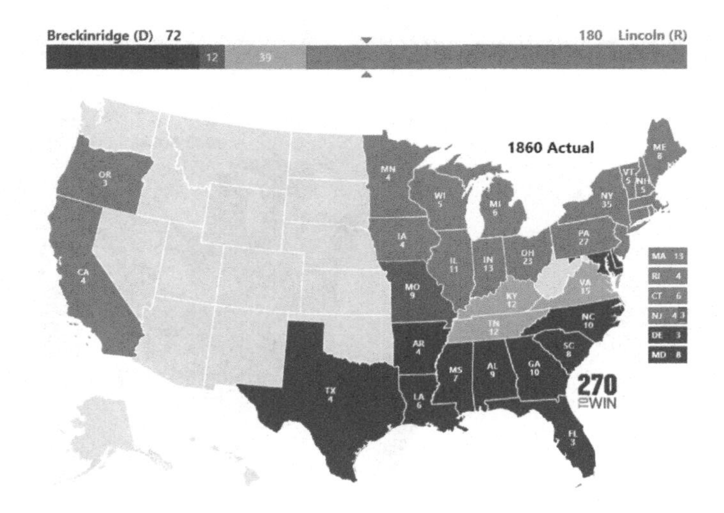

An even quick look at the electoral maps above leads one to conclude that the calcification of regional parties, representing the special interests of North and South respectively, tracks well with the descent into conflict without compromise.

The Civil War came about because GOP, industrial-nationalists were not alone in creating the political crisis. Although not often mentioned in mainstream American history texts, Southerners exercised a willful blindness and illogical hope that the Constitution and national political system could or would protect their rights and liberties. In other words, Southern leadership was determined to work within the Constitutional system, foolishly maintaining that that system could work as it was designed and tested in the anti-Federalist and Jeffersonian fires of the past. States had substantial rights within this federation, did they not? The Tenth Amendment said so. The Senate would block the democratic impulses of the Northern dominated House, as it was designed to do, would it not? The provisions of the Constitution and subsequent laws passed by the federal Congress would actually be executed and not be ignored, subject to the whims and will of Northern locales? Wishful thinking. John Calhoun spoke with immense authority from that same Senate's floor about how the theory of concurrent majority was baked into the Constitutional, political order, and many heads from various regions of the country nodded. Sorry though, Calhoun was dead in the spring of 1850 and with him, Southerners should have realized that the Constitutional framework was failing to protect minority rights. On that same Senate floor, just six years later, Calhoun's fellow countryman Preston Brooks would cane Massachusetts Senator Charles Sumner nearly to death. Decorum Senators! Decorum!

If not the Senate then, well, perhaps the Supreme Court would serve as the bulwark against "Northern tyranny"? The Southern reaction to the Dred Scott decision demonstrated just how unreasonable and misplaced Southern trust in the mechanisms of the federal government really was.

Richmond Enquirer
Richmond Enquirer
@RichmondEnquirer

"A prize, for which the athletes of the nation have often wrestled in the halls
of Congress, has been awarded at last, by the proper umpire, to those who have justly won it.
The nation has achieved a triumph, sectionalism has been rebuked, and abolitionism has been
staggered and stunned."

Mar 10, 1857 · Richmond, VA

270 Retweets **12** Quote Tweets **2,099** Likes

To review, in 1857, the Taney Court ruled in the case *Sanford v. Scott*, that Dred Scott, a Missouri slave, legally remained a slave despite having been transferred to Illinois (a free state) and Wisconsin Territory (free territory) for a time. Thus, in one fell swoop, the majority of the Taney Court upheld the non-contingent rights of slaveholders over their human property AND struck a near-fatal blow to federalism—and the powers that were in the South, rejoiced! Again, by stating that Dred Scott was still a slave, regardless of the law (and for that matter), the time and the space which Dred Scott occupied, the Taney Court invalidated the whole idea that Northern states could independently outlaw slavery. What a weird case that served as a prelude to Northerners advancing nullification while Southerners called upon univocal application of federal law! But, that is precisely what transpired in its aftermath.

The Civil War came about because of such glaring, ideological inconsistencies—and the ultimate champion of such ideological inconsistencies was Abraham Lincoln.

The truth is, Abraham Lincoln was, at best, agnostic on slavery and, was most certainly, a true believer in nationalism. As a free soiler Whig, Lincoln patterned his politics after those of Henry Clay. As a Republican after the dissolution of the Whig Party, Lincoln pursued the interests of his new party and some Northern Democrats as well—to the exclusion of other Americans. Lincoln was all in on advancing Clay's American System and preserving the gains of that system to Northern whites. In his unsuccessful campaign for the U.S. Senate in 1858, Lincoln had to parry Stephen Douglas's attacks that he was a miscegenist, i.e. someone who believed in the mixing of the races. He stated time and time again that he believed that the black race was inherently inferior. Lincoln may have envisioned an America without slavery, but certainly not one wherein blacks and whites

Well, How 'Bout That?

Check this out: The Fugitive Slave Act and subsequent Dred Scott decision had both the Wisconsin legislature and state supreme court speaking for nullification and concurrent majority. The latter went so far as to invoke John Calhoun himself, in the famous Ableman v. Booth *case of 1859: "That this section confines the appellate powers of the supreme court strictly within the limits of the constitution, provided such appellate powers exist, or are given at all, I believe has never been seriously disputed. Mr. Calhoun, in his "Discourse on the Constitution and Government of the United States," when commenting on the section in question, and the clauses of the constitution granting and defining the judicial power, says, "The question is thus narrowed down to a single point. Has Congress the authority in carrying this power into execution to make a law providing for an appeal from the courts of the several states to the supreme court of the United States?"*

could live together in peace. He advocated for displacement and recolonization of blacks. What a champion of human rights!

He did speak out against slavery as an institution when in front of the most agreeable audiences. Most importantly, though, Lincoln worshiped the notion of Union—that propositional state with its Constitutional republic—that was Lincoln's Church. The nation was sacred. The United States was one and indivisible no matter how much history and reality smacked him in the face of the opposite, in that no one at its founding in 1776 or 1788 would have declared it as such, nor did the vast majority of his own contemporary Americans hold that the Union was perpetual and indissoluble. He quoted from Scripture to support the Union; he defied logical consistency to defend it. For example, in the same 1858, he declared:

"A house divided against itself, cannot stand.' I believe this government cannot endure permanently half slave and half free. I do not expect the Union to be dissolved--I do not expect the house to fall--but I do expect it will cease to be divided. It will become all one thing or all the other."

Jun 16, 1858 · Springfield, IL

And sure enough, within two years, he was openly advocating for the ratification of the Corwin Amendment which would have protected slavery, per individual state fiat, in perpetuity. All of one thing, or all of another?! Right...

Why did Lincoln venerate the Union to the point of excluding from his mind the possibility of actual federalism? Why, to Lincoln, was the prospect—then reality—of secession such an intractable evil? To my mind, only historian Tom Woods has presented a cogent explanation for this; namely, that the Hegelian zeitgeist of Lincoln's time (the 19th century) was toward the consolidation of nation-states, for example, in Germany and Italy in Europe, and not their fragmentation. If the Union was all that Lincoln had convinced himself it was—advanced, democratic, modern, ingenious, incorruptible and sacred—then it needed to be preserved at all cost. I simply add here a corollary of sorts to Woods's keen insight and analysis: Lincoln could not reconcile the mercantilist nature of the national economy—one that was clearly exploitative of the South—with the prospect of an independent South. To force Northern mercantilism upon (cringe) an independent Southern Confederacy would be to deny the legitimacy of the American Republic's break from Great Britain, four score and four years before 1860. No, the South would need to remain within the Union—both in its economic and political instantiations. After all, the Union was the political arrangement by which Southerners exercised representative power. By doing so, they consented, win or lose on various votes and measures. This is why throughout the Civil War, Lincoln never admitted to the reality of Southern secession. To him, the Confederacy was a demonic illusion, an irreality. Sure, when it was convenient for him during the war, as we will see, he treated the Southern states as independent territories. But, conceptually, for his own faint nod to logical sanity and consistency—the Civil War was an illicit, internal rebellion which would be resolved by "the better angels of our nature."

To sum up then, the major, underlying causes of the Civil War were as follows:

1. De-evolution of the Whig Party
2. Intent of Northerners to Maintain Dominance over National Political Economy, i.e. Tariffs, American System
3. Willful Blindness of Southerners that Washington could protect their Rights, Liberties, Provincial and Peculiar Institutions (including slavery)
4. Nationalism as an Assault on Federalism (Dred Scott)
5. Lincolnian Nationalism

The two events that provided the sparks to the powder keg of toxic ingredients above were John Brown's Raid on Harper's Ferry in 1859 and Lincoln's election in 1860.

First, on John Brown. Best to say first what John Brown was not. John Brown was not the radical egalitarian we were all taught he was in school. He was not at peace; he was not sane. He was, instead, a white supremacist in his own right. Brown, who in 1847, wrote in the person of "Sambo", pushed the common, abolitionist take on blacks: Blacks were inferior. Slaves were paradoxically too free, that is to say, in their mannerisms, in their drink, dancing, and sensualities. Blacks—free and in bondage alike, but especially slaves in the South—craved "silly novels and other miserable trash... expensive gay clothing". They were slavish more so in their culture and timidity towards whites than in their actual legal status. If blacks were to advance and slaves to be free, they would have to adopt higher, dignified, white culture and, violence of course. Condemn John Brown for his 19th-century version of reverse cultural expropriation as you will and should, but he was consistent on the whole violence thing. Believing that "[h]oliness does not consist in mystic speculations, enthusiastic fervours, or uncommanded austerities..." Brown took his anti-slavery crusade to the West. In May 1856, John Brown and his sons dragged five pro-slavery settlers out from their homes in Pottawatomie Creek, Kansas and hacked them to death with broadswords in front of their families. Undeterred and undetained, three years later, Brown launched his ill-fated raid on the federal armory at Harper's Ferry, Virginia. It was Brown's hope that his attack would inspire a general slave insurrection across the South. In that, it failed miserably. Federal troops under the command of Major Robert E. Lee suppressed the rebellion, Brown was apprehended and hung. John Wilkes Booth witnessed the execution.

The raid at Harper's Ferry convinced Southerners of various classes that the time of Northern abolitionism consisting merely of fiery rhetoric and political maneuvers was over. Abolitionists aimed to bring the fight against slavery to the South, and as Georgian Senator (and future Confederate Secretary of State) Robert Toombs declared in reaction to the Raid from the Senate floor:

"It (the Federal Government) has already declared war against you and your institutions...defend yourselves! The enemy is at your door, wait not to meet him at your hearthstone; meet him at the doorsill, and drive him from the Temple of Liberty, or pull down the pillars and involve him in the common ruin."

January 1859 · Washington, D.C.

130 Retweets **17** Quote Tweets **4,800** Likes

Abraham Lincoln campaigned on an industrialist, protectionist platform. His support from abolitionists was at best lukewarm; he was a huge disappointment to Frederick Douglass. He was the best and most viable choice to secure executive power for Northern interests. Lincoln's political career and rhetoric up to 1860 proved—at least in Southern eyes—that he would be an implacable and uncompromising foe to the South.

He was elected president in the most unimpressive of ways, with just a sliver of the electoral votes needed and an underwhelming 39.7 percent of the popular vote—albeit, his name did not appear on many Southern ballots.

Because of Brown's raid and Lincoln's victory, poor and middle-class white Southerners moved away from their traditional antagonism toward the elite, slave-holding planter class and towards siding with said elites. Suspiciously excluded from every analysis that I have laid eyes on is a treatment of how much antebellum whites—rich and poor alike—retained the ardent independent, pugnacious spirit of their ancestors. It is almost as if academics have closed their minds to the notion that white Southerners were not just knuckle-dragging neanderthals who reveled in enslaving and dominating blacks. To them, their world, lives, property and freedoms were at stake, in a way no different than in 1776:

"The tea has been thrown overboard. The Revolution of 1860 has commenced."

Dec 20, 1860 · Charleston, SC

4.5K Retweets **1.1K** Quote Tweets **31.3K** Likes

Well, How 'Bout That?

The most recent and persuasive scholarship on the relations between poor and non-slaveholding white Southerners, free blacks, and slaves dispels the apocryphal contention that these groups were generally at odds. Hostilities did break out, but mostly when the slave economy (supported by the planters) appeared to operate to the exclusion of poor whites. Otherwise, as historians Jeff Forret and Timothy J. Lockley point out, poor whites and blacks—free and enslaved—often engaged in robust and cooperative economic and cultural exchange. Proof of this rests not just in deep historical and archeological dives, but in the fact that rich white Southerners openly worried about and lamented such open cooperation leading up to the Civil War. John Brown, therefore, did more to advance the notion of white supremacist unity across class lines than any Southerner-rich, poor, and in between—ever could.

We know one thing: Whites across class ranks supported federalism more than perhaps ever before, distrusted Northern intrusions perhaps more than ever before; and that vehement affinity for state and local autonomy moved them toward secession. Most whites in most Southern states had the franchise. There was overwhelming popular and legislative support for leaving the Union. They dropped like flies: South Carolina seceded unanimously in convention in December 1860, followed by Mississippi, then Florida and so forth and so on until by the beginning of February, Texas had made it seven states gone from the Union. It was truly government of, by, and for the people, even in the states wherein blacks outnumbered whites, such as South Carolina. Those who had the most to lose, those with the most land and (other peoples') skin in the game, exercised their fundamental rights to no longer associate or assemble with those absolutely bent on ridding them of both by national fiat.

War was hardly inevitable by April 1861. Abraham Lincoln made sure it came about nonetheless and regardless of the flowery assurances that all he wanted was for his American, "dissatisfied fellow-countrymen" to drop their rebellion.

South Carolina had sent delegates to Washington to negotiate about what to do with federal installations and government lands located in the now independent South Carolina. This included, of course, Fort Sumter guarding greater Charleston. Lincoln's own Secretary of State, William Seward, urged him not to supply federal troops at the fort so as to avoid war. Lincoln did so anyway in a move not unlike that of old President Polk with the liminal lands of Texas and Mexico: Act per se in a peaceful manner, the optics

Soapbox

As to whether South Carolinian slave holders and other Confederate slave owners should have held such political power, such "property rights" is an ethical question. In the opinion of this anarcho-capitalist, I would argue they **should not** ***have. However, as a historical, legal and Constitutional question, the question was—from both Northern and Southern perspectives outside those of the abolitionists—settled. Slavery was an American institution older than the republic itself. Protection of it was enshrined with the Constitution, and the Supreme Court of the national government had affirmed the inviolability of slave owners' rights to their property in*** **Dred Scott v. Sanford.** ***The Union's president-elect supported the Corwin Amendment that would have cemented slavery's legality in the South*** **in perpetuity.** ***Again, it ought to be emphasized here, the continued impossibility of a multiregional republic wherein the North invoked the supremacy of the national government on all issues and then allowed states to thwart its laws and decisions, and a South that intractably favored federalism only to then invoke the authority of a Supreme Court case to justify its continued membership in said Union. At some point, gigantic and innumerable inconsistencies matter.***

being that nothing was done in a provocative way. Then, when the expected violent pushback (blowback?) would inevitably take place, Lincoln could then declare that defenseless Union troops were aggressed upon by the secessionists. Finally, stoke and enflame anti-Southern sentiment in the North, portraying all secession (despite the entirety of the country's past) as an un-American and dangerous disease that must be stomped out at all costs. And the costs were sure to be enormous.

On Friday, April 12, 1861, Confederate forces under the command Pierre-Gustaf Toutant Beauregard (he was obviously Irish—just kidding, but he was handsome like his name) fired on the Union garrison at Fort Sumter. The commander of the Union troops was none other than Major Robert Anderson, Beauregard's artillery teacher at West Point. The fort was taken without any deaths on either side. Virginia, Arkansas, North Carolina, and Tennessee then all seceded due to the Lincoln Administration's aggressive actions. The war was indeed on from that point.

Total War; Totally Avoidable Carnage

Manassas. The Peninsular Campaign. Shiloh. Manassas again. Antietam. Fredericksburg. Chancellorsville. Vicksburg. Gettysburg. The Wilderness Campaign. Cold Harbor.

Manassas or Bull Run ensured the war would be a long drawn out affair. At Shiloh in Tennessee, there were almost 24,000 casualties in two days. Antietam was the Saratoga of the Civil War, i.e. its most pivotal battle and turning point of the war. Robert E. Lee hoped to accomplish two things there beyond owning the field: 1) Motivate Marylanders to secede from the Union and begin a further succession of border states to secession, and 2) Deal a blow to the Union on ostensibly Union soil so as to gain valuable national recognition and support for the Confederacy from Britain and France. Neither materialized as Lee's Army of Virginia limped home after the military stalemate. At Fredericksburg and Chancellorsville, the Confederate forces delivered humiliating losses to the Army of the Potomac, led at that time by a continued motley crew of hapless Union generals. Chancellorsville, however, was the epitome of a Pyrrhic victory as the South lost its best commander in the war, Thomas J. Jackson, who had inspired the "rebel yell" at Manassas two years earlier and who had stood atop his horse like a stonewall despite the onslaught of Union fire. It had to be that he died from friendly fire in the fog of war. Union seizure and occupation of Vicksburg on the Mississippi, "the Gibraltar of the South", ensured that a major objective of the Union's "Anaconda Plan" was achieved—Ulysses S. Grant and David Farragut controlled the river and thus severed the vertebrae of the Confederacy.

Gettysburg represented the Army of Virginia's furthest incursion into the North. The battle could have gone either way, but thanks to a bunch of Iowa and Illinois farm boys who held a "thin blue line" under the command of a former English professor from Maine, Joshua Chamberlain, it was a Union victory. In the Wilderness Campaign in Northern Virginia that followed, Lee fought out of desperation a hit-duck-run campaign in the faint hope of moving the already shaky Northern voter sentiment and the will to continue the fight. He failed despite his martial brilliance and that of his subordinates. U.S. Grant fought a war of attrition against the Army of Virginia. He realized that the Union's advantage was in resources and men, and he threw both with vigor right at his enemy. Blood and guts campaign it was: At Cold Harbor in Virginia, the Union army lost 13,000 men in the course of a twelve-day defeat. However, eventually cornered at Appomattox Courthouse, Lee surrendered his command of the Army of Virginia to Grant.

Those were the famous battlefield casualties. They were soldiers who, by and large, had signed up to fight either for the preservation of the Union or for Montgomery, Alabama; Jackson, Mississippi; Rome, Georgia, and thousands of other Southern towns, cities, and hamlets. This, of course, would exclude those conscripted into the war by the first American draft, ordered by Lincoln. So, in probably the most egregious infringement on human rights a government can perpetrate against its citizenry—namely forcing men to go off and die in the slaughter of war—Lincoln, the great emancipator, supported and enforced such. Draft riots broke out across the North, especially in Manhattan where Union troops from Gettysburg restored order after a week of violence and race riots in 1863.

The war ravaged the country, especially the South where the bulk of the fighting took place. In many ways, the "Civil War" was the first truly modern war in human history; the adjective "modern" being used in the most pejorative sense possible. General William Tecumseh Sherman deployed tactics in his famous "March to the Sea" of total war. For Sherman and Union leaders, the lines between Southern combatant and Southern civilian were so blurred as to become nonexistent—such is the sad outcome of the existence of modern nation-states. A Southern farmhand was paying taxes to the Confederacy. A Southern woman was raising Southern babies and maintaining the homestead. A Southern boy was a potential rebel soldier. They could, therefore, be starved out. Their homes burned. Raped. War is hell, Sherman rightly quipped, and he brought more of the flames. The South would not recover for decades. The war and following Union occupation devastated the South to such a degree that the quality of life regressed by a century. It has been shown that the effects of famine--the scarcity of foods, medicines and salt--rendered Southerners vulnerable to plagues of typhoid and dysentery, as well as hookworm and pellagra; the latter two stunted Southerners' growth and left many of them with symptoms of debilitating lethargy and dementia.

Well, How 'Bout That?

In point of fact, the Union dismissed nearly all considerations of what classically defined the practice of a just war. Non-combatants—meaning the innocent, or non-threatening—could never be targeted by military forces. The Anaconda Plan called for the immediate, indiscriminate naval blockading of the South, which was designed to so maim the Southern economy that the general Southern will to fight would be crushed. Major-General Benjamin Butler ordered his troops occupying New Orleans and its environs to treat Southern women as "wom[e]n of the town plying [their] avocation[s]," i.e. prostitutes. When he was not busy giving the green light for rape, Butler was impugning Jews in New Orleans as Christ-killers. What a gem! Add in Sherman's total war campaigns and these deplorable predations led the Papal States under the leadership of Pope Pius IX to side with the Confederacy and condemn the Union during the war.

Beyond the moral turpitude of Union Army actions and psychological scars that would last lifetimes, in the North, communities and families were destroyed by the horrifying deaths of husbands and fathers. Like their Southern adversaries, many of those who did return home did so with gangrene, addictions to morphine, bore one or more prosthetic limbs and worse, amputated spirits. All to the end of forcing people to stay in a political union of which they no longer wished to be a part. What a catastrophe.

Blue, Gray, and Red Pills on the American "Civil" War

It is hard to determine which set of widely held, apocryphal beliefs regarding which integral period of American history has caused the most damage. Damage in terms of acquiescence to and compliance with the state; damage in terms of situating and supporting current misguided worldviews, philosophies, and ideologies. But, misunderstandings about the nature and execution of the Civil War have to be somewhere in the top three, along with the American Revolution and (oh God, wait until we get there...) the New Deal.

The bluest of the blue pills pertaining to the war follow the same insidious and asinine, WWE, good guy versus bad guy, banal, and simplistic formulae. They are taught as truths in the government's schools, and so they are widely known.

The war was fought to liberate slaves in the South. The Confederacy seceded solely to protect slavery. All Northerners were good abolitionists, horrified by slavery and deeply concerned about the plight of the slave. The United States is "one nation, indivisible". Abraham Lincoln was a swell guy whose idealistic belief in the sanctity and infallibility of the Declaration and Constitution pushed him on this crusade to save the Union and the slave. Republicans were altruistic. Andrew Johnson was the devil incarnate. So was Jefferson Davis. The list goes on and on.

Here's the verifiable truth: The War of the Two Americas, the War of Northern Aggression, the War Between the States—whatever you want to call it—was fought for the continuation of Northern political, imperial, and economic domination of the South, and for that matter, the West too. Power had been effectively centralized in Washington despite the "federal" nature of the Constitution, and once the decidedly Northern-based GOP controlled the national government's levers, they were never to relinquish them. Sure, Northerners, as they had always done, looked down upon Southern culture, with all of its gambling, licentiousness, and fun. The major white abolitionists were abject Puritans who wished to redeem the whites of the South from the corruptive influences of the culture as much as if not more so than they pushed to liberate the slaves. The war was about power—political, economic and cultural—as such, it was a progressive war even before the conception of American progressivism as a concerted movement early in the following century.

You need proof. Well, here it is.

Let's start with dear old Lincoln. Honest Abe was anything but. He was a calculating political actor who was the faithful handmaid of all of the plutocratic power brokers in the North. Just as John McCain would never see a war he did not like, Lincoln never saw a tariff hike he did not like. He professed a deep reverence for the Declaration of Independence, the notion of equality (of rights) of white men, and the Constitution. The Union was his church; democracy his holy writ. He was willing to commit hundreds of thousands of men and unheard of treasure to defending his chosen religion of centralized nationalism. If he would not have been assassinated by the end of the war, his sainthood would be of nothing because then his opportunistic political allies (who more often than not believed he was a dull-witted incompetent) could not make a martyr out of him for their own ambitious ends.

Given the level of universal sacrifice he demanded, Lincoln had to sell this war to the Union populace. His major value proposition: preservation of the national union. What he avoided with every fiber of his being was ever even hinting at the idea that the conflict had anything to do with slavery.

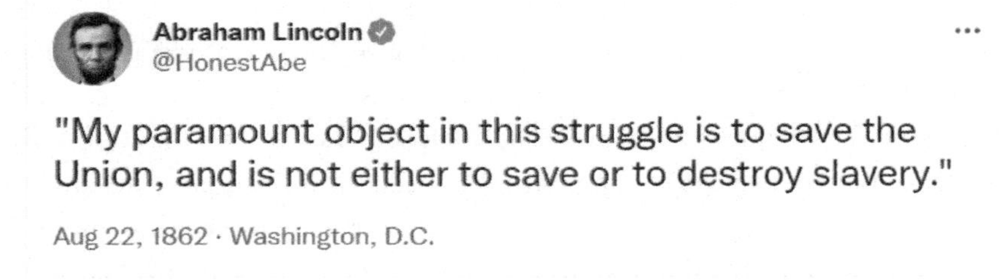

If that were not clear enough, Lincoln continued in the same letter to Horace Greeley:

> If I could save the Union without freeing any slave I would do it, and if I could save it by freeing all the slaves I would do it; and if I could save it by freeing some and leaving others alone I would also do that. What I do about slavery, and the colored race, I do because I believe it helps to save the Union; and what I forbear, I forbear because I do not believe it would help to save the Union. I shall do less whenever I shall believe what I am doing hurts the cause, and I shall do more whenever I shall believe doing more will help the cause. I shall try to correct errors when shown to be errors; and I shall adopt new views so fast as they shall appear to be true views.

And in his conduct of the war, that is the only thing upon which he remained consistent.

Lincoln faced an interesting dilemma that would have left anyone who was not a true believer in the centralized nationalistic cult, in a state of inertia. It was nothing but a minor speed bump to him. It pertained to the nature of the war; the logic of it being this: The war was to preserve the Union and the republican political order created by it by the Constitution. But, in order to crush what Lincoln preferred to call a rebellion of the Southern states instead of a true secession (something Lincoln believed to be an impossibility according to his most ardent defenders like James McPherson), Lincoln abused the very Constitution he viewed as sacrosanct time and time again. These were not minor but fundamental contradictions. One is left only to conclude that Lincoln held a head-scratcher as a principle: In order to save the most perfect Union and the document of its very conception, he had to subvert it. The Constitution was such an inviolable, holy document that it needed to be set aside in a time of crisis. Of course, where the allowance for a dictator can be located in the document itself is anyone's guess.

My favorite Lincolnian abuse of the Constitution and the Union's political order came in the form of an episode involving the aforementioned Benjamin Butler, who before he was encouraging soldiers to abuse Southern women (while able-bodied Southern men were away, of course) in New Orleans, operated at the beginning of the war in Virginia. Recall that, from the very beginning of his term, Lincoln jailed Confederate sympathizers, including the mayor of Baltimore, in the then still extant Union. He denied them the right to a speedy trial or any trial at all because, well, they were not guilty of any real crime. This was such a clear violation of the writ of habeas corpus that the Supreme Court ruled on the matter:

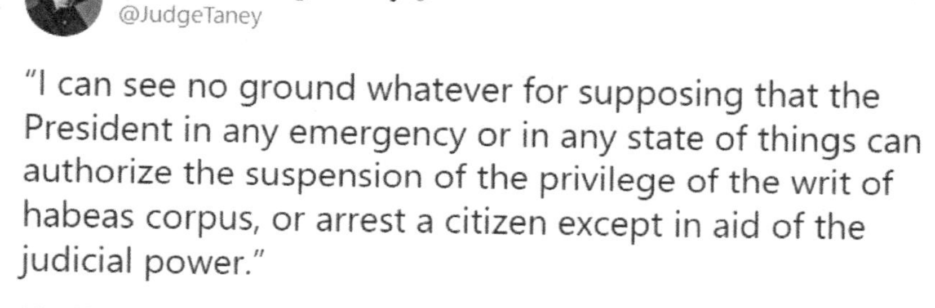

Lincoln just ignored the ruling. So much for the beautiful separation of powers and checks and balances in the Constitution.

Now defenders of the Administration chime in here that the writ of habeas corpus may be suspended in times of rebellion or invasion when "the public Safety may require it." Thus, Lincoln was in fact consistent: While no invasion had taken place, a rebellion as he defined it was on, and from Lincoln's point of view the public safety required it.

Wrong. Two problems here. First, the suspension clause as it is nicknamed today can only be enacted by Congress. It was up to the legislature's determination—not the sole executive's—whether or not a rebellion was transpiring or that the public's safety was at risk. Second, and here's the big one, if Lincoln made the legal determination that rebellion alone was occurring and that justified his suspension of habeas corpus, then he totally contradicted himself when he gave permission to Benjamin Butler to take runaway slaves as contraband of war.

In 1861 in Virginia, after returning runaway slaves back to their farms and plantations per the *Congressional, federal Fugitive Slave Act*, Butler began taking the slaves.

He sold the move to Lincoln as a war measure. Butler made the slaves do menial, uncompensated labor. Lincoln then approved the act, all in contravention of a federal law, not to mention the fugitive slave clause *within the text of the original Constitution*. Next, when in a dispatch a Confederate commander challenged the legality of appropriating slaves, Butler attempted to justify the confiscation of property on different grounds to his army superior, General Winfield Scott:

The Lincoln administration just could not get its story straight. Either the Confederate states were in rebellion, which would allow the administration—with Congressional approval—to suspend basic liberties, like the writ of habeas corpus, *or* the

Confederate states did legally and in reality secede and did form their own state, as Butler attests here. But, it cannot be both!

In the end, these contradictions and inconsistencies only validated what Southerners had complained about for decades prior to the conflict: The North was willing to twist, bend and then outright ignore the text or imagine into existence elements of the Constitution to further Northern regional interests at the cost of the South.

The true character of a regime is revealed when little to no opposition stands in its way, either from a suspicious citizenry or a contingent of said Americans' representatives.

Examine the laundry list of laws passed by the Union federal Congress once the Southern states that joined the Confederacy no longer had representation in the legislature.

Gone was the last obstacle to total Northern dominance. Not one but two unconstitutional income and revenue acts were passed. The Confiscation Acts of 1861 and 1862 allowed for the uncompensated seizure of any and all Southern properties—from fellow Americans or foreigners? Who knows. Just how woke and understanding were the Congress and Lincoln himself in enacting the Anti-Coolie Acts of 1861? "Coolie" was a wicked racial epithet for the Chinese. In it, Congress aimed to both limit Chinese emigration and punish Chinese workers already stateside in the West. This act reveals what much of the regional conflict prior to the war was about; just like the Wilmot Proviso before it, the Union Congress showed in the Anti-Coolie Acts that it was intent on monopolizing the labor market for white, Northern workers. The Legal Tender Act of 1862 and National Banking Act of 1863 allowed the national government to fund the war through controlling the money supply and mandating payments in (for the first time in American history) fiat currency "greenbacks". In other words, through money printing and attendant inflation, Washington taxed without tax legislation, because onerous, forthright tax bills would have been met with resistance in the North. The Homestead Act of 1862 was a gigantic, fraudulent land giveaway that encouraged rapid white, Northern settlement of the West. All this was done at the expense of American Indians who lost large tracts of their ancestral lands. After the war, part of that massive Union Army would be deployed to the West to kill or forcibly assimilate as many Indians as necessary to ensure that land transfer to whites was complete. Finally, Congress spawned the Pacific Railway Act of 1862—boy, was this Congress sure busy in passing bills that had little to nothing to do with winning the war! The Pacific Railway Act empowered, subsidized and emboldened railroad companies to steal as much land as possible and lay barely functional track in the most haphazard and inefficient of ways. Because land grants depended on the speed and area of laid track, in Utah where the Central Pacific line was to connect with the Union Pacific line, the two companies constructed parallel track for miles past the would-be conjunction point. Add in vast ecological destruction (the government paid the Union Pacific more should it blow up mountain sides with dynamite for unnecessary tunnels) and an equally unnecessary race war between the mainly Chinese-Union Pacific workers and the mostly Irish-Central Pacific workers, and this act had all the true markings of a national initiative: waste, fraud, wealth inequality, environmental disaster and racial war.

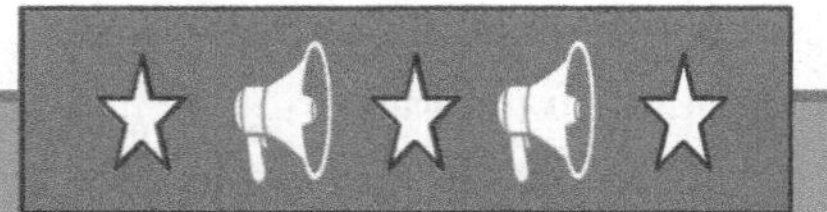

Soapbox

Perhaps what makes both Confiscation Acts all the more nefarious—setting aside of course the blatant disregard for the 4th and 5th Amendments—is that their name proposes the notion that government does anything else but confiscate.

But what about the Emancipation Proclamation and the Gettysburg Address?

The Emancipation Proclamation, it is true, did not effectively free one slave because as even the semi-informed will say, where Lincoln had jurisdiction (the border states and those areas of the South under Union Army occupation) he did not free the slaves, and where he had no jurisdiction, (the states and areas in "rebellion") he aspired to do so. More significant is that Lincoln was unabashed in his aims behind the Emancipation Proclamation. It was an executive order in which Lincoln claimed that he had the power to create and execute manumission due to his position as the commander-in-chief of Union forces. One might wonder, correctly, why he did not pursue legislation through Congress to that effect. The answer is as simple as the question: He did not have enough representative support to do so—in the *Northern dominated Union Congress*. As an executive act then, the Emancipation Proclamation reads like a military order, because that is precisely what it was. So as to expedite the end of the war in favor of the Union, it was designed to inspire a massive slave exodus and revolt in the Confederacy. This would cripple the Southern economy and increase defections from the major Confederate armies as Southern troops would be compelled to return home.

Jefferson Davis saw through it all:

"[The Emancipation Proclamation] affords to our whole people the complete and crowning proof of the true nature of the designs of the party which elevated to power [Lincoln], and which sought to conceal its purpose by every variety of artful device and by the perfidious use of the most solemn pledges on every possible occasion."

Jan 13, 1863 · Richmond, VA

3.7K Retweets 752 Quote Tweets 23.2K Likes

Lincoln had resolutely declared before and again during the war that he had, "no purpose, directly or indirectly, to interfere with the institution of slavery in the states where it exists." Indeed, this was not some altruistic move. Davis rightly viewed this as a step to incite a race war in the South at a time in which most of the fighting aged men were off at war. President Lincoln and his administration did what they were apt to do throughout the war: Use the slaves as pawns, then treat them as encumbrances, then use them as their own slaves, then deploy them as weapons against the South so as to obtain the GOP's own political ends.

The supposedly brilliant Gettysburg Address alludes to this in the most awkward and illusory of ways.

...our fathers brought forth, on this continent, a new nation, conceived in liberty, and dedicated to the proposition that all men are created equal. Now we are engaged in a great civil war, testing whether that nation, or any nation so conceived, and so dedicated, can long

> endure. We are met on a great battle-field of that war. We have come to dedicate a portion of that field, as a final resting-place for those who here gave their lives, that that nation might live. It is altogether fitting and proper that we should do this.
>
> But, in a larger sense, we cannot dedicate, we cannot consecrate—we cannot hallow—this ground. The brave men, living and dead, who struggled here, have consecrated it far above our poor power to add or detract.
>
> The world will little note, nor long remember what we say here, but it can never forget what they did here. It is for us the living, rather, to be dedicated here to the unfinished work which they who fought here have thus far so nobly advanced. It is rather for us to be here dedicated to the great task remaining before us—that from these honored dead we take increased devotion to that cause for which they here gave the last full measure of devotion—that we here highly resolve that these dead shall not have died in vain—that this nation, under God, shall have a new birth of freedom, and that government of the people, by the people, for the people, shall not perish from the earth."

Read carefully through that text. It is as baffling and hypocritical as it is brief. Look at the logic (?) in it: The cause of the Union effort in the war was to guard the idea, before the world, that representative government works, that somehow a Union victory would affirm both the universal right to self-governance and the efficacy of republics the world over. Yikes. By November 1863, Lincoln was claiming that the cause of the war was to guarantee the right of self-determination and "a new birth of freedom"—whatever that meant. But, here's the rub: At Gettysburg, Lincoln deployed tens of thousands of men—just as he did at every battle in the war—*to prohibit* government of the people, by the people, and for the people. Southerners had rejected the notion that the government in Washington, far away from most of them in terms of distance and disposition, still possessed any mandate to rule over them. He seems to be utterly blind to the fact that he spoke at the dedication of a cemetery to the fallen, a cemetery where Union *and* Confederate dead alike were interred. It was Lincoln's nationalistic obsession to crush self-determination that led to all of their deaths. To claim then that the Union troops fought and died there to defend some sort of spirit of democracy, is sheer lunacy. Quite the opposite was true: Confederate troops fought and died throughout the war for the right of political self-determination.

Scores of newspapers said so at the time, and they were not just in the South. Regarding the reshaping, or what we might call today, "the evolution" of the main objective behind the war, the *Harrisburg* (Pennsylvania) *Patriot & Union* decried:

"We pass over the silly remarks of the President; for the credit of the Nation we are willing that the veil of oblivion shall be dropped over them and that they shall no more be repeated or thought of."

The *Chicago Times* was no less critical:

"The cheek of every American must tingle with shame as he reads the silly, flat, dishwatery utterances of a man who has to be pointed out to intelligent foreigners as the President of the United States."

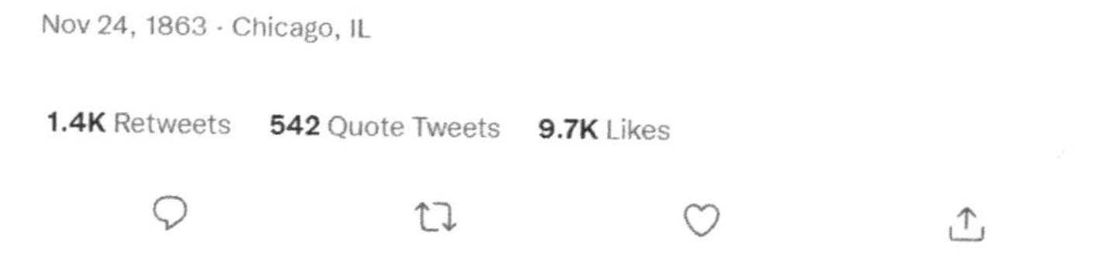

And for the icing on the cake, the *London Times*:

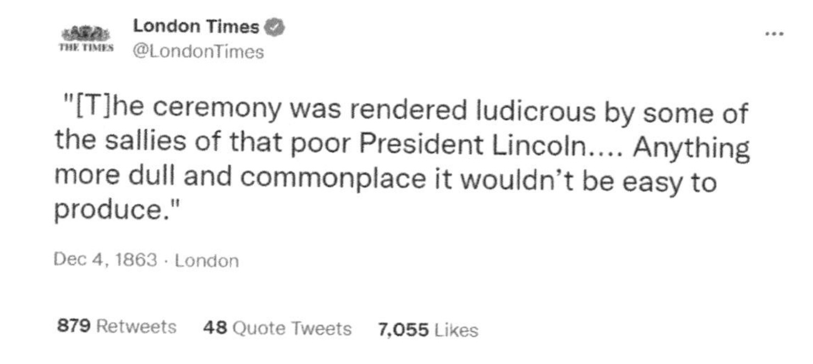

In truth, the Union government fought the Civil War (let us grant it the name here) in order to reimpose and safeguard the established Northern political and economic order of dominance over the rest of the country. Its triumph not only obviated any possibility of secession—no matter how egregious the future actions of the national government against the states—but also crushed any legitimacy behind traditional American principles such as those contained in the Principles of 1798, general federalism, American distaste for imperialism, local autonomy, limited taxation and free markets. When John Wilkes Booth assassinated Lincoln at Ford's Theater on Good Friday, 1865, the Republicans who had the most at stake in the political monopoly won by the war, found the perfect martyr for their cause. The propaganda machine went full bore into Lincoln hagiography and shrines were soon erected to both Lincoln and the national government, the two forever inseparable and demanding of our eternal reverence.

The backfire of all backfires: Booth's last words, according to the Union troops who shot him were, "Useless, useless." It was even worse than that.

4
Reconstruction, Industrialization, Empire and Depression, 1865-1939

Recolonization

There is an irony in the Lincoln assassination in that John Wilkes Booth eliminated the one Republican who seemed most poised to treat the Southern states in a relatively conciliatory manner after the war. Before his death, Lincoln had pushed to extend his ten-percent plan which permitted reentrance to the Union with full representation in Congress should just ten percent of a (formerly) Confederate state's voting population swear an oath of allegiance to the Union and agree to slave emancipation.

It is something of a motif in history that assassinations backfire ultimately for the cause of the assassin. The plot against and then murder of Lincoln allowed Radical Republicans in Congress to capitalize on Northern resentment and enmity toward the entire South and thus recast national reconstruction into a process of punitive recolonization.

Thaddeus Stevens and Charles Sumner built the Reconstruction regimes postbellum to achieve, as Stevens put it, the complete and continual "ascendancy of the Party of Union"—that is the Republican Party—over the national government. In a political sense then, Reconstruction amounted to a bold gerrymandering of the country. There would be one party rule—this time not through consensus but through force.

Mind you, few of these initiatives increased the standard of living for the now freedmen in any marked way, and as Reconstruction ended with a thud with the Compromise of 1876, it is clear that the freedmen were convenient pawns to be surrendered at the moment in which backing them would mean less national power for Republicans. It was an easy choice.

The 13th Amendment outlawed slavery only to leave freedmen little to no choice but to engage in sharecropping, a system that left the freedmen in perpetual debt slavery, with many of them working on the same plantations upon which they were once enslaved. In point of fact, despite all of the supposed efforts—including that of the first welfare program in American history, the Freedmen's Bureau—if one would have visited the South with the mission of attesting to black standards of living, let's say in 1850 and 1870, there would be little difference. The 14th Amendment followed President Andrew Johnson's repeated vetoes of previous civil rights bills and granted universal citizenship to freedmen and attendant civil rights. In so doing, the Republicans in the federal government used the freedmen to further crush federalism since in the original Constitution, it was the decided function of the states, not the federal government, who determined the citizens of the various states. So as to clarify that civil rights included the right to vote—in all elections—the Congress proposed, and a limited number of states ratified, the 15th Amendment. The freedmen would go on to constitute a major voting block for the Republicans, transforming the formerly solid Democratic states into Republican ones.

It must be pointed out that for all of the legislation of the era coming down from Washington that ostensibly aimed to protect the freedmen, when it came to defending the fundamental right of freedmen to—you know, get up and move out of the South—Stevens, Sumner, Morrill, and their ilk did not lift a finger. To do so would have endangered their main objective of retaining perpetual political power. When Redeemer (read white segregationist) governments retook power in the various stages of Reconstruction and passed black code laws severely restricting black freedom of movement, no national act nor court decision invalidated them. Even northern states like Illinois enforced anti-vagrancy laws aimed to stem any tide of freedmen into the state. The former slaves were no longer legally slaves, but they were bound nonetheless to the land and would have to suffer the same consequences of national policy—including food and salt famines resulting in widespread malnutrition and disease—as for their poor white counterparts: *Plus que ça change...*

Understandably, this analysis stands at odds with almost everything you have probably read in a standard and approved U.S. History textbook. Without relying on that as proof of veracity, allow me to rest my case on the less-than-altruistic motives of the Radical Republican establishment in Washington with some thoughts on the Compromise of 1876.

After eight years of mismanagement and rampant corruption in Washington under successive Grant administrations, members of his own party passed a resolution in Congress to preclude a third Grant term in 1876. As a result, the Republican milquetoast governor of Ohio, Rutherford B. Hayes would run against the Democratic nominee, Samuel Tilden. Tilden had made a name for himself by prosecuting organized, state-aided (is there another kind?) crime in New York City. In a remarkably close election, disputed electoral votes from three Reconstruction states—Louisiana, South Carolina, and Florida—and one other, Oregon, would decide who the next president would be. In all of the Southern states, the popular vote favored Tilden only to have Reconstruction Republican carpetbagger and scalawag officials deny the legitimacy of the vote. In turn, they refused to register electoral votes for Tilden.

Well, How 'Bout That?

Hayes started a long string of GOP presidential nominees from Ohio. Even Grant had been born there. Because of their relative lack of achievement, charm, or panache, a parody of a Shakespeare quote circulated about them in the Gilded Age: "Some men are born great; Some achieve greatness; Some are born in Ohio."

The resolution: In the most unconstitutional of ways, the leaders of both political parties created an Electoral Commission to determine the ultimate outcome of the election. It was made up of 8 Republican officials, 7 Democratic officials. You might pause here and ask: Were the Democrats really that bad at math or were they that convinced that they might persuade at least two of the GOPers to abandon their partisanship and side with them to get Tilden into office? The truth is neither. Democrats conceded to the lopsided Commission in a quid quo pro for the ages. Obviously, Rutherford B. Hayes—despite losing the popular vote to a nominee of a party that had been burdened with the toxic brand of secession and one that had been, for all intents and purposes, legally suppressed—would be the next president. In return, Reconstruction would end. The Union troops who, at various points in the effort, had placed whole regions of the South under martial law, who protected Freedmen's Bureau officials, who enforced protection of blacks under laws like the Ku Klux Klan Act, would be removed from the South. That's right: When the Republicans came to that fork in the road of Reconstruction, forced to choose between protecting the freedmen and maintaining the spoils system or maintaining power in Washington, they sold the freedmen again down the river. Nuts and bolts—they got screwed. And so did Tilden, of course.

And We All Shine On, Sort of...: The Gilded Age

Even though Reconstruction or Recolonization/Occupation of the South ended abruptly, there is significant overlap between that era of American history and the next of import, the Gilded Age.

I posit that this is the most interesting period of American history to study due to the almost poetic contradictions of the era and the fact that—just like one's historical perspective on the Great Depression of the 1930s—whatever take you have on the Gilded Age determines one's worldview today. The reverse is true as well: If the preference is to the left, everyone on that side of the political and ideological spectrum views the Gilded Age exclusively through the exploitation lens. If on the right today, there is a reflexive defense of big business, a defense often lacking proper nuance. It was either the worst of times or the best of times. The truth, however, lies somewhere in between: For most Americans, it was the best of times, that is, relative to past periods. Explosive economic expansion raised the American general standard of living to impressive heights, and no, wealth was not pooled only into the hands of monopoly-owning, trust-baby fat cats. Scrouge McDuck was not a real person/animal, doing backstrokes in his pool of gold coins. No doubt the Rockefellers, Carnegies, and Morgans of the world attained enormous wealth, but in as free a market system as the United States has ever had, the benefits of mass production and ingenious efficiency redounded to the lower classes at the same time that Standard Oil, U.S. Steel, and Northern Securities Trust secured huge market shares.

When Mark Twain famously dubbed the era as "gilded"—meaning something covered in a thin layer of gold that disguises a base, cheap metal—he said perhaps more truth than he knew at the time. Certainly, there was criminality, corruption, scandal, virulent vigilantism (lynchings reached a climax in the Gilded Age), and race wars from coast-to-coast, city-to-country. At the same time, however, a lot of good transpired especially in a country just ravaged by civil war. The main cause for the good was gold. It was not some surface level, thin veneer. In that, Twain had it wrong: Gold was the base, fundamental cause of prosperity.

My suspicion, confirmed by observation of other history teachers, for why the Gilded Age receives such short shrift in survey courses is that; to understand the true essence of the period, economics is a prerequisite, and sound economics is avoided like the plague. Furthermore, an economic-historical approach to understanding the Gilded Age blows up the leftist and certainly progressive narrative that the excesses of the period justify government intrusion and regulation of production, consumption, exchange, property—in other words, all human agency.

If your knowledge of the period consists of Howard Zinn's diatribe against the robber barons, your 10th grade reading of Upton Sinclair's *The Jungle*, and a few heart-wrenching photos of New York ghettos by Jacob Riis, well you have been sold an elaborate albeit extremely limited story by government schools.

Sep 7, 1904 · New York, NY

876 Retweets **111** Quote Tweets **4.4K** Likes

How convenient; the same institution that controls the curriculum and very functionality of those schools seeks to emphasize the evil that transpires should it not be in control of society.

Good historians are all about distinctions, and economic historian Burton Folsum provides an essential one for understanding the Gilded Age; that is to say whether we should characterize the Rockefellers, Carnegies, Vanderbilts, Stanfords, etc. as crooks or as just really successful entrepreneurs. To summarize: there were *political* entrepreneurs and *market* entrepreneurs. The former deserve our just disdain; the latter our just lauds and appreciation. Political entrepreneurs used their sway or connections in government to game the system by attaining insider information to which only the state was privy or by urging for protectionism and regulation so as to harm competitors in their given field. Sometimes, like in the case of the railroads with the Pacific Railway Act, political entrepreneurs benefited from direct subsidies, indirect easy credit, or precise and timely deployment of the U.S. Army to clear out any unwanteds in their way.

The case of Crédit Mobilier stands out. It had a French name because, especially at the time, French names sounded fancy and sophisticated. Crédit Mobilier was a finance company through which the government allocated funding to the Union Pacific company for the construction of the transcontinental railroad. Its directors engaged in a dual-pronged scheme to bilk the federal government and private investors simultaneously. By 1867, Oakes Ames, a Congressman himself, directed the company and orchestrated the fraud. Congress paid $94,650,287 to Crédit Mobilier to fund the Union Pacific project, while Crédit Mobilier incurred (certainly hyperbolized) costs of only $50,720,959. That's quite a windfall for the directors! Not only that—the heads at Crédit Mobilier employed a Ponzi scheme from the beginning. When selling or at times granting—especially to federal officials—shares and bonds in the company, the directors made sure to issue an enormous rate of return once those initial investors liquidated their holdings. Word got around to the general public (let's call them the "B" and "C" groups of investors) and the price of Crédit Mobilier stock continued to ascend with demand. However, only the "A" grouping of initial investors and company directors would see a dime. The monies from the secondary and tertiary investor groups were used to pay off the "A" group; by the time the B and C investors caught wind of the scheme and attempted to sell, their paper was worthless—all returns and principle, gone. The *New York Sun* newspaper uncovered the intricacies of the scheme and reported that several individuals had lost their life savings—one man to the tune of $19,000 (the equivalent of $400,000 today)—in the swindle. And, The Sun named names. Several high ranking officials in the Grant administration and heads of major committees in Congress were implicated. Even future president James Garfield was said to be connected. But, despite mountainous evidence and an enraged public, to the shock of no one, not one of those of the powerful and connected were brought up on charges, faced jail time, or even lost their positions in Washington. After all, there would have been no such thing as Crédit Mobilier without Washington. The company presented itself as a private enterprise when in reality it is what scholar Michael Rectenwald has dubbed, a "governmentality". The American taxpayer and especially later investors in the company were the victims of abject criminality.

Well, How 'Bout That?

Rectenwald, an ostracized New York University professor, has done yeoman's work in his various books to destroy the notion that large tech companies today, especially Google, Twitter, Facebook, and Apple, are somehow private companies. They receive huge government contracts to mine data and perform other services. They work in concert with one another to quell political dissent and even, as is utterly apparent now in 2022, steer the outcome of national elections.

Contrast that with the activity of the great market entrepreneurs of the period. It was their foresight, ingenuity, and genius that produced the bubbling spring of prosperity inherent to the era. Armed with advanced industrial machinery which some of the magnates themselves re-engineered and refined so as to further augment efficiencies, these men who built modern America competed in the open market to produce quality goods the public desired at ever decreasing costs. John Rockefeller, Andrew Carnegie, James Hill et al. did not amass oil, steel, and chemical monopolies by doing what we *suspect* all monopolies do. Monopolies must engage in predatory pricing, right? In other words, monopolies and monopsonies (corporations that act as the only buyer of a material or good) can only exist because they are large enough to undercut competitors by lowering prices, taking a short term hit. Then, the weakened competitors are forced to sell to the behemoth, which then at some critical point raises prices once the behemoth company dominates the space. Finally, the monopoly can lower the quality of the goods or services it's peddling because the competition has been wiped out.

But here's the thing: There's no evidence that the supposed monopolies, ranging from Standard Oil to the Great Northern Railway, engaged in such practices. After all, if they had to any degree engaged in so-called predatory pricing, commodities, goods, and service prices would have risen significantly during the Gilded Age. They did the opposite: Prices plummeted. Rockefeller's cheap kerosene saved sperm whales—whose oil was previously used to light the lamps of the rich alone—and general literacy rose exponentially as a result. People could afford to read at night. His inexpensive and readily available petroleum literally fueled the second industrial revolution in America. Without Carnegie's Homestead Works out-producing every other major European competitor by wide margins, the architectural marvel of skyscrapers, like those that characterize the metropoleis of today, would not have been built. James J. Hill maximized the benefit of Cyrus McCormick's reaper. His Great Northern Railway and attached shipping empire ensured that Midwestern grain could be sent to feed hungry mouths as far away as East Asia. Hill provided incentives to frequent and heavy freight customers, and his venture was extremely lucrative, that is, until his whole comparative advantage in pricing was wiped out by Congress's ruinous, socialistic Hepburn Act of 1906.

This is not to say that the mostly market entrepreneurs remained consistently so throughout their lifetimes. For example, Andrew Carnegie urged and cajoled representatives in Congress to pass protectionist measures against foreign steel. Such is the allure of temptation when it appears that the state is for sale to the highest bidder. I would contend that Carnegie made up for such sins against capitalism when he became one of the most avid and acerbic critics of American overseas imperialism during his lifetime.

Two final, sure-to-be-scandalous thoughts before proceeding onto analyzing further aspects of the Gilded Age beyond purely political economy. First, and stay with me here: The whole notion of a monopoly is illustrative of the unfortunate but natural animosity and non-complementarity of free societies and the governments that rule over them. In a truly free market, monopolies are impossibilities. You read that last sentence correctly. Monopolies are non-entities in a truly capitalist system—the only way they can come into being is through government action. Think about it. The only means by which one corporation could come to control 100% market share within an economic sector, or even, let's stipulate, so dominate a sector to the tune of 75+%, would be through offering the very best of goods or services at the absolute lowest cost to consumers, AND it would have to do so in perpetuity. The very moment a corporation failed to do so in the slightest, that would be the entry point (again, in the absence of state prohibitions against others entering said field) that competitors would rise up and challenge the supposed monopoly.

How ironic then, this second point. If as proven above, in a totally free market, competition is always baked in, then how backward and nonsensical are governmental anti-monopoly, antitrust laws?! Antitrust advocates argue for the state, which is the only institution that ensures monopolization, to then regulate them out of existence! I'll let Tom Woods deliver the final knockout blow to the Marxist insanity and justification for antitrust laws:

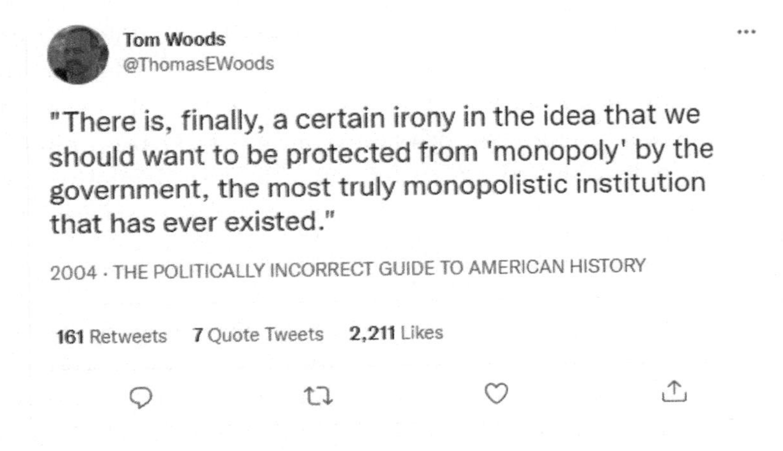

Indeed, well before and then during the implementation of antitrust legislation in 1890, the mostly free market, big businesses of America were offering a seemingly endless array of staple as well as new products to American and global consumers. Prices fell. Wages increased. And those wages increased not because a central bank created and pushed easy money and inflation: People worked less yet were compensated more because valuable capital flowed into innovative industry, and no one was left guessing as to the worth of that capital. For the most part, federal administrations and Congresses resisted calls to move the dollar off of a pure gold standard. Individuals and enterprises could save and delay their consumption and their savings would actually appreciate in value. What a wild concept, so utterly foreign to Americans today.

Politically speaking, the Gilded Age was an era of small government. But, that did not stop the two major parties from warring ruthlessly for control of the cash cows of Congress and the White House. Establishment and approved textbooks lament this legislative and regulatory inaction, dubbing it the age of political paralysis. Statists detest when the state is anything less than ubiquitous and divine.

It is an odd phenomenon though: At the very moment that there was broad policy agreement between the parties, especially after Reconstruction, Democrats and Republicans fought tooth and nail for control over state capitals and Washington itself. Such is the allure of power, but it was also that, since in the 1876 election, Republicans realized just how tenuous their grip on government was. Desperation fueled electoral animus. Should Republicans lose control of Congress and the presidency for the first time since prior to the Civil War, gone would be their control over the spoils system and the way they had deployed it to buy votes since the war to end all American wars ended. Republicans bought votes through the pension system. It was Washington's worst kept secret that lucrative and inordinate benefits went to both actual Union veterans and voters who simply claimed to have been veterans. The Republicans delivered on the pensions. Men who claimed they were drummer boys at Antietam certainly could not have been since they were born in 1864. Embryos—though fully human—make very poor drummer boys. The only way such payments would continue was with continual GOP dominance. Political entrepreneur magnates like Mark Hanna in Ohio willed the bezzle to continue: Their fortunes relied upon deep state connections.

By 1880, the corruption of one-party rule ran so deep that enough power players in the GOP realized that, at the very least for optics, a reform-minded candidate ought to win the nomination for president. James Garfield of Ohio had a true rags-to-riches story. Accounts of his connection to Crédit Mobilier failed to discredit him. He won a narrow victory in 1880 and appeared poised to implement some reforms. As a result, Charles Guiteau, who had labored long and hard for the Garfield campaign, shot the president at a Washington train station. Garfield had refused to give Guiteau a plum government job. Guiteau was so convinced of the rectitude of his act that he not only expected Vice President (and notorious plutocrat) Chester Arthur to award him with a position but also implored other disaffected Republicans to pay for his legal defense—after all, he had done what they only wished upon poor Garfield.

In the following years, Congress and Arthur did initiate some reforms aimed at the obvious offenses of the spoils system. For example, the Pendleton Act created the Civil Service Commission which was designed to rule out pure cronyism in federal appointments. Still, the Commission amounted to a federal agency of the federal government vetting candidates for the federal bureaucracy. In other words, it was a promise of the federal government to hold itself accountable, when, in reality, Washington operated in ways indistinguishable from the organized crime rings that arose during the era. Just as with William Marcy "Boss" Tweed in New York, the bilking of the public could only transpire with the active hand-in-glove relationship between criminals in and out of government. Talk about a public/private venture!

Grover Cleveland= BOSS

The national political fray into which Grover Cleveland entered in earnest in 1884 consisted of the fight over which party controlled the levers of Washington, over which party operatives could ensure continual re-election and ascendency of power given that they could sow the plunder of government onto their loyal constituents. There were two unintended benefits to all of this; first, because Republicans had so dominated the executive branch and its ever-growing, already extensive tentacles, they busied themselves warring with each other in intra-party factions. The result: the "Stalwarts" and "Half-Breeds" underappreciated national political sentiment for classical liberalism and general reform—not of society, but of the state. And, secondly, the internal squabbles kept them from enacting sweeping domestic or foreign policy legislation. Inertia in government tends to tie the state's hands and fists. Good.

By the time he had won the Democratic Party's nomination for the presidency in 1884, Cleveland had served as mayor of Buffalo and governor of New York, the Union's most populated state. The leader of the Half-Breeds, James G. Blaine, won the GOP nomination. The knives were out during the campaign, especially when Blaine supporters discovered that Cleveland had fathered a child out of wedlock. Now, granted: Today that would be a non-story, but back then, in somewhat Victorian America, fornication and illegitimacy were still scandalous. Newspapers first in Buffalo then in Chicago, then nationwide ran with the story. Even worse, later in October 1884, Maria Halpin claimed that Cleveland had raped her. Whatever the case may have been, it certainly amounts to a late 19th century "he said vs. she said" moment. While Halpin claimed rape, Cleveland doubted his paternity. Cleveland responded to the revelation in the most unsavvy of ways: He admitted to an affair. In point of fact, for the entirety of the boy's life (cue Diana Ross's 'Love Child') Cleveland provided for his possible, illegitimate son.

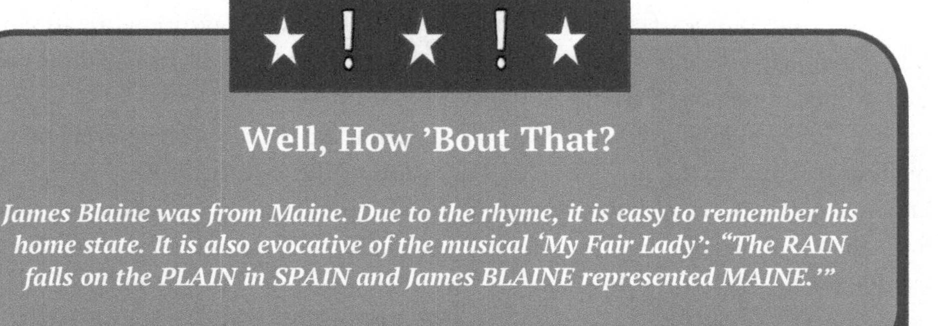

While that story did not stick to Cleveland and harm his popularity in the end, the Mulligan Letters saga stuck to Blaine like stink on feces. Note to those of you who wish to have a public career or profile beyond your non-blue checkmarked Twitter account: If you're planning on engaging in graft, do not write down instructions to collaborators (in

Blaine's case, one James Mulligan) and then write, "Kindly burn this letter" at the end. This is what is called a sloppy cover-up. Mulligan blabbed to newspapers, and almost a decade later, their ink stain still stuck with Blaine. His attempt to explain away the letters in 1884 was even worse than his initial cover-up:

By "kindly burn this letter" I wished to have the paper be fuel in order to provide warmth to the dirty Irish Catholic Mulligan household.

No corruption here: I care for the heathen Irish. I'm half heathen myself...

Aug 4, 1884 · Blaine Mansion, Dupont Circle, Washington, D.C.

Cleveland carried New York and squeaked by in the election. For the first time since James Buchanan back in 1860, the Democrats held the White House.

Now, it would have been easy—indeed it was anticipated—that with Cleveland at the helm, Democrats would encourage the same graft that had typified the previous Republican administrations. For example, Cleveland and his party could avail themselves of the attendant popularity won by continued veterans' pension payments. The Republican Senate would be more than happy to oblige since they would be re-elected too. Everyone except Southern Democrats were on board.

Nope.

Cleveland was an ardent believer in extremely limited government: He maintained that the Constitution and the example of American history prescribed nothing else. It was in his first months in office that his political integrity shined through. He vetoed pension bill after pension bill. And while he did, in part, continue the spoils system by handing Democratic cronies bureaucratic jobs, he cut government spending to such a degree that there were fewer ghost-payroll positions for them to fill. He favored small government frugality and understood that the state represented, for the most part, a gigantic wrench always prone to throw itself into the workings of an otherwise smooth-running American capitalistic engine:

"The public Treasury, which should only exist as a conduit conveying the people's tribute to its legitimate objects of expenditure, becomes a hoarding place for money needlessly withdrawn from trade and the people's use, thus crippling our national energies, suspending our country's development, preventing investment in productive enterprise, threatening financial disturbance, and inviting schemes of public plunder."

Dec 6, 1887 · Washington, D.C.

34.9K Retweets **3.7K** Quote Tweets **198.2K** Likes

These were not the musings of an ill-informed political hack who simply attuned his positions to the fancies of the majority. Cleveland was a man of letters and thought. He was a voracious reader. Famously too, he engaged in lengthy debates with the intellectual giants of his age, either in person or through letter chains; that is, when he was not devouring one or more of their works.

Soapbox

The best disputation of all Cleveland shared with Lysander Spooner. It was within this correspondence between a Constitutional minarchist president and a radical anarchist that we peer through the window to see what was at the heart of the Gilded Age—a debate about just how small to non-existent government ought to be. There is no mention of the state's messianic role of resolving all of the difficulties and tribulations bound up in the human condition. Instead, the two men hammered away at what social and political conditions most accelerated human freedom and flourishing. I was born in the wrong time, I suppose...

Of particular interest and sway were the works of sociologists and economists who denounced what had, for almost all of American history since Alexander Hamilton, been taken as political economic law. Ever since Hamilton did the most British of things and pushed a tariff bill through Congress so as to protect and foster American manufactures, it was taken as a given that tariffs benefited domestic industry. By design, tariffs allowed domestic manufactures to raise prices and yet maintain a decided price advantage over foreign goods entering the U.S. market. That's all to their advantage, is it not?

As a Northern Democrat, mayor of an industrial city and governor of New York, Cleveland had remained supportive-to-agnostic regarding the tariff until about the middle point of his first term as president. However, after reading the theorists of the time and re-examining the efficacy of the tariff himself, he went from doubter to doubting be. That is to say that, Cleveland reversed his position on the tariff and in doing so, risked much of the political support he had won in the North from tariff-fundamentalists. There would be a price for this, and yet out of principle, he in turn advocated for a drawn down then complete elimination of the tariff system. Cleveland did so because, in a very Jeffersonian way, he sincerely doubted the Constitutionality of tariffs given the general welfare clause, and he understood that tariffs were in the end not beneficial but deleterious to the very interests they appeared designed to aid. Finally, there was a substantive issue that divided the parties.

Cleveland concluded that tariff policy and general protectionism harmed the American consumer, laborer, *and* producer. How so? It's quite clear how tariffs harmed consumers: They artificially increased the cost of goods. They hurt the laborer because laborers made up the bulk of consumers and protectionism provided a hindrance for competitors entering the industrial sector. But, how in the holy name of Moses were producers themselves injured by tariffs—the very policies they defended with all of the vigor of rabid self-interest? Using the work of thinkers like William Graham Sumner at Yale, Cleveland argued that tariff policy did not take place in a vacuum. Foreign powers engaged in retributive trade policies by placing tariffs on American goods entering their respective markets. So at the very moment that the United States was rapidly gaining on Great Britain for the title of manufacturer-to-the-world, the federal government was promoting what amounted to neo-mercantilism. Mercantilism=the dumb idea that just won't die, no matter how many times one drives the wooden stake of economic sense through the heart of it. Cleveland advocated for a voluntary, open, and uninhibited global free market which he knew would benefit Americans of every class. He then appealed to the producers themselves: Tariffs raised the prices on goods of all sorts in what we refer to today as the supply chain. From minerals, to steel, to locomotives, to the rails they rode upon; from lumber, to wagons, to the furniture Americans sat upon; from the fields, to the derricks, to the petroleum that engines ran upon—tariffs raised costs on all of the various stages of production. Whatever gross gain industrialists *presumed* they won for themselves through protectionism was lost and exceeded in the net costs that resulted from higher steel costs for the railroads and skyscraper architects; from the higher lumber costs for coopers and carpenters; from higher oil costs for machinists and engineers. Americans were creating untold wealth because of the remarkable division of labor and the specification of the processes of production. What the tariff did was diminish the net return on that by acting as a veiled tax on all of the various levels of production.

That tax led to an actual federal surplus of revenues by 1888. That's right, you read that correctly—*surplus*. Washington took in more than it expended. None of this sat well with Cleveland, not just because he knew tax was a usurpation and a burden on the booming market; in fact, those surplus dollars were denominated in gold and not the fanciful fiat wishes of a central bank. The dollar ensured deflation instead of inflation. That's right; for the government and individuals alike, just sitting on the savings accrued greater value as time progressed. There was no need to engage in gambling and high-risk speculation. Saving was profitable in and of itself. Allocating to capital instead of engaging in immediate consumption increased wealth. Furthermore, because of the strict gold standard, capital and labor did not blindly guess as to the value of stuff, whether it be labor output or common goods and services. Prices were rather stable and if and when they moved, they tended to go down while incomes proceeded upward. I know—it is like an alien world from another dimension for us today.

But just how far was Cleveland willing to stand on the principle of limited government when a significant push arose for intervention when tragedy struck? It is easy to propound laissez-faire minarchism when seas are calm. Not so when, let's say, a natural disaster strikes as it did in Texas in 1886-1887. Drought had wiped out Texas farmers. In response, Congress passed a bill to appropriate $10,000 from the federal treasury to buy seed to help out those disaffected by the drought. What a goodwill gesture; but as a later White House occupant would remark, there is nothing easier than spending other people's money. Cleveland vetoed the bill, asserting:

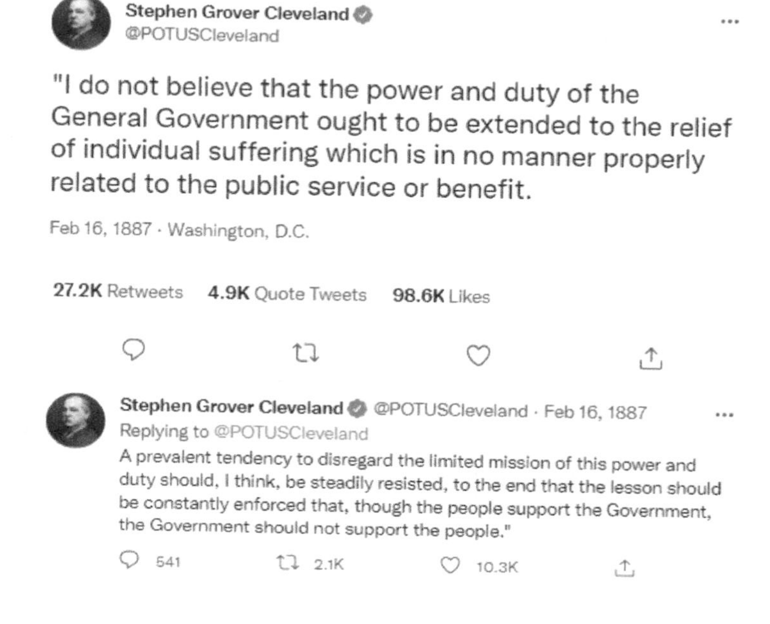

There was no delegated power in the Constitution that empowered the national government to carry out such welfare, no matter how well-intentioned. In addition, Cleveland viewed such measures, regardless of the amount of appropriation, as contravening the true meaning of the general welfare clause. Finally, he rightly concluded that such state action created the moral hazard of crowding out voluntary, private charitable contributions of Americans who would come to the aid of their fellow citizens in need. His assertions proved prescient in this regard when private aid to Texas farmers far exceeded the $10,000 that was on the line.

Today, lazy critiques of laissez-faire and Constitutional political economy amount to strawman arguments that equate free market advocacy with atomistic, agorist theory. Whoa—that sentence requires some explanation. Put another way, libertarianism does not require everyone to go at it alone. What it does deny is any institution's or any individual's ability to transgress upon anyone else's person or property. Cooperation is at the core of economic liberty, but said cooperation cannot be forced, and both the degree to which one enters into free exchange and those with whom he chooses to engage, cannot be determined by anyone except the parties to the arrangement.

Cleveland knew that "leaving people be", *pace* John, Paul, George and Ringo, really were words of wisdom.

The Golden Fruits of Freedom

Burgeoning wealth created immense economic opportunity and new social avenues for groups that are often overlooked by typical historians of the Gilded Age. Women's true liberation came not because of marches and protests of the American Woman Suffrage Association or the Anti-Saloon League. Women exercised independence and agency because they found economic opportunities apart from men in the bubbling economy of the era. Demand arose for women to work in occupations beyond the traditional teaching, nursing and domestic services traditionally allotted to women. They became clerks, shop owners, and managers, especially in the expansionary and diversified American economy. Women's fashion related this change in status attributable to the functioning of a generally free market. Those in the upper classes imported wares from Europe and added their own, often practical flourishes. Gone were the crinoline, wired dresses which were anything but functional at work. Women's clothing instead became more subdued and utilitarian. More and more women attended college to the point in which one out of every five university students was female by 1900. Quite the gains since very few women went to college in 1870.

American painters took note of the changing gender roles. Take a look at John Singer Sargent's painting *Mr. and Mrs. I. N. Phelps Stokes.*

The painting ought to have been titled, *Mrs. I.N. Phelps Stokes and Some Guy (Maybe Mr. Stokes) in the Background.* Here, a strong, confident and vibrant young wife appears ready to engage in some form of newly dignified work. Women's liberation in

America came with capitalism.

That was in the world of the urban bourgeoisie in America, what historian Thaddeus Russell calls the realm of "formal culture". But, what of women in the realms of "informal" or popular culture? It was in "ordinary" or what one might call "profane" America that women truly exercised immense power and shaped culture. And, the greatest of power brokers were the madams of bordellos.

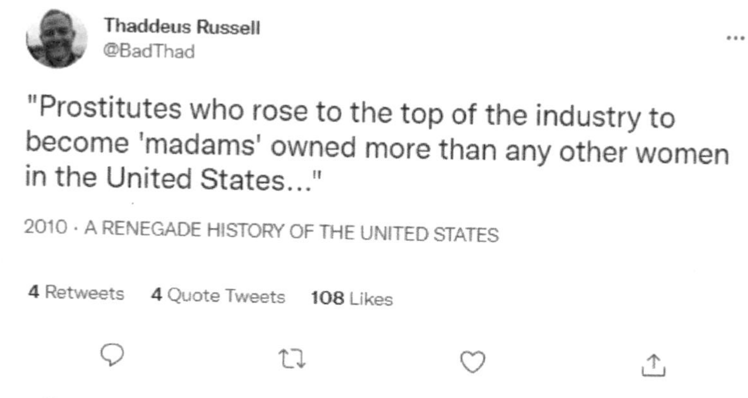

Russell continues:

> Indeed they were among the wealthiest people in the country, especially in the West. "Diamond Jessie" Hayman began work as a prostitute in the gold country of the Sierra Nevada foothills in the 1880s, then moved to San Francisco to become one of the most successful prostitutes in the city's history. Hayman's three-story brothel in the Tenderloin district of San Francisco included three fireplaces, a saloon, a champagne cellar, and fifteen suites filled with imported furniture. She provided each of her employees with a $6000 wardrobe that included a fox fur coat, four tailored suits, eight hats, two dress coats, twelve pairs of shoes, twelve pairs of gloves, seven evening gowns and seven negligees. Hayman earned enough money from her business to buy several parcels of land in the city. After the 1906 earthquake..., Hayman and the other madams provided food and clothing to the thousands left homeless. She died in 1923 with an estate worth $116,000.

Prosperity, really, freely and rightly gained, created conditions by which positive effects or externalities resulted for society. Voluntary and trusted exchange with the attendant division of labor emerged as the boot of government was removed from the neck of a populace that pined for, craved for, and then relished autonomy. This was true for women in the oldest and newest of professions. This was true even for black Americans who established prosperous businesses whether white folks wished to avail themselves of such services or not.

Don't Call It a Comeback; He'd Been There Four Years

By 1888, Grover Cleveland remained generally popular with American voters but deeply hated by the political class in Washington. Republicans in particular were beholden to political entrepreneurs who, despite Cleveland's articulate arguments regarding the myopic nature of tariffs, remained unconvinced. So movers and shakers like Mark Hanna and Matt Quay looked (where else?) to Ohio by way of Indiana to find an empty suit as the GOP nominee in 1888. They found Benjamin Harrison to be pliant enough for their liking. He had name recognition. What they did not fully know was that ol' Ben's presidency would produce as little good as that of his grandfather who served for only a few months as chief executive, William Henry.

Tippecanoe and tariffs too. Though Cleveland beat Harrison in the popular vote in the election, Harrison secured New York and the electoral majority. Once in office, replacing my man, Grover Cleveland, Harrison delivered on the graft. He signed a bill to annex Hawaii. He signed the McKinley Tariff Act into law, which raised tariffs to an incredible 49.5%. He feigned concern about supposed monopolies and virtue-signaled/signed the toothless Sherman Anti-Trust Act. Perhaps worst of all, Harrison buckled to the wants of Republican politicos who pined for the electoral support from farmers and debtors and signed the Sherman Silver Purchase Act in 1890. The Congress under Harrison doled out those Civil War pensions again and spent like, well, the money was not gold anymore. It was dubbed the "Billion Dollar Congress". In doing all of this, Harrison turned Cleveland's surpluses into considerable deficits and set the stage for an economic panic with which his successor—whoever he would be (?!)—would have to deal.

Soapbox

I have often wondered and debated in my head which Sherman brother did the most damage to the country during their earthly sojourns, William or John? William did it primarily with the sword and John with the pen, but both inflicted enormous damage upon the republic. I'm leaning toward John, but I'm willing to be swayed otherwise.

Oh for the days of 1892, and for that matter, 1992, when the best rap song up to that point was still a hit on the radio—LL Cool J's *Mama Said Knock You Out*. Is it reaching to note that this track features the line: "Don't call it a comeback/I been here for years/Rocking my peers/Putting suckas in fear/Making the tears rain down like a monsoon/Listen to the bass go boom/Explosions, overpowering/Over the competition, I'm towering"? I think it is centennial serendipity.

Gary Richied
@garyrichied

2021 · Twitter for American History

4 Retweets **1** Quote Tweet **25** Likes

Unfortunately for Cleveland, he would spend the bulk of his second term cleaning up the economic mess created by Harrison and the Billion Dollar Congress. Their spending had turned Cleveland's old surpluses into deficits, and the monetization of silver (bimetallism) achieved what would be the calling card of the lurking but not yet existent Federal Reserve Bank. Cheap silver, that is, cheap relative to gold, drove out the use of gold as money and pushed people to hoard it. Malinvestment and expansion in the economy took place. Skepticism abounded then about the actual value of the bimetal dollar and foreign investors, mainly from Britain, sold off their holdings in the United States. Fear struck depositors who moved to get their savings out of banks; in turn, major banks across the world, from London to Chicago failed or suspended payment because they had run out of reserves. The corresponding credit crunch halted both the artificial and natural expansion of the economy. Within the course of a year, from June 1892 to June 1893, the total money supply in terms of specie, Treasury paper, national banknotes, and national and state bank deposits, fell by 6.3 percent. Thankfully, Alan Greenspan, Ben Bernanke, Janet Yellen, and Jerome Powell were not around to, like bad magicians, perform their one trick. The powers that be did NOT engage in wild fiscal and monetary policy. They did the opposite. Cleveland and the new Congress allowed prices to clear, the bad investments to go under, and then repealed the Sherman Silver Purchase Act in order to buttress the value of the dollar. Confidence was restored. The banks that survived the panic were incentivized to and then did build up their reserves. And, in the most amazing occurrence of the entire episode, when the U.S. Treasury was on the verge of running out of other people's money to spend, rather than plunging the country into a prolonged depression by increasing taxes, Cleveland accepted a meeting—hat in hand—with J.P. Morgan and August Belmont in 1895. During that rendez-vous, Morgan and Belmont agreed to credit the federal government to the tune of $65 million in gold.

Well, How 'Bout That?

Concurrent with these damaging financial waves, financiers in Chicago were constructing the World's Fair to end all World's Fairs. The 1893 World's Columbian Exposition celebrated the best of the industrialized world's achievements. While Erik Larson's Devil in the White City *(2003) succeeded in reminding moderns of the size, scope, importance and drama of the fair, aside from some passing remarks, more needs to be done on just how the fair was financed. In other words, would Chicago have even won from Congress the ability to host the fair if its big money men like Charles Yerkes, Marshall Field, and Philip Armour did not have access to easy money and credit thanks to bimetallism? Secondly, did the continual expense of the fair at all contribute to the diminishment of bank reserves and the drying up of credit elsewhere? Given the paucity of Chicago newspaper reports on the looming banking and economic crisis, most Chicagoans and Fair visitors from around the world remained as blissfully unaware of the Panic of 1893 just as all too many single female attendees were ignorant of a serial killer targeting them as the Ferris Wheel spun for all those months. It was only at the end of the fair that people grew knowledgeable of both. *Note: I should really get some cut from Larson or something for all of this promotion of his book.*

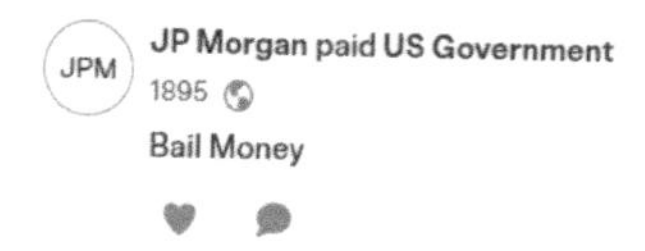

That's right: In 1895, independent businessmen bailed out the federal government, not the other way around. The economy roared from that point on, sound reinvestment ensued, and the value of the dollar jumped in a deflationary environment to reward savers and workers.

Of course, Cleveland and those last Jeffersonian Democrats allied with him were vilified from that point forward, for supposedly becoming the tools of plutocrats and robber barons like Morgan. The charge stuck to such an extent that, at least in the arena of national politics, the next presidential election would put a tariff-loving, crusty Republican (McKinley) against an outright inflation maniac, Populist-Democrat William Jennings Bryan.

Dear Grover deserved much better. I know there's some space left on Mount Rushmore; or better, just get Lincoln and Roosevelt off of there altogether. Plenty of space then.

Race and the Race for Empire

Social Darwinism was the dominant social and cultural ideology of the Gilded Age. The aforementioned World's Fair of 1893 in Chicago itself affirmed the notion that various ethnicities and racial groups were more biologically fit than others to survive and thrive in the modern, industrial world. Western nations, with their engines of production, gained the center stage. Of great and foreboding inclusion was the German Empire's choice to include a Krupp Company cannon as part of its national pavilion. When fired out to Lake Michigan, the reverberation from the largest artillery piece ever assembled was said to shake and damage neighboring buildings and blow out windows at great distances. The arms race was on but so too was the race for empire. Meanwhile, black Americans were barred from entrance into most of the fair attractions, that is, outside of the Midway wherein a Dahomey Village, a Street in Cairo, and a Pygmy exhibit displayed those respective peoples in their native environments in what amounted to a human zoo.

The same German state busied itself with obtaining and developing colonies in Africa and the Pacific; what with the numerous and sundry similarities—historical, cultural and linguistic —that people in Frankfort shared with the Herero tribe in South-West Africa or the Samoans in the South Pacific. I hope by now you can detect biting sarcasm emanating from your author. From the American perspective, given social Darwinism, it appeared understandable if not totally acceptable that European powers like Germany, Britain,

France and Russia had been able to assemble massive and diverse empires, but come on, sparrow fart countries like Portugal and Belgium (!) had them as well. Belgium! Belgium didn't even exist as a state until 1830, and despite its size and youth, its king was nonetheless tasked with "civilizing" (translated from the Flemish, "civilizing" means "to murder, rape, and plunder") the Congo.

American schemers and politicians viewed Manifest Destiny and the dissolving of the frontier as a sure sign that the superiority of "American civilization" proved the need for the United States to enter into the overseas imperial contest. After all, not doing so would seem to limit the global impact of spreading ideas like the deified "democracy". At the very least, inaction would render the United States a minor player in the world. If only Europeans had been more impressed by the rampant and wanton genocide and destruction that Americans wrought in North America against Indian populations!

What I am getting at here is that American dispositions to race and empire at home and abroad differed little. In both settings, a narrative formed with its own terms borrowed from across the Atlantic: the American intelligentsia, political class and media establishment really bought into the ideas of engaging in civilizing missions, humanitarian efforts, and the white man's burden. Take out Rudyard Kipling, and the warped justifications for perpetual American empire today remain the same.

After the Civil War and for well into the 20th century, the federal government waged outright war against non-compliant tribes in the West. The unrelenting waves of white settlement in the West convinced the still independent tribes that war was the only means of resistance. At the same time, American Indian attacks against settlers and recalcitrance at resettlement upon reservations appeared to justify U.S. Army responses, no matter how disproportionate. U.S. Army raids led to George Custer's demise at Little Big Horn in 1876. At Wounded Knee in 1890, the U.S. Army mowed down about 300 Indian men, women and children after a deaf man refused to surrender his gun to U.S. authorities. It is unknown if Black Coyote (the deaf man) had ever read or even heard of the Constitution or the Second Amendment. However, it is likely that he had rightly concluded that laws written on paper are only as good as the will of a citizenry to force the government to uphold them. He simply resisted because the soldiers were transgressing against his natural right to hold property and the concomitant right to defend himself. The campaigns against the Sioux, Pawnee, Cheyenne, Apache and numerous other tribes amounted to the 19th-century version of 20th-century blowback. I wonder how Ron Paul would have fared against McKinley et al.

There's an old story from the absolutist days of French history that is quite relevant. At the low ebb of Protestantism in 17th century France, at a point in which Huguenots comprised less than 4 percent of the population and had been relegated to the status of second or third class citizens in mostly impoverished hamlets along the southwestern coast of France, Louis XIV issued the Edict of Fontainebleau which revoked his predecessor's Edict of Nantes. Francis I had granted Protestants limited freedom to worship at Nantes; at

Fontainebleau, Louis XIV called upon the forces of his state to openly suppress and persecute the tiny Huguenot minority. Why? Louis XIV knew the Huguenots were of no threat to him. But, reasoned Louis XIV, their very existence in his realm, a realm wherein his univocal authority was to be felt in every inch of France upon which sunlight fell, such tolerance of a dissident minority betrayed the very notion of absolutism. Even passive civil disobedience was anathema to absolutism.

Passive, voluntary disassociation with American civilization and democracy by Native Americans, Blacks, the Irish, Jews, Catholics, and Mormons in North America and eventually Hawaiians, Cubans, Dominicans, Filipinos and Puerto Ricans abroad proved more intolerable to the American state and formal culture than any minority to a French king. After all, the French king and Ancien Régime were backward and arcane. American democracy was refined and enlightened. Enlightened. Why would anyone not submit given the superiority of American civilization and institutions? Changing allegiances and identities required first bayonets and then gunboats. *C'est la vie impériale, n'est pas*?

Imperial life was something to which the South had, sadly, grown accustomed. But, Southerners white and black had lived and operated under the yokes of tariffs and disinvestment for decades postbellum. For blacks in the Gilded Age, the second civil rights movement in American history (the first was Reconstruction) took hold with two prominent, albeit very different leaders and with divergent visions for black liberation.

Booker T. Washington was born a Virginia slave in 1856. At the age of 25, he founded Tuskegee Institute in Alabama in order to educate blacks mainly in vocational trades. Students learned advanced techniques in carpentry, masonry, and printing, among other disciplines. The school's ostensible mission was an extension of Washington's practicality; blacks were to continue to advance in occupations and markets already afforded to them. Washington did not hold that segregated or predominantly black areas of economic activity required white support, influence or activity. Should acceptance of blacks in greater and predominant white society occur, it would occur due to the prosperity generated in the black community. With prosperity, it could be shown that blacks could function and contribute to greater American society. In the end, whites would provide investment capital and support to black institutions.

It should be noted that—for the most part—the nuanced and historically accurate description of Washington's philosophies and approaches to civil rights is not expressed nor evaluated in the general media of history education. Not in standard textbooks. Not in documentaries shown by lazy and ill-informed teachers. Instead, what tends to be overly emphasized is Washington's approach to black rights vis-a-vis whites, labeled *post hoc* as "accommodation". It should be emphasized that Booker T. Washington himself *never* used this word to characterize his work and approach. But, because his more gradualist, pragmatic approach is often contrasted with the more radical, integrationist, and ultimately socialistic take of W.E.B. DuBois, Booker T. Washington is cast as something of an Uncle Tom from this era.

Washington outlined his course of action—what later opponents would determine as inaction—in his famous address at the Cotton States and International Exposition in Atlanta, Georgia, on September 18, 1895. Again, only after the fact was the speech dubbed the "Atlanta Compromise". He appealed to blacks in the most quoted line of the speech:

That is to say, in whatever circumstance you may find yourself, do not dream of lofty, unrealistic goals, like studying esoteric philosophy at Oxford or Berlin—instead, increase your skills and human capital in the industries and occupations readily available. Improve your lot where you are, and gradually the civil rights restrictions and violations imposed upon black communities would be eliminated.

In May 1896, the Supreme Court of the United States decided the *Plessy v. Ferguson* case. The majority decision established the judicial precedent of "separate but equal". So long as a state provided equal accommodations, public institutions could be legally segregated. The court found no power provided to the national government in the Constitution to impose integration of the races only, per the Fourteenth Amendment, to ensure equal protection under the law to people regardless of race. It was an odd and rare case of judicial restraint and agnosticism on social Darwinism, and that fact, in reality, is why the decision is regarded today as so evil. To some extent then, the Plessy case reinforced the Washington approach to civil rights. Since integration would not be legally enforced, blacks would continue to build up their own institutions and prosper in a parallel society, one that could operate unencumbered by the racist limitations, Puritanical mores, and predominantly white institutions of the era, especially government.

Soapbox

The genesis of the case is of great interest here: In 1890, the State of Louisiana passed the Separate Car Act which required railroad companies to provide separate accommodations for whites and blacks. For economic reasons, the very railroad upon which eventual plaintiff Homer Plessy rode to spark the case/protest had earlier petitioned against the law because it required more cars on their trains and thus more compulsory, inefficient expense. Plessy refused to leave the designated white-only car in New Orleans, was arrested, and a trial ensued that through the appeals process would ultimately land in front of the nine robes in Washington. In that decision, the Fuller Court ruled in a 7-1 decision that while the "equal protection under the law" clause in the Fourteenth Amendment provided legal equality to blacks, the federal government possessed no power to create or impose actual, social equality. In areas of public accommodation, so long as there were equal spaces provided for black people, the individual states of the Union could legislate as it pertained to the social reality of segregation. "The [plaintiff's] argument also assumes that social prejudices may be overcome by legislation, and that equal rights cannot be secured to the negro except by an enforced commingling of the two races. We cannot accept this proposition. If the two races are to meet upon terms of social equality, it must be the result of natural affinities, a mutual appreciation of each other's merits, and a voluntary consent of individuals." Note: The Court was right! The right to assemble entails the right to exclude, or better discriminate in today's parlance. Power to legislate as to the localized application of that right in public spaces redounds to the states per the Tenth Amendment. No one thought about whether integration could be imposed upon purely private institutions. Note take two: All of this complicated mess was totally avoidable in my ideal Ancapistan (the Anarcho-Capitalist Utopia). In such a world, there would be no state government coercing a transportation company to segregate its seating. The company would simply respond to the true democracy of market forces and like the East Louisiana Railroad Company wanted back in 1890, not racially segregate. Problem solved. There would not be a perceived further need for a distant, centralized government to impose another injustice in order to attempt (poorly and authoritatively) to remedy the first. But, let's entertain the possibility that in Ancapistan racial segregation became widespread because for whatever reason there was a high concentration of racist assholes living in one area. Such an injustice would be easily resolved through the process of competition, either at the level of another railroad company entering the market, or by the existence of neighboring communities that were much more prosperous thanks in large part to not being majority racist assholes. The oppressed racial group could get up and relocate—probably not comfortably by train however...

W.E.B. DuBois was born into a well-heeled, established, mixed-race family in Great Barrington, Massachusetts in 1868. He attended college. He studied abroad at the University of Berlin. He returned to Harvard and earned his doctorate in history. He was the first black to do so.

DuBois was, early on, a supporter of Booker T. Washington. As time passed and after the Plessy decision, DuBois became increasingly convinced that Washington's approach ceded too much ground. In other words, from DuBois's perspective, blacks should not relegate themselves to vocational education and training when white colleges could afford a classical, liberal arts education to capable blacks. For DuBois, integration was not limiting or prohibitive to black economic and social advancement—it was a necessity. Gradualism would not do. It truly was accommodating to white supremacy. The faster segregation in all forms could be crushed and even forced integration ensue, the faster blacks would have a larger share in the prosperity being generated in the United States at the time.

The two means by which DuBois wished to achieve integration and equality for blacks were through the media and the courts. Both would accelerate the process. In 1905, he purchased a printing press and published the *Moon Illustrated Weekly*. The journal disseminated the opinion pieces of black intellectuals, who like DuBois, belonged to the Niagara Movement opposed to the accommodationist approach. Several other publications followed. In August 1906, at Harper's Ferry on the 100th Anniversary of John Brown's birth, DuBois proclaimed at the Second Niagara Conference:

"Today, two classes of Negroes...are standing at the parting of the ways. The one counsels patient submission to our present humiliations and degradations; ...The other class believe that it should not submit to being humiliated, degraded, and remanded to an inferior place. ...[I]t does not believe in bartering its manhood for the sake of gain."

Aug 15, 1906 · Twitter for American History

273 Retweets **24** Quote Tweets **989** Likes

No more turning the other way while segregation continued to impoverish blacks. No more of the spirit of permissiveness to lynchings, so long as whites would feel compelled to give handouts to blacks. No more of this wretched apartheid.

The press, eventually through DuBois's magazine *The Crisis*, represented the persuasive arm of the Niagara Movement. Meanwhile, the National Association for the Advancement of Colored People (NAACP) engaged in legal battles to rapidly advance the cause of integration. Both black and white, the main members of the NAACP were DuBois disciples and lawyers who collaborated to end racial lynchings and break down barriers for blacks in education and employment. Blacks were to obtain real civil rights and equality in an immediate fashion. The time for gentle persuasion was over.

Soapbox

Admirable, justified and necessary radicalism for the time. However, before we go canonizing W.E.B. DuBois as the moral leader and hero of the period, it needs to be emphasized that DuBois was no man of the people. He was an early, fervent, and later unapologetic supporter of eugenics. He openly advocated for the weaning out of genetic flaws and deficiencies, especially from the black community. He pushed for abortion and sterilization, and later lauded the Bolshevik government in the Soviet Union for its efficiencies and success in maximizing the production of workers. An early Soviet dupe of whom Walter Duranty might be proud.

Both approaches—those of Washington and DuBois—ended up falling short, particularly by the end of Booker T. Washington's life in 1915, of achieving the desired ends of obtaining for blacks the attendant and expected outcomes of the 13th, 14th and 15th Amendments. Blacks were widely considered naturally inferior to whites, throughout the country, not just in the South. Blacks habitually had basic civil liberties negated; government officials at all levels, federal, state and local actively negated these rights. The Armed Forces would be resegregated by Woodrow Wilson. Blacks were all but entirely shut out of government jobs. Unions, with state sanction and support, locked out blacks from jobs in trades. All of these shortcomings would highlight the need for a third civil rights movement to come in the 1950s and 1960s.

Perhaps the most important takeaway here is how under the leadership of Martin Luther King, Jr. and others, that third major civil rights movement of the 1950s and 1960s successfully incorporated and skillfully deployed the approaches and tactics of both Booker T. Washington and W.E.B. DuBois. In retrospect, in examining King's work, when an audience appeared more receptive to an "accommodationist" message—he served that up. When an audience needed to be encouraged, awakened, or goaded into action, the verbiage of DuBois was deployed.

Back to the West and far beyond for a moment. The educated and political classes maintained a disposition toward Indians remarkably similar to their disposition toward blacks. The preference was for the minority races to live in separate, parallel societies. To the extent that there might be interaction with the dominant civilization, appointed externs among the Indians and blacks conducted affairs. Those externs needed to be made white. Whatever smacked to whites to be the residual effects of Indian or black culture—those features needed to be eradicated.

Take the example of the Carlisle School for Indians in Pennsylvania. The motto of the government school came from its founder:

This message was at the core of Manifest Destiny fueled imperialism. There was no possibility of bringing civilization to savages without violence, but the ends justified the means. And, the ends were glorious and salvific. Imperialism is humanitarian, don't you know?

Attached to that humanitarian impulse and justification were commercial interests. It should not come as a surprise to anyone that while the North American frontier was disappearing, American industrialists looked beyond it to do as British industrialists had done before them. Production of durable goods, from McCormick reapers to Schwinn bicycles required newer and larger markets in which to sell them and everything in between. Now, the peaceful and altogether just way in which to open up foreign markets to American goods was to have private, corporate envoys go abroad, engage in voluntary contractual exchange, secure shipping rights and port access, and then proceed with global trade. But, let's face it: That takes a long time, requires negotiation, currency valuation, learning languages and customs—the whole process consumes a lot of energy and effort. Ockham's razors then were the bayonet and the gunboat: Why not do as political entrepreneurs in Britain and France had done for ages? Get the Congress and White House to deploy the military to "secure American interests", which always meant and still means creating a monopoly on trade within some foreign territory. Best to have an unwanted contingent of

American merchants and traders in the country beforehand, as was the case in Hawaii. In an amazing twist there, due to the McKinley Tariff Act (1890), white American sugar growers were being undersold because the tariff was assessed on their product when it arrived on the West Coast. So, in 1893, said growers staged a coup against Hawaiian Queen Liliuokalani and inserted themselves as the de facto government. Old Glory was raised over Honolulu, and the Americans in the old Sandwich Islands pined for American annexation and tariff parity. It would have to wait. Grover Cleveland had just taken the helm in D.C. Cleveland—along with his other prudential and sagacious positions—was a staunch anti-imperialist. In spite of vocal calls to annex Hawaii, Cleveland rebuked the growers and attempted to reinstall Lilioukalani as queen. Hawaii would be annexed under *President* McKinley just five years later. So, McKinley's legislation created conditions for the takeover of a distant, overseas nation, and once he was in position to do so, he did what his industrial and commercial benefactors desired. Quite the system. If it wasn't part of common parlance to call it government, we would rightly identify it as organized crime.

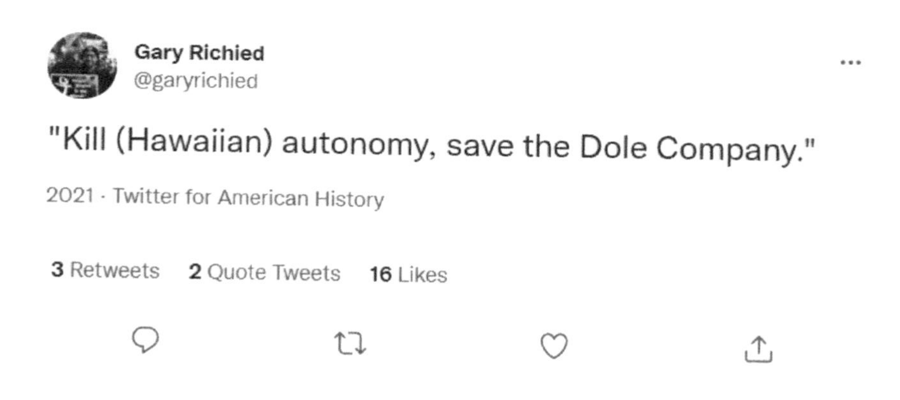

Of course, it did not stop with Hawaii. William Jennings Bryan and his new Populist-Democratic Party knew it would not stop with Hawaii.

By 1896, the Democratic Party had undergone a metamorphosis. Out of favor were Cleveland and his Jeffersonian Democrats and in was William Jennings Bryan, with his fiery Christian oratory and an equally fiery rhetoric condemning the wealth brokers in American society. When he accepted the nomination for the presidency in Chicago in 1896, he articulated his worldview in his famous "Cross of Gold" speech:

Powerful stuff. The speech cast the capital class and the political class as Pontius Pilate and the workers of the country and even world as Jesus Christ Himself. Gold was the weapon of the workers' passion, the attribute of their collective martyrdom. So long as the U.S. Treasury insisted upon a strict gold standard for the dollar and in turn refused to inspire inflation, the laborers of the country would be oppressed. Recall why Bryan advocated for bimetallism: By introducing silver for redemption for the dollar, the value of all dollars would be lessened, just as had happened in previous instances in American history. Inflation provided relief for debtors, especially those debtors whose livelihoods seemed to require debt financing, such as farming. Agriculture is a very seasonal economic sector. Most of a given year is dedicated to production with the expenses of seeding, cultivation, and harvest. It is only after the last of those phases that farmers see what they hope to be a windfall of revenue to be devoted to the payment of previous costs and then some extra. If inflation increased, the nominal dollar amounts would be repaid to banks and financiers, but the actual value of those dollars would be much less. Again, debtors LOVE inflation; creditors HATE inflation.

Along with bimetallism, the Democratic-Populists espoused a number of other positions. Populism and nativism went hand-in-hand in the era; immigrants were thought to drive down the price of labor, so Bryan and his party argued for strict immigration controls. They railed against imperial designs overseas—again, for largely nativist reasons. Populists called for the direct election of U.S. Senators, a graduated national income tax, and government ownership of railroads and communications companies.

Well, How 'Bout That?

It is really amazing to see how the Populists' platform was absorbed into the Democratic Party's platform in such short order and so completely that within a decade or so, the progressives among the Democrats succeeded in owning the old Party of Jackson. Through skillfully espousing established, Democratic positions and those of the radical Populists, Progressive Democrats codified all of the aims of the Populists except their anti-imperialism, which for Progressives, represented a non-negotiable. Remaking the United States was never enough; their ideas and programs were universally applicable and effective in their minds. Stay tuned to when the Populists and Progressives run afoul of one another, and William Jennings Bryan sees the light in 1915.

Bryan lost in the first of several presidential bids. He would go on to lose in 1900 (against incumbent President William McKinley again) and in 1908 as well. Like Henry Clay, he was always the bridesmaid, never the bride. Despite the electoral losses, the appeal of Bryan's famous whistle-stop campaigning and fiery populist rhetoric would grow to a crescendo in the Progressive era.

What Populist-Democratic electoral losses guaranteed were more aggressive and expansionist foreign policy initiatives. The simultaneous and further crumbling of the global Spanish empire proved too alluring for aspiring imperialists in Washington, even if their President McKinley dragged his feet on the matters. McKinley understood that empire meant war. McKinley—as the last of the Civil War veterans to become president—understood that William Tecumseh Sherman was right: War is all hell. But was it a hell through which yellow press magnates like William Randolph Hearst and Joseph Pulitzer, and was it a hell through which politicos Theodore Roosevelt and Henry Cabot Lodge were willing to put other people and their sons? Certainly.

Theodore Imperator

About that Theodore Roosevelt. It is wise to spend extended space here to study the biography of Theodore Roosevelt because he is such a transformational figure in American history. Whereas the McKinley presidency served as a bridge between the one shore of the 19th century Gilded Age and the Progressive Era of the 20th, Theodore

Roosevelt raced from the old era into the new and then blew the bridge to kingdom come in order to ensure that the United States would never retreat back.

Theodore Roosevelt Jr. was born in Manhattan in 1858. He was a weak and asthmatic boy who fondly recalled the late night carriage rides his grandfather and father took him on in order for Teddy to breathe more easily in the less fetid air of a slumbering city that supposedly never slept. The tens of thousands of horses in the city did indeed sleep, so the enormous piles of manure did not grow as quickly. The Roosevelts were extremely affluent. Teddy was able to accompany the family on trips to Europe and Egypt. When he was hiking in the Alps, he realized that his respiratory health seemed to improve the more he exercised. He would later claim that he was able to whip asthma simply through physical exertion and personal determination.

When he was not on journeys across the Atlantic, young Theodore busied himself with capturing and killing animals in order to study their anatomy and physiology. Modern psychologists identify this as a common trait among psychopaths and serial killers. In fact, detectives discovered in 1896 that juvenile animal killing was a known pastime of a young H.H. Holmes, the serial killer who victimized so many in Chicago in and around the World's Fair in Chicago in 1893. Roosevelt himself took in the fair in 1893 and walked away further convinced of American grandeur.

Roosevelt had a whirlwind of an adult life. He graduated from Harvard and attended Columbia Law School for a time. He served as a New York State Assemblyman. After the tragic death of his mother and first wife (on the same day no less), he headed out to Dakota Territory and tried his hand as a cattle rancher. He soon returned to New York, worked for the Civil Service Commission, and later became the city's Police Commissioner. He was the epitome of a micro-manager in both positions; and in the climate of rampant organized crime and commensurate graft, maybe he was just what was needed at the time. The *New York Sun* called him "irrepressible, belligerent, and enthusiastic".

He did seem to possess limitless energy. While occupied with these various and sundry public offices, he found time to read, voraciously. One of his favorites happened to be one of the favorites of the imperialists of the period—Alfred T. Mahan's *The Influence of Sea Power Upon History*. TR was something of an accomplished naval historian himself, and Mahan's work supported Roosevelt's long running thesis. Great civilizations, they held, all had one thing in common: A powerful and prodigious navy. And, if the United States was to take her rightful place as the greatest power among the nations, she too would have to build a great fleet in order to, of course, defend a great empire.

When McKinley defeated Bryan in the 1896 election, to the surprise of some, Roosevelt accepted the position of Undersecretary of the Navy. It was something of a demotion. Republican elites and power brokers were already weary of this New York climber and firebrand. At the same time, Roosevelt saw it as an immense opportunity. The actual Secretary of the Navy, John D. Long, was not a very active, hands-on bureaucrat, and that afforded Roosevelt a great deal of room to openly advocate for war with Spain and run the office himself. Whatever you think of Roosevelt—and I happen to loathe the man—he certainly was idealistic and opportunistic.

As history would have it then, after years of the yellow press pining for war, with the Cuban *insurrectos* against the Spanish being compared to George Washington and John Hancock, and with the sinking albeit probably planned combustion of the U.S.S. Maine in Havana harbor in February 1898, war fever swept the country. Roosevelt was in a paradoxically focused delirium. For weeks before McKinley asked Congress for a declaration of war against Spain, and while McKinley worked toward a diplomatic solution, without Long or McKinley's knowledge or consent, Roosevelt was telegraphing the Pacific fleet commander, Commodore George Dewey, to get ready to attack the Spanish navy in Manilla. That's right: The Undersecretary of the Navy had inserted himself as commander-in-chief in his own right. For TR, despite all of his education and scholarship, leaders needed to act decisively. There was a brief moment for thought, but when that short time passed, he was all action.

Teddy (I like calling him that since he hated the moniker) planned and then hastened the execution of his "splendid little war". In hindsight, it is still a marvel that for all of the stated reasons to go to war with Spain—freedom for Cuba, human rights, and all that jazz—the first military action in the war was in the Philippines. Dewey's fleet destroyed the mostly wooden ships of the Spanish navy in the Pacific just a week after the U.S. declaration of war. Boy, Manilla sure is far from Havana; even further from Santiago or any other Cuban point of interest. The primacy of the Philippine theater demonstrates what was and is rather self-evident: Justifications for the war represented just platitudes and excuses for the United States to seize what remained of the 19th century's version of the sick man of Europe.

Teddy quickly resigned as Undersecretary of the Navy—his job was done. He rushed off to Tampa, the departure point for the U.S. invasion of Cuba. He formed the famous Rough Riders, ensured that he would be one of the first in Cuba but then last in battle, glorified his participation in the American capture of San Juan Hill, and ensured that the propaganda rendered him a war hero. After all, he lacked only one thing on his resumé for the presidency—military hero, vanquisher of the unwashed Gauls/Spanish. Caesar himself would have blushed.

The Spanish sued for peace, and hostilities ended on August 12, 1898. Spain ceded Guam and Puerto Rico to the United States. Cuba gained its pseudo-independence. The fate of the Philippines would be decided in the subsequent Treaty of Paris.

This left time for an open, public debate on the notion of American imperialism. Should the United States enter full bore into the imperial contest and colonize a place and subjugate a people like the Philippines and the Filipinos with whom Americans had no historical or cultural ties? If the United States did not, would Germany or another imperial power step in? Were the Filipinos naturally fit for self-governance?

The Anti-Imperialists were a motley crew of strange bedfellows. They included in their ranks steel magnate Andrew Carnegie, labor union stalwart Samuel Gompers, literary giant Mark Twain, muckraker Jane Addams, and Massachusetts senior Senator George Frisbee Hoar. That has to be the best non-nicknamed figure in American history. He sounds like a 1970s, not 1870s hippie who refused to share the preferred flying disk of the era. In any case, he often found himself on the right side of issues, and this was certainly no exception. Hoar's opposition to the annexation or colonization of the Philippines was all the more significant because Massachusetts junior senator, Henry Cabot Lodge, was the BFF of Roosevelt and a strident imperialist.

To be sure, the anti-imperial movement united the diverse crew above thanks to a variety of divergent, respective reasons. Some thought it unconstitutional since there was no discussion of Filipinos ever gaining parity with U.S. citizens through eventual statehood. Others argued on the principle that it was ahistorical and unbecoming of the United States, having once thrown off the yoke of imperial rule to become a coercive empire in her own right. In addition, would not the United States become simply a new Spain to the Filipinos, natives who just months before, allied with American soldiers to liberate the archipelago? There were less altruistic reasons as well. Some anti-imperialists roused nativist sentiment and framed colonization as resulting in an influx of "inferior" peoples to the United States. Gompers and other labor leaders feared the possible or probable flood of cheap laborers to the United States, laborers who would drive down the general price of labor to the detriment of union workers. Gompers's otherwise existential foe, Andrew Carnegie, even offered to buy the Philippines to no avail:

Still, McKinley saw no other alternative than annexation of the Philippines as a United States territory, and he threw his political weight behind ratification of the Treaty of Paris in the Senate. By the slimmest of margins (57-27 for, ⅔'s vote was needed to ratify), the Senate approved the bill.

Seeing that the Americans were no longer liberators but occupiers, Filipine patriots under Emilio Aguinaldo went to war again—this time against the Americans. They utilized the same guerrilla tactics that had proven so successful against the Spanish. And, just as the U.S. Army had engaged in heinous practices to subdue Native Americans at home, so too Filipine combatants and innocents alike suffered under the brutal hand of American occupation. In a tragically ironic twist, American forces under butchers like Arthur McArthur (terrible name and yes, Douglas's daddy) routinely tortured captured natives and ushered any suspected insurrectionists into concentration camps that eerily resembled those that the Spanish had established for the Cuban freedom fighters at the start of this whole mess.

So much for the pacification and civilizing of the "half-devil and half-child" as Kipling called the Filipinos. Andrew Carnegie was having none of it:

If only it had stopped there. Before the Philippine-American War concluded in mid-1902, over 4,200 American soldiers had died. Some 20-30,000 Filipino combatants lay dead. Ten times that number of Philippine civilians were killed, either through being directly targeted in combat or by the dysentery and cholera epidemics that ravaged the concentration camps and impoverished cities and countryside due to war.

Theodore Roosevelt was there—certainly not in the Philippines—but back in the halls of government, applauding it all. While occupying the governor's mansion in Albany and then as Vice-President under McKinley, American corpses returning home and Filipino corpses in mass graves left him undeterred. In point of fact, the insurrection seems to have emboldened Roosevelt all the more to support American imperialism. The savages' savagery indicated their desperate need for American enlightenment and civilization. All the more important then, from Teddy's point of view, was the mission to perfect American domestic life and rid it of the perceived evils of the day. That is to say, through hard work and principled exertion, Roosevelt believed that government ought to function as the mechanism by which America's "asthmas" would be resolved.

Teddy long believed that for the duration of most of his life, government had ceded too much ground, too much authority to private interests and private markets. There was for Teddy an inordinate imbalance, even a mutated antagonism, between, for example, homesteader entrepreneurs and the environment, especially in the West. The federal government—with superior leadership of course—could and ought to serve as an arbiter and referee in such matters. As to capital and labor, well, gone was the presumption that a free market provided opportunities for mutual, beneficial exchange in hiring and employment. No. Laborers were being exploited, and the federal government possessed the means and responsibility to regulate such dealings. Sure, that arcane document of the Constitution made no mention of any of these positive authorities being held by any of the branches of government, but that was precisely what made it so arcane. What America needed was what Teddy would call a "square deal", and by God or some other power—including his own sheer will—TR was to provide it.

On September 6, 1901, Leon Czolgolz, a disaffected anarchist shot President McKinley in the stomach while the President was greeting visitors to the Pan-American Exhibition in Buffalo, New York. Emma Goldman was one of the few anarchists even to defend the act. The Vice-President happened to be in upstate New York as well, vacationing in the Adirondacks. When he was alerted that McKinley had been shot, he boarded a train for Buffalo. McKinley died nine days later, and TR assumed the presidency.

Well, How 'Bout That?

Even fellow anarchists made the previously popular Goldman into an absolute pariah, to such an extent that she took on a pseudonym and retired (for a time) from public life. In other words, there was a concerted effort to destroy Goldman's public persona as much as there was to destroy Czolgolz himself. He was hastily tried, received an inadequate defense, was convicted, and then after his electrocution, acid was poured onto his body in a sadist act by his jailers. H.H. Holmes's body received more dignity. Perhaps the first commandment of the American state oligarchy: Thou shalt never attack the idols we place before thee.

Soapbox

That train ride from the Adirondacks has become something of folklore. Roosevelt biographer/hagiographer Edmund Morris (Theodore Rex, 2001) used the occasion to imagine in the most graphic of terms, what TR must have been thinking on his descent to Buffalo. To be sure (?), he peered out his train car window and encountered the coal smoke stacks and devastated forests. He gandered upon coal miners, working as hired slaves of mining conglomerates, besoot with blackened cheeks and lungs. And, he aimed to do something about all of it. Because that was all that was needed—a strong man to do something about it. If only the problems were all at the apparent, surface level. If only the human condition were so easily and simply remedied.

For all of his education, for all of his self-identification as a man of letters, for all of the clear thrills he received from campaigning on the back of trains, TR was not fond of negotiation or persuasion. He was a man of action and force. He viewed the Constitution as an impediment to progress, a kind of elastic cookbook for government which offered a basic recipe for the nation, one with which he needed to tinker. Modern times, modern empires required expedient and transformative moves, not horse-trading in Congress or subtle, gentlemanly diplomacy. America did not ask for the imperial presidency, but with McKinley dead and Theodore Rex at the helm, that is precisely what they got. Executive power has only continued to grow ever since.

The Big Scepter

The Roosevelt regime was one in constant motion. Roosevelt would not have had it any other way, and never was there an admission that his administration could not juggle transforming American foreign and domestic policy at the same time. We mortal historians, however, do prefer categories, so permit me to assess foreign matters first.

During the Spanish-American War, in 1898, the U.S.S. Oregon took several weeks to steam from the Pacific, around the southern tip of South America so as to engage the Spanish in the Caribbean theater. By the time it finally arrived, hostilities with the Spanish were already winding down. For Roosevelt, this just would not do.

For decades, Roosevelt had advocated for an isthmian canal, and there was no time like the present to make it a reality. No stranger to cooking up a war in place of negotiations and peace, TR consequently signed a treaty with the British to give the United States a free hand in digging and owning a canal. When Columbia drove a hard bargain with the American regime to dig in its province of Panama, Roosevelt inspired a Panamanian war for independence, intercepted the Columbian navy with a presciently than serendipitously located U.S. squadron, installed the French director of the previous canal company as the first foreign minister of Panama, signed a treaty with that French director/foreign minister which granted the canal zone to the United States, and ordered the canal to be dug beginning in 1904. All in a few years work: TR reveled in the feat and the means by which it came to fruition:

Well, How 'Bout That?

That French director and eventual foreign minister of Panama was a type *known as Philippe Bunau-Varilla. Fascinating life in that he slipped, maneuvered, inserted and lobbied his way into windfalls of private and public largesse. He was an international political entrepreneur, who had an eye for opportunity (public larceny) and an equally keen sense of who he needed to hire to get the job done. When a Congressional debate ensued about whether Nicaragua or Bunau-Varilla's Panama site should be chosen for the canal, Bunau-Varilla hired Roosevelt crony William Nelson Cromwell to lobby Congress. Senators and Representatives received generous "encouragements" and even stamps featuring an active volcano in Nicaragua. Congress—due in large part to these inducements—voted to pursue the Panama option as a result. For his work and success, Bunau-Varilla arranged to pay Cromwell an unheard of sum of $2.8 million or around $80 million today.*

"I took the Canal Zone and let Congress debate, and while the debate goes on the Canal does too."

Mar 23, 1911 · Berkeley, CA

1.1K Retweets **208** Quote Tweets **3,867** Likes

After winning the election of 1904, Roosevelt just could not help himself but to jaunt off to Panama to help in the process:

Emperors of the world's emerging powers rarely stop at meddling just in their own continent. Why stop there?

In response to constant and numerous instances in which Central and South American republics defaulted on European creditor loans, Roosevelt announced his Corollary to the Monroe Doctrine to deal with the typical European response which consisted of blockades and an occasional firebombing from the sea. From 1903 onward, the United States would intervene to ensure that German, British and Italian gunboats no longer appeared in Caracas harbor (as they did that year) or any other Latin American port. United States bureaucrats would manage the necessary payments to European financiers from the coffers of caudillos. It is difficult, save outright colonization, to envision a more paternalistic and social Darwinistic policy. Such interference and impingement on the sovereignty of these nations would inspire anti-Yankee sentiment that lives to this day in Central and South America, as well as the Caribbean.

No nook or cranny of the world could be hidden from old TR's scope.

From the beginning of 1904, Russia and Japan waged war against each other as the two nations contended for Pacific territories as well as commercial dominance over parts of northern China. Roosevelt offered to mediate the end of the war, a conflict that, to the surprise of many observers, saw the lightweight Japan whip the heavyweight Russia in successive battles. The war was so unpopular back in St. Petersburg that massive protests almost culminated in the removal of the czar and did crescendo into the famous Bloody

Sunday massacre in 1905. At the same time, Japan, a resource and fossil fuel-starved power, felt the economic drag of modern warfare. Both powers were war-weary by the autumn of 1905, but Japan appeared victorious. It was the Japanese who therefore left the negotiations resulting in the Treaty of Portsmouth with a sense of disappointed resignation. Despite the fact that Japan had gained a clear upper hand in the war, Roosevelt fashioned and supported a ceasefire that resembled more of a stalemate.

Back in Japan, news of the disproportionate concessions to Russia in the treaty moved masses of citizens there to protest, then riot, then engage in widespread arson in what is referred to today as the Hibiya incendiary incidents. Over two days, various parts of Tokyo burned. Rioters especially targeted individuals and buildings associated with the foreign ministry, Russian Orthodox Church, and American missionaries. The proud Japanese people had suffered hardship for the better part of two years, not to mention tens of thousands of Japanese casualties for little in return.

To say Roosevelt's mechanizations were accidental, or to claim this move speaks of Roosevelt's desire for equanimity is to betray his constant modus operandi of careful calculation, especially whenever it came to imperial aspirations. The truth is that Roosevelt forecasted Japan, not Russia, as being the United States' sole imperial rival in the Pacific. From the Treaty of Portsmouth to Pearl Harbor, in a nearly ceaseless fashion, tensions between Washington and Tokyo continually rose.

On October 11, 1906, San Francisco moved to legally segregate Japanese immigrant and naturalized students from white students. News of the new laws reached Japan and resulted in outrage from the Japanese public and government alike. Always the micromanager, TR agreed to intervene, and through a gentlemen's agreement, promised to pressure the California school boards to rescind their segregation moves. In return, the Japanese state committed to halting the issuance of passports to Japanese laborers bound for the Western United States.

Next, in a typically Rooseveltian move of measured goodwill, one that contained a poorly veiled message of strength and attendant intimidation, President Roosevelt ordered the U.S. Navy to set out on a worldwide, paradoxical peace tour featuring the most modern warships. But, since the Great White Fleet was indeed painted white so as to signify that the American forces were pure in their intentions, well, the Japanese nor any other global power need worry.

But worry the Japanese did. When the Great White Fleet docked in Yokohama harbor, Japanese schoolchildren greeted their American visitors waving Japanese and American flags. Makeshift gates were erected throughout the city through which parades featuring American sailors and dignitaries passed. At the same time, the Japanese military and imperial government hastened to war plan for an eventual conflict with the United States. Largely as a result of this "goodwill" mission, the Japanese government committed to a prodigious military buildup, so much so that by 1921, almost one-third of the entire state budget was afforded to naval expenditure.

Global ambitions and micromanaging have costs. Of course Roosevelt himself would be long dead before the ultimate payment came due. His distant cousin would not, however.

Time to turn back the clock a bit then and address Rooseveltian domestic policy. Roosevelt was the antithesis of the old guard Cleveland Democrats who wished government to be as non-intrusive and thus, Constitutional, as possible. Whereas Cleveland Democrats viewed government as lacking sufficient knowledge by which to guide American society and the country's economy, given the innumerable value decisions made by the tens of millions of Americans in a given day, Roosevelt held that smooth, sophisticated, and scientific operators could direct (maybe nudge) those collective decisions in what he believed to be the right direction—the moral direction. This is the foundational, core belief of progressivism as a political ideology. Progressivism is Puritanism under new, secular, and scientific management. And, TR believed himself to be the smoothest of such operators. Others who dared, like the reform movement figures of the mid-19th century, to engage in their own social missions—the so-called muckrakers—TR demeaned as "flubdubs" and "mollycoddles". In other words, Donald Trump was not the first nor will he likely be the last American chief executive to make up insulting monikers for his political rivals. Admittedly though, Trump was the best at it.

Roosevelt considered what he called "the monopoly problem" the most pressing issue of his day. It should be noted, however, that he was not against the existence of all so-called trusts or monopolies, just those that he believed had gained too much dominance over their respective market shares by too many irreputable means. What constituted "too much" and "irreputable means" according to TR was anyone else's guess. Did it mean a company that had a 50.1 percent market share? 75%? What about those corporations which had engaged in aggressive acquisitions and marketing? What was "too aggressive"? Those questions were to be answered by TR alone and then the apparatus of the executive bureaucracy was deployed to break up the bad trusts.

This is precisely what happened in the case of J.P. Morgan's Northern Securities Trust. Roosevelt's Attorney General Philander C. Knox (a horrible name if ever one was given—sounds way too close to philanderer) filed a federal suit against Northern Securities Trust, and in a case that rose all the way to the Supreme Court, Knox was able to convince 5 of the 9 justices on the bench at the time that Morgan, Hill, and Rockefeller had broken the law by creating a railroad acquisitions company in the State of New Jersey, wherein state law had already asserted the legality of such corporations. This was not just a blow to laissez-faire economics; this ruling and interpretation of the Sherman Anti-Trust Act of 1890 was a loss for federalism. The result: A private enterprise was forcibly broken up by the federal government despite the fact that nowhere in the Constitution is such a power delegated to the legislative much less executive branches. The case provided precedent that allowed Roosevelt and Knox to file anti-monopoly suits against Standard Oil, meatpackers in Chicago, and James Duke's American Tobacco Company. Even after these victories over big business, Roosevelt still wanted to put more teeth into the Sherman Anti-Trust Act—and this is indeed a less than veiled insult I'm leveling at him because A) I don't like him and B) because TR had some ugly, prominent gibs. The President's allies in Congress authored and advanced sweeping anti-trust legislation, but many of the bills never made it to a vote. The House and Senate were still populated by enough Clevelandites and older Republicans for whom Roosevelt represented a progressive bridge too far.

Well, How 'Bout That?

In this climate of uncertainty pertaining to which of his companies and interests might be regulated to death next, per TR's whims, J.P. Morgan created a campaign slush fund for TR's reelection in 1904. Morgan himself contributed $150,000 to a man who had destroyed his largest enterprise. Interesting, is it not, that the same tycoon who under Cleveland had bailed out the federal treasury was, under Roosevelt, throwing his financial support behind the same man? Let me clarify the implication then: Morgan and allied barons gave huge sums over to the Roosevelt campaign in 1904 in order to gain TR's favor. If there is a more dramatic shift from the era and spirit of market entrepreneurialism to pure political entrepreneurialism, I know not of it.

Of course, opposition from Congress proved little more than a speed bump to TR enacting his transformative agenda. Throughout his nearly two terms in office, the President pushed through his "Square Deal" agenda for labor and his environmental conservation initiatives largely through presidential fiats, otherwise known as executive orders. Andrew Jackson—no shrinking violet—issued 12 total. Abraham Lincoln, 48. My man Cleveland issued a total of 253 over eight years. That's a lot, but it pales in comparison to Theodore Roosevelt's 1,081! And, one needs to look beyond the sheer number of executive orders and investigate the typical nature of these orders.

Take a random executive order by Grover Cleveland, or for that matter some random 19th-century president like Rutherford B. Hayes or James K. Polk or Franklin Pierce. Invariably, because these presidents understood the strictures inherent to the executive office, the executive orders pertain to inconsequential and trivial matters. Often, there was a ceremonial nature to them. For example, in his first term, Cleveland issued an executive order that all federal officeholders take a moment of silence in respect to a Civil War general who had passed away. Needless to say, the republic would survive with or without the execution of these orders. Now, examine some typical Rooseveltian orders. An executive order with TR's signature from August 9, 1902, set aside a segment of Nebraska for use by the federal Department of Agriculture for an experimental tree growing program. Tree-hugger or not, this is not insignificant, especially when one considers that this amounts to unconstitutional eminent domain by the federal government. Most disturbing, that is if one examines the list of all of TR's executive orders, is the number of those pertaining to exempting certain federal bureaucrats from Civil Service Commission examinations aimed at determining their relative merit for said positions. So, at the very time in which the federal government was asserting its authority and augmenting its jurisdiction over ever-increasing aspects of American life, TR was shielding those in positions from legislative or judicial oversight of those bureaucrats' worthiness and competence. In effect, TR was just enlarging the spoils system while at the same time giving it a glossy but altogether optical and not substantive sheen of professionalism. The bureaucratic, unwieldy and corrupt behemoth that exists today as the executive branch was established under Theodore Roosevelt.

How did he get away with this? Roosevelt offered, or more so resurrected and then fed steroids to the political justification for almost unchecked executive power, a theory first advanced by the aforementioned Jackson. The president was the sole office that the bulk of the nation's voters elected. Therefore, the president alone was a unique voice of "the American people". If you want to get all Rousseauian, it was the president and the president alone who could represent the general will of the country, not the provincial tastes and regional allegiances found and expressed through Senators and Representatives.

In the fall of 1902, Roosevelt was presented with the perfect opportunity to flex his self-established, royal power. For months leading into that autumn, the anthracite coal miners had engaged in a strike to which there appeared no resolution as winter approached. The vast majority of American homes depended on such coal to heat their homes, not to mention, the locomotives that ferried freight throughout the country—including raw materials like coal—relied upon coal as fuel. Roosevelt moved to interject himself into the negotiations, even as the aforementioned Attorney-General Knox informed him he had no authority to do so. Roosevelt formed a commission to resolve the matter, and invited the mine operators' representative, George F. Baer, and the charismatic United Mine Workers' union head, John Mitchell, to Washington. When impasses continued to thwart a compromise, Roosevelt, who clearly favored the young labor firebrand Mitchell to the stodgy and aristocratic Baer, threatened to order the U.S. Army in to run the mines, because, you know, soldiers make excellent miners and operators.

Labor pulled out the big guns for the commission. The famous Chicago attorney Clarence Darrow argued on the side of the miners. The poor wages, the occupational hazards, the black lung, and the overall crushing poverty of the miners required action. And in typical, Darrow fashion, he appealed not to legal statute and reasoning, but instead relied upon rhetorical flourishes and idealistic appeals:

"We are working for democracy, for humanity, for the future, for the day will come too late for us to see it or know it or receive its benefits, but which will come, and will remember our struggles, our triumphs, our defeats, and the words which we spake."

Oct 23, 1902 · Washington, D.C.

721 Retweets **51** Quote Tweets **3.5K** Likes

The strike ended in late October and a winter featuring a coal famine was averted. The commission granted a 10% wage increase for the miners and a 9-hour workday. The commission moved that the coal mine operators did not need to recognize the United Mine Workers. In other words, the owners were not forced to collectively bargain with the union. That's it. It was, by and large, a win for labor, but more so, the arbitration on the part of Roosevelt established a destructive precedent upon which justification would be found for federal intervention into any and all capital and labor disputes. With the president, after all, being the voice of the American people, one need not look into a crystal ball so as to determine on which side the chief executives would fall in future incidents.

Roosevelt dominated in his election bid in 1904. For TR, this decisive victory in what he considered a sort of plebiscite emboldened him further in his progressivism. It was in TR's second term when most of the lasting damage was done. In 1905, Roosevelt empowered the Interstate Commerce Commission with new and expansive authorities, including the power to arbitrarily examine the books of any business engaged in activities across state lines. 1906 was a particularly active (read ruinous) year as Congress passed the Hepburn Act, the Meat Inspection Act, and the Pure Food and Drug Act. The Hepburn Act destroyed businesses whose competitive advantages rendered for customers and consumers alike better goods and services at cheaper prices—all in the name of "fairness and equity". Recall, rail rates had long been in the crosshairs of Populists like William Jennings Bryan. Short of nationalizing the railroad companies, the Congress used the Hepburn Act to universalize freight rates and thus prohibited transport companies from granting coupons or discounts to farmers and businesses who used the trains with great frequency and magnitude. In other words, Congress destroyed the whole business model of men like James J. Hill, owner of the Great Northern Railway, who won the loyalty of his frequent customers with considerable discounts. His business model was so efficient that he even passed savings onto ship lines which were taking foodstuffs from his Seattle railroad terminus and shipping Midwestern grain all the way to Asia. Thus, by crushing Hill's model, the costs of all freight increased, efficiency decreased—as competition fell—and exports of grain to Asia declined as well. Congress and the president may have been well-intentioned, though I doubt it, but even if one was to concede the point, the Hepburn Act did nothing to aid American farmers, American workers, or foreign peoples.

That, indeed, is at the malignant heart of Progressivism as an ideology. Progressives abandoned and dismissed (and still do today) a long held and self-evident truth about economics. Any true study of economics, any accurate assessment of human action must encompass what the great Fredéric Bastiat referred to as the seen and the unseen. Progressives like Robert LaFollette and Theodore Roosevelt legislated simple and myopic fixes to perceived problems, won acclaim from populists for acting in the interests of the disadvantaged lower classes, and always ended up exacerbating the sometimes real but just as often imagined, problem. They had neither the minds nor inclinations to study the unseen and the end effects of their policies.

James Ostrowski provides an even better definition of progressivism—one that I was going to save until the treatment of the Wilson years, but I find just can't wait:

> Progressivism. A mindset about politics that has no rational basis; is utopian; favors the use of democratic government force to solve problems; holds that government force will produce a better result than voluntary society and the marketplace; has no theory of costs, or denies and minimizes the costs of its proposed solutions; is a form of self-help therapy against existential angst; and has no limiting principle and therefore tends toward creeping totalitarianism.

The Meat Inspection Act (1906) is the epitome of a progressive law. Moved by the gripping, yet fictitious, hyperbolized and fantastic yarn spun by Upton Sinclair in his novel, *The Jungle* (1906), the plight of workers in the country's meatpacking plants regained Washington's attention. Newspapers ran numerous (almost univocally unconfirmed) reports of contaminants in canned meat ranging from mice feces to sawdust. Something, it appeared, needed to be done. So, Congress crafted the perfect progressive bill, of course to the great pleasure of the giant meatpacking companies in Chicago and Cincinnati. TR signed the bill into law, and the cost required all meat producers to meet the new federal standards. The law created yet more federal agencies, ones that of course, continue to lumber on to this day, the Food Safety and Inspection Service (FSIS) and Food and Drug Administration.

Well, How 'Bout That?

It is a myth that the meat packing industry went on unregulated until 1906. Long had the big meat firms (that's funny to say) encouraged state inspection. The increased costs of meeting inspection standards fell heavily upon the smaller firms. That all being said, Upton Sinclair was a charlatan, a quack. And a blind socialist one at that—they make the worst kind of quacks. Truth is that, the federal government's own report from public meat inspectors already on the ground in Chicago years before 1906 declared that none of the government inspectors, "ever registered any complaint or [gave] any public information with respect to the manner of the slaughtering or preparation of meat or food products." Even TR dismissed him as a flimflammer: "I have an utter contempt for him. He is hysterical, unbalanced, and untruthful. Three-fourths of the things he said were absolute falsehoods. For some of the remainder there was only a basis of truth." Finally, fellow traveler but actually talented author, Sinclair Lewis, wrote to Sinclair himself, decrying the former's obsession with denouncing critics as "evil and capitalist-controlled sp[ies]". Yet, to this day, Upton Sinclair's works are utilized by the left as gospels proving the necessity of the interventionist state.

Who could afford the new compliance costs for the inspections? Well, certainly not your small or even midsize butcher operations. Nope; Swift and Armour and other major meatpacking trusts could. So the law was written so as to ensure the continued dominance of the big boys in the meatpacking world because their small competitors would go out of business. Swift, Armour, Wilson, et al. could absorb the increased costs of production in the short term and then, when their smaller competitors were eliminated, they could raise the prices with their increased market share. Wild, is it not, that in a truly free market, predatory pricing is a non-entity, a figment of socialists' imaginations. However, in a quasi-free market, where the government exerts command and control functions, predatory pricing becomes a reality. Furthermore, the major meatpackers received a sheen of approval from the U.S. government for their products, from meat inspectors who possessed no clear incentive to provide careful quality control.

The Pure Food and Drug Act (1906) might, however, be the worst of the trio. Contained therein is the clear genesis of the federal government's arbitrary and often racist regulation then prohibition of the use of certain narcotics. It was the beginning of the American War on Drugs.

Roosevelt "conserved" land and natural resources by confiscating state lands. In any other circumstance, this is called theft or eminent domain, but for Ken Burns, this form of legalized plunder was "America's best idea". In all, TR enlarged National Parks and Forests to the tune of 230 million acres, roughly the landmass of Texas and Michigan combined. What an awful precedent in that, so long as the federal government has veiled its land and resource grabs as having some remote connection to "conservation" or "environmental protection" (as if the government is good at either), it has continued in its land avarice almost unabated. In a weird numerical twist, today, federal lands comprise 230 million acres of Alaska alone, accounting for 60 percent of the state.

All that was left to put a coda on the Roosevelt presidency was a domestic economic panic, and one arrived in 1907. The president's critics dubbed it "Roosevelt's Panic", and the name stuck. It is a historically accurate moniker, at least in an indirect way. Roosevelt's own Treasury secretary, Leslie Shaw, had for two years prior, illegally operated the U.S. Treasury as if it were a central bank. He issued huge credit lines to major, crony U.S. banks far in excess of the gold reserves held by the entire banking system. Inflation resulted in 1905-1907. In turn, a bank run ensued due to widespread and well-placed fear that principles in accounts were in danger. This fear only worsened when, for a time, Shaw's Treasury permitted major banks in Chicago and New York to suspend specie payments to depositors. In other institutions outside of the banking cartel, this would mean—full irony here—that they would be "bankrupt", out of business, or as they say in Hamburg, *kaput*. Not so for connected banks. They could keep operating despite not having funds to operate. In response to cries that something be done, Shaw insisted that he be given regulatory omnipotence over the entire financial system. Such is the hallmark of bureaucracy: create or imagine a problem and then demand that you alone possess the antidote.

Congress demurred. Roosevelt's Panic ended as quickly as it hit. However, it provided the necessary pretext for the government to do with finance what it had accomplished with the meat industry under Roosevelt. In two short years, bankers assembled to create their own legislative restructuring of the banking system, one that would work to capitalize gains and socialize the risks they would take. Six years later, it would be mission accomplished.

The Odd Thrupple: The Next Two Progressives

William Howard Taft succeeded Roosevelt in the Oval Office. Although Taft performed as a progressive executive—he actually requisitioned more federal lands than Roosevelt had—he just wasn't transformative enough for today's American historians in academia. Most texts refer to him as the "listless progressive", not only as a jab at his physical girth but also his tendency to stall sweeping state action if such moves smacked of blatant unconstitutionality. Such 19th-century anachronism landed Taft out of favor with progressives of his time, including Roosevelt, who soured on Taft quickly and led a public relations campaign against him, like a scorned, petulant child, from Europe.

Roosevelt's campaign worked to split the GOP into two distinct camps: Roosevelt asserted himself at the head of the progressive wing while Taft and anyone who didn't like TR, formed a sort of old guard branch of the party. To be sure, the members of the Old Guard were not principled like the Cleveland Democrats; they were political operatives through and through, but they also saw progressivism as an all-consuming wave of leftism in which they refused to be totally swept.

Division in the Republican ranks opened the door wide open for the Democrats to win in 1912. That election pitted Taft as the incumbent against Roosevelt, who ran under the Progressive Party banner, against the Democratic nominee, Woodrow Wilson. In the debates and missives exchanged during the campaign, it is clear that all three candidates for the presidency attempted to outdo one another in a race to the left. They posited that the country was in a progressive mood, as if a spell had been cast over everyone from the Rappahannock to the Colorado by William Jennings Bryan, Herbert Crowy, and Robert LaFollette—a "charmed" progressive trio if there ever was one.

Wilson won in a runaway. In fact, Roosevelt came in a distant second; Taft in an embarrassing third with a total of 8 electoral votes. Turns out that winning only Vermont and Utah in a presidential election is not a path to victory. Democrats swept to victory in the House and Senate as well.

Wilson believed himself to be armed with a decisive political mandate from the American people. The former president of Princeton University and governor of New Jersey espoused progressivism with religious fervor. Through wise, centralized, and ubiquitous statecraft and leadership, Wilson held that the federal government could be the catalyst for a new American way of life, an elevated and more sophisticated one; a way of life that was a marked departure from the Gilded Age, where pools of wealth seemed only to concentrate in the hands of a few. According to American historian John Garraty, Wilson pontificated that:

John Garraty
@HistorianJG ...

"The federal government could best advance the course of social justice... by modernizing the special interests and privileges that allowed business to flourish."

1995 · THE AMERICAN NATION: A HISTORY OF THE UNITED STATES, 8TH ED.

83 Retweets **1** Quote Tweet **932** Likes

I like that description of Wilsonian progressivism because Wilson never called for the *elimination* of special interests; no, he maintained that the special interests could be governed—or as Garraty put it "modernized"—so as to direct the country to achieve progressive goals. Government on the other hand, per Wilson, could function in the most altruistic and beneficial of ways:

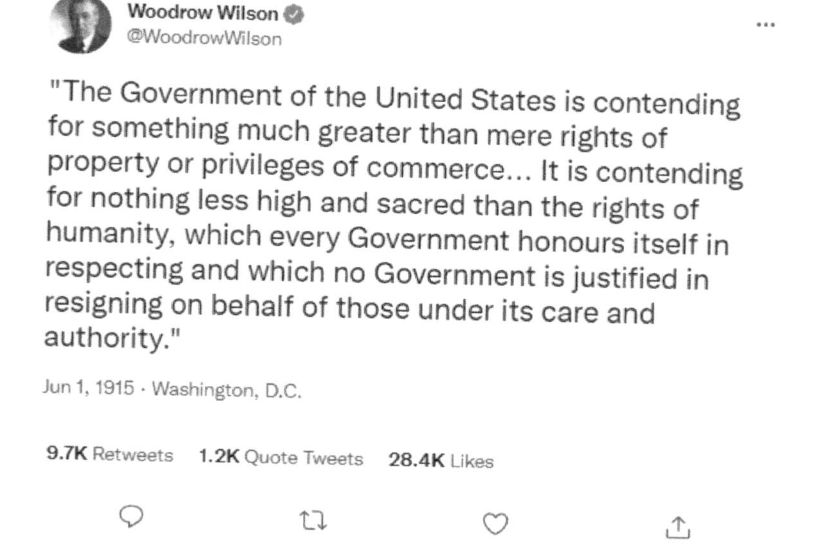

If TR was the primary progressive, and Taft was the listless progressive, then Wilson was to be the aggressive progressive. No one adhered to the doctrine that the federal government must be the engine of social change and economic equity more so than Woodrow Wilson.

He dubbed his legislative program, the "New Freedom". As to what was so wrong with the old freedom, well, that was anyone's guess. Here's mine: The old freedom entailed individual autonomy and self-ownership in the classical sense. It allowed you to move where you wanted to go, consort with whomever you consort with, work in whatever field you wished, and devote the fruit of that life and labor to whatever pursuit you desired. Progressives wanted and still want none of that. That being said, one must credit Wilson with good branding. I mean, who really wants the "old freedom" with all of its Constitutional restrictions and laissez-faire inequalities when the "New Freedom" was sitting right there, a gift from the new president and Congress?

Spider-Man (?) Scales the 'Triple-Wall of Privilege'

This "New Freedom" could only be realized should the federal government assert itself into reforming what Wilson liked to call the "triple wall of privilege": tariffs, banks, and trusts.

Let's take them in order. Early in 1913, Wilson worked to pass the Underwood Tariff Bill, which called for drastic reductions in tariff rates. Now, I know what you are probably thinking. *Oh, just because you hate Woodrow Wilson with a passion you seem to only reserve for Lena Dunham and those knock-off Oreos that bedevil grocery shelves and the occasional cookies 'n cream ice cream brand, you're not going to give Wilson credit for doing something good like lowering tariffs, which you lauded Cleveland for doing some pages ago...* Yeah, that's right. I detest the man. I think it should be required that every time his name is uttered or his picture shown, ominous sound effects should play in the background. I'm not going to hate Woodrow Wilson any less than I do because of the Underwood Tariff Act and here's why: The decline in tariffs came with an inordinately heavy price; namely, because tariffs made up the main revenue stream to the federal government, once they were reduced, the new federal government-behemoth that Wilson was creating needed a new revenue source. That would come in the form of a national income tax. Intent matters, and while Wilson took one very small step forward in reducing protectionism, he concurrently created conditions for a transformation in legal plunder, otherwise known as taxation. Any remaining Constitutional and legal hurdles to a national income tax were done away with through the ratification of the 16th Amendment, the first amendment to the Constitution since freedmen were granted the right to vote in 1871. In point of fact, the reduction of the tariff from 40% to 26% was so inherently tied to this taxation scheme that the Underwood bill was just one piece of the larger Revenue Act of 1913, which placed a then "modest levy" on incomes over $3000 per annum.

It did not stay modest for long. By 1917, the national income tax brought in more revenue to the federal government than all tariffs. Essentially then, Wilson and the progressives in Congress in 1913 revolutionized the established order of national taxation that had existed—albeit with a few brief challenges during the Civil War and Reconstruction—since 1789.

Transformations did not end there. For Wilson, the social and economic inequalities that persisted in the United States existed not as a result of human nature and comparative advantages that some Americans had over others in the marketplace. The injustices came about because of greed and market failure. And, so what if such inequities did emerge from nature? Wilson and progressives warred against nature. These were intellectuals by and large who perceived themselves ordained to right the injustices wrought by the free market and traditional, voluntary society.

No institutions did more to maintain those inequities than the banks, according to the progressives. Since 1910 when a cabal of representatives of the richest men on earth, including representatives for the Rothchild's, Rockefeller's and Morgan's, convened on Jekyll Island in Georgia to reimagine the world's financial system, many of the same progressives had pined for the favorable day in which the designs from Jekyll could be implemented. As it turns out—shocker—the interests of progressive politicians wishing to curry populist favor by reining in the banks, and the interests of the uber-bankers wishing to further enrich themselves, were very compatible. Remaking the financial system could be immensely beneficial and lucrative for both parties. Wilson and his allies would be viewed as secular angels, reforming the system that seemed to keep the rich, rich and the poor, poor. Meanwhile, the bank magnates could do to banking what the meatpackers had done to the food industry back in 1906. The legislation that emerged from Jekyll Island in order to mature into the Federal Reserve Act of 1913 was designed to accomplish three things for this most unholy of alliances: 1) Monetize the debt of the national government so as to remove fiscal restraints from any of its most costly endeavors. 2) Capitalize reward while socializing credit risk. 3) Wipe out competition to the big banks by wiping out the small banks.

The Federal Reserve System has accomplished what it was designed to do. Of course, it was not sold to the American public in this manner. The whole plot was surreptitious from the beginning: The six attendees at Jekyll Island, including Senator Nelson Aldrich, did not even admit to their presence at the meeting until well into the 1930s. Advocates for the Federal Reserve bill promised that the new Federal Reserve System (not a Bank of the United States—it was carefully marketed as "non-political") would put an end to that nasty economic boom-bust cycle that proved so ruinous to so many ordinary Americans in the country's 19th century past.

How so? Remember the notorious panics, during which asset bubbles popped, investors lost savings due to natural market corrections, the same asset prices then bottomed out, and finally the rich swept in to grab them at artificially low costs? Whether in land, railroad stocks, or government bonds, some government action (often war) had resulted in a misallocation of resources, easy credit was afforded to lenders, and artificial valuations boomed. When investors realized in 1819, 1907, and every panic in between that the actual value of the asset fell far short of the cash price of the bubble asset, a wild sell-off began, runs on banks and bank failures proceeded and then economic recession resulted as credit dried up.

Senator Aldrich, the Jekyllites, Wilson, and Senator Carter Glass (who drew up the final bill) sold the Reserve System as the magic solution to the banking and currency system. No more panics! No more booms and busts for the benefit of the rich in both crests and troughs. The new Federal Reserve Board and its 12 regional reserve district banks would control the production of money notes and disperse them to banks which were required to keep a percentage of their reserves with the Fed. More importantly, the Federal Reserve would have the power to raise and lower the general rate of interest. That's right: a pseudo-private, government created and appointed board would determine the price of money. Price fixing of money, if you prefer. When said board determined that an artificial boom was taking place, it would make access to credit more restrictive—like turning down a hose spigot—by raising the cost of money, i.e. interest rates. In turn, should the country face an economic downturn, interest rates would be, effectively, lowered to encourage increased borrowing, consumption, and expansion.

Central to the Fed's very existence was the long held progressive assertion that there was something inherently wrong with the operation of the free market. Thus, in their minds, the only institution powerful enough to remedy a recession created by the free market was a state mechanism which consisted of an independent consortium of experts. These experts would possess the otherworldly foresight of knowing the exact point at which market prices were too low or too high. The Fed was empowered to set the rates at which private banks loaned money to one another. How so, without a total takeover of already established financial institutions? The Fed would set a federal funds rate, that is, a rate of interest at which banks could take out loans from the Fed directly. This would function as a sort of rate ceiling.

For example, let's say that the Federal Reserve directors determine that a recession (which, per Keynesian economics *always* takes place because of irrational "animal spirits" that cause a reduction in consumption) is about to transpire. The Fed responds by reducing the interest rate by one or more percentage points, let's say from 6.00% to 5.00%. Again, should a bank wish to acquire more credit in dollars, it could acquire them from the Fed at the new rate. However, this—let's call it, *financial intrusion* by this megabank—would, in turn, incentivize other banks to lower the interest rate at which they loan money to each other to just below the new 5.00% mark. The other banks' rates must be less than the 5.00% funds rate or else banks desirous of credit could just go to the Fed for loans. The corresponding rate reduction is meant to inspire lending, because, in point of fact, credit becomes cheaper. Lenders—both institutional and individual— face lower costs for taking out credit. This extrinsic manipulation of interest rates "gets cash and savings off the sidelines (i.e. savings)" and gets it deployed into the market. Companies expand. Individuals and families spend more. Production of goods and provision of services increase to meet the new demand. Economic crisis averted? Maybe. Many, like the bosses of United Cigar Stores Co., drank the kool-aid so completely (with their Monte Christos?) that they believed economic downturns of any kind were rendered anachronistic:

"Properly administered, the new currency system will do much to ward off any disturbances of national business confidence and panic should under this new system become effete."

THE NEW CURRENCY LAW A FORERUNNER OF BETTER TIMES

Dec 24, 1913 · Twitter for American History

34 Retweets 5 Quote Tweets 571 Likes

The reduction in interest rates, presumably, could stave off an increase in unemployment, followed by a decrease in demand, then a decrease in production—an economic death spiral according to Keynesians. The inverse, supposedly, would hold true for when the economy might become overheated. Should demand and consumption range too high and asset bubbles emerge in various industries and sectors resulting in overproduction, the Fed would tighten the spigot of credit by raising rates. Such a move would disincentivize people from taking out loans.

Soapbox

I apply the Gamaliel principle to the Federal Reserve, which, I suspect even the Jekyllites would have found acceptable: We should know the Fed by its works. How has it performed as the solution to economic booms and busts? Well, since its inception—very poorly. From the Roaring 20s to the Great Depression (the ultimate boom and bust) to the economic crisis of stagflation in the 1970s, then the Great Recession of 2008-2009, the Fed's record is, at best, checkered. If, indeed, the original goal of the Fed was to cause, deepen and extend the booms and busts, or the periods of economic peaks and valleys, then it has been remarkably successful. It would be living according to its nature. As it is, however, the Fed has created and overseen—no matter who has been on the various boards; no matter who is the Fed Chairman—the largest, most historically unprecedented transfer of wealth from the lower and middle classes to the already wealthy.

To end the Fed is a most just imperative.

But, as the great Ludwig von Mises pointed out, the Fed's price-fixing on money hinders or at times cripples the capacity of the market to, through the innumerable transactions that occur in a given day, set the natural price of, well, anything. In other words, there is no substitute for natural price discovery, as Mises pointed out:

"The ultimate source of the determination of prices is the value judgments of the consumers... There is no such thing as prices outside the market. Prices cannot be constructed synthetically, as it were."

1940 · HUMAN ACTION · New York

4,305 Retweets **154** Quote Tweets **35.7K** Likes

No one—including the supposed demigods at the Federal Reserve—can determine the proper prices of money and hence, the proper prices of everything else. The Federal Reserve bill's destructive conceit has crushed the value of the dollar and exacerbated income inequality since the Fed's inception since the Federal Reserve is anything but an independent body of financial seers and soothsayers. They are instead political operatives who, almost without exception, are incentivized to induce and sustain a persistent boom and avoid, like the plague, a corrective bust while they are in office. Their decided penchant, therefore, is to keep interest rates artificially low, which results in destitution for earners, consumers and savers.

Soapbox

Readers whose interest I have piqued in this explanation of the Fed, its history, operation and results, are encouraged to read the works of the masters of the Austrian school of economics, the only school of economics extant today to possess an accurate explanation of the Fed's manipulations. Because of the length and difficulty of the seminal texts in this area (ex. Mises's Human Action *and Murray Rothbard's* Man, Economy and State*) it is worthwhile to consume the more accessible works of economist Robert Murphy in* Choice: Cooperation, Enterprise, and Human Action *and Ron Paul's* End the Fed. *If you really want to be scandalized and read a book that you're really not supposed to read, check out* The Creature from Jekyll Island *by G. Edward Griffin.*

No matter. Congress passed the bill on December 23, 1913, and an enthusiastic President Wilson signed it into law on the same day.

On to trusts, the final portion of the triple wall of privilege.

In 1914, Congress passed the Federal Trade Commission Act. By this legislation, Congress empowered the president to appoint a federal investigative team whose sole purpose was to build evidence and cases against supposed monopolies. As I have noted in the past, when a new bureaucracy is created by government, and that bureaucracy has an expressed purpose, the clear and proven tendency of that office is to affirm its *raison d'être* (reason for being). The War Department (when it bore a proper name) guess what (?!)—seeks to go to war. The Treasury Department proves its worth to the powers that be in Washington by finding ways to finance kleptocratic expenditures. The Federal Trade Commission, of necessity then, tended toward finding malevolent trusts at every turn. Fair "trade" after all could only be achieved with the federal government determining just how just business practices were.

The law itself along with the Clayton Anti-Trust Act (1914) granted the Commission sweeping authority, including the power to order companies to cease and desist their business practices. A scan of some early decisions of the FTC in the several years following its creation illustrates what a broad and arbitrary government power grab this all was.

In 1916, a Philadelphia textile and print company known as A. Theo Abbott & Co. committed the cardinal sin of selling a new cloth they dubbed "cilk", a cotton-based fabric that nonetheless featured the sheen of authentic silk. The FTC determined that because a number of their clients believed they were getting actual silk, the Abbott company had engaged in unlawful business practices. Damn the directors at the Abbott Company for their puns, and damn teachers for not teaching cloth merchants the proper spelling of silk! Another good one: in 1917, the FTC charged the United States Gold Leaf Manufacturers Association with monopolistic practices such as garnering approximately 50% of the gold leaf market. Oh, the horror! As to why 50% is some magic market share number that makes a company a monopoly and not a good, honest enterprise—well, who knows? Why not 45%? 70%? The ill-defined powers granted to the FTC in the Act permitted the Commission to divine the exact market share that transformed a company into a monopoly. And then, my favorite: the case of Buddha Tea Company from Philadelphia. You see, the Buddha Tea Company head honchos were determined to be inveterate robber baron criminals because they incentivized the purchase of their teas and coffees by giving coupons and prizes to various customers. Oh, the horror! They too were investigated and fined.

In essence then, the FTC assumed the role of a national fairness-in-business police force. *Caveat emptor* (let the buyer beware) was dead because if you had the means and connections to reach the FTC in Washington, you could sick the Commission on businesses and competitors you simply did not like, or, for that matter, whose demise would benefit your own enterprise.

The Clayton Anti-Trust Act went several steps further. It was basically the old railroad Hepburn Act (1906) writ large. It outlawed price discrimination, interlocking directorates (wherein men served on several corporate boards), and cartelization. However, while Congress forbade business owners from collaborating in a cartel, labor unions were exempted from the same practices. In other words, large labor unions could engage in aggressive actions and create powerful consorts without fear of prosecution. So elated and moved was Samuel Gompers—head of the American Federation of Labor—by the decidedly anti-capital and supposedly pro-labor Act that he declared:

Hard to believe, but Wilson and the 63rd Congress followed up those rabidly anti-market and unconstitutional acts with several more. The LaFollette Seamen's Act (1915) regulated the compensation and working conditions of sailors and portsmen. The Federal Farm Loan Act (1916) created federal farm loan banks from which farmers could obtain long term loans at more favorable interest rates than the market offered. The Workingmen's Compensation Act (1916) awarded government employees pay while off of work due to job-related injuries.

All of this sounds good, right? Wrong. All three acts had serious and ultimately unjust consequences. The Seamen's Act increased the cost of international trade and thus the overall price of goods for the American consumer. The Farm Loan Act led to malinvestment, additional risk-taking, and agricultural overproduction that would cripple the average farmer after the boon that was World War I. When the war ended, the demand for U.S. grain, for example, plummeted and so too did the price for grain. Farmers were left destitute well *before* the Great Depression. Finally, the Compensation Act encouraged corruption among federal employees and served as a system for dispersing federally funded disability insurance. Consequently, federal employees became a protected class of workers and—not unlike what the Republicans had done with Civil War pensioners during the 19th century—federal employees became loyal voters of the Democratic party.

All of these acts were massive intrusions into the operation of the free market. Their effects were felt by Americans of all stripes and situations and rarely were these effects positive in any meaningful way. Americans were more taxed and more regulated than ever before, and yet while wages did increase from year to year from 1912 to 1916, the purchasing power of those wages actually *declined* by 1916. Americans were taking home more money but monetary and price inflation stifled a rise in the general standard of living.

Well, How 'Bout That?

As it pertained to organized labor, the Bureau of Labor Statistics reported that: "While the increase in the rates of wages of organized labor in 1916 over 1915 was greater than the increase in any one-year interval as far back as 1907, yet the increase in 1916 fell short of the increase in the retail prices of food in the year. In 1916 the retail price of food as a whole was 12 per cent higher than in 1915, 11 per cent higher than in 1914, 22 per cent higher than in 1910, and 39 per cent higher than in 1907. As retail prices of food increased to a greater extent last year than wages, the purchasing power of wages con-sequently was reduced. From 1912 to 1915, inclusive, wages main-tained practically a uniform purchasing power, measured in food, but the abnormal conditions of 1916, while advancing wage scales over 1915, **increased retail prices of food so much more that the purchasing power of wages declined about 6.5 per cent within the year."**

The government created a hostile environment for small and big businesses alike. Even the superior American cola company, Coca-Cola, fell under the scrutiny and oppressive gaze of the feds. From 1914-1916, agents from the FTC and then the Department of Justice led investigations into Coke's business models and threatened expensive legal action against the company. It was determined that Coke had increased its market share and resulting profits by refusing to sell Coca-Cola to retailers who dealt in competing cola drinks. The FTC found that Coke officials had "maliciously intimidated" competitors by filing lawsuits against them for attempting to brand themselves as Coke—which is quite the irony in that the government was complaining about *Coke's* attempts to hurt companies through exhaustive legal proceedings. Coke had engaged in "excessive advertising" (whatever that means), issued rebates based on total annual sales, and "slandered the character" of competitors in the soft drink space. To be sure, calling a business opponent's product inferior and then engaging in proactive, aggressive marketing were hallmarks of Gilded Age economics. Such practices—common since the Commercial and Industrial Revolutions—had contributed to the greatest production of wealth and sharpest rise in the global standard of living in human history. The government's intrusions left Asa Candler, Coca-Cola's chief executive, apoplectic. According to historian Mark Pendergrast, an expert on all things Coca-Cola, including the actual Coca-Cola formula:

"Candler could hardly be blamed for feeling persecuted. He must have felt that the American government had gone mad, abusing him for being an astute businessman who employed aggressive promotion and reasonable concern to protect his product's good name and integrity."

2000 · FOR GOD, COUNTRY AND COCA-COLA · Atlanta, GA

178 Retweets **25** Quote Tweets **991** Likes

Wilson and the progressives in Congress had constructed a bureaucratic, managerial sate that, by 1915, had slipped its claws into the once invisible hand, and with the full weight of a chainmail glove, sought to guide and direct the American economy.

Soapbox

For this massive intrusion into the functioning of American society, Wilson is widely lauded in modern American history textbooks. Several tomes stand out, but the most fawning has to be the popular The American Pageant, *now in its 17th (!) edition, by historians Thomas Bailey, David Kennedy, and Lizabeth Cohen. Hope you're seated for this. Regarding Wilsonian domestic policy, they write, "Energetically scaling the 'triple wall of privilege,' Woodrow Wilson had treated the nation to a dazzling demonstration of vigorous presidential leadership. He proved nearly irresistible in his first 18 months in office." Good lord! Woodrow Wilson is not the 19-teens version of a political-virtuoso Spider-Man! His programs did nothing to diminish any inequity that existed in the United States—in fact, they provided state cover for the very institutions that created privilege. Spider-Man my ass.*

Basket Case Foreign Policy

As myopic and ultimately counterproductive Wilsonian domestic policy was, it still cannot shake a stick at his galactically stupid and ultimately murderous foreign policy.

In 1914 and again in 1916, Wilson ordered military incursions into Mexico with the most paternalistic and self-serving aims. Civil war, regime change and general instability threatened American business interests there, as well as the personal holdings of some American elites, including press magnate William Randolph Hearst who owned an estate south of the border larger than the size of Rhode Island. Without Congressional approval, much less declarations of war, Wilson ordered the U.S. Navy to occupy Veracruz in 1914, saying that the U.S. mission and evisceration of Mexican sovereignty would help Mexico, "adjust her unruly household."

Wilson's paternalistic imperialism did not stop at Chiapas:

U.S. forces invaded and occupied Cuba, the Dominican Republic, Haiti, Honduras, Mexico, and Nicaragua at various points during his tenure. These incursions produced immense hostility against the United States—"anti-Yankeeism" that persists to this day in Latin America and the Caribbean— and these interventions did nothing to preclude the rise of ruthless, sectarian dictatorships and civil wars within these nations.

All that being said, Wilson's serpentine actions as chief executive before, during and after World War I proved catastrophic, especially if one hoped to see a resurrected and stable Europe after the war.

World War I was an unimaginable bloodbath. When the powder keg of Europe exploded in the summer of 1914, all of the powers of Europe waged modern war against one another. It was cataclysmic. The Concert of Europe, established and for the most part achieved at the Congress of Vienna a century before it, blew up into a cacophony of murderous abandon. The alliance system and imperialism ensured that a conflict that had started with a Serbian terrorist's (Gavrilo Princip) assassination of an Austrian archduke (the *Thronfolger*, Franz Ferdinand) in Sarajevo, quickly turned into a global war.

While the war was sure to transform the existing political order, it did much more to destroy the individual lives of its participants; the willing and unwilling alike. Terms that are common parlance today, terms whose connotations have changed over time, can nonetheless trace their denotative origins back to World War I. "Shell-shock" became an actual, diagnosed medical condition as men came back from the front and the trenches psychologically crippled for life from the relentless artillery shell explosions to which they were exposed. The term basket case—used today in order to describe the insane—was first used to describe the horrifying and all too numerous occurrences in which soldiers returned home missing all of their appendages, thus, they had to be carried around in large baskets.

Americans overwhelmingly felt relieved to have had no direct part in it. They had been spared the slaughter and wanted to keep it that way. Moreover, American farmers and manufacturers benefited from the voracious national appetites of the belligerents for everything from American grain to American iron. It should be noted—as the war went on—there would be no possible way in which the European powers could finance the war without abandoning the international gold standard and, consequently, relying upon fiat currency. The war efforts were exhausting to the point of extinction, and there just were not enough reserves to pay for it all. The government printing presses roared, and with hard money deemed a relic of the increasingly distant past given the historical rupture that was the Great War, governments lost any semblance of the real strictures that previously constrained them. As the masterfully insightful anti-war progressive Randolph Bourne declared:

I would simply add that the "health of the state", justified in war, becomes the bane of all peoples during war, and beyond. Since World War I, so long as a government could claim that any existential threat endangered the nation, the elites of supposed democracies have readily metamorphosed their regimes into totalitarian oligarchies with permanent, dictatorial powers. Hence, in our modern times since World War I, the connotative but altogether accurate meaning of "democracy" is doing what those elites deem necessary. Historian Paul Johnson concurs:

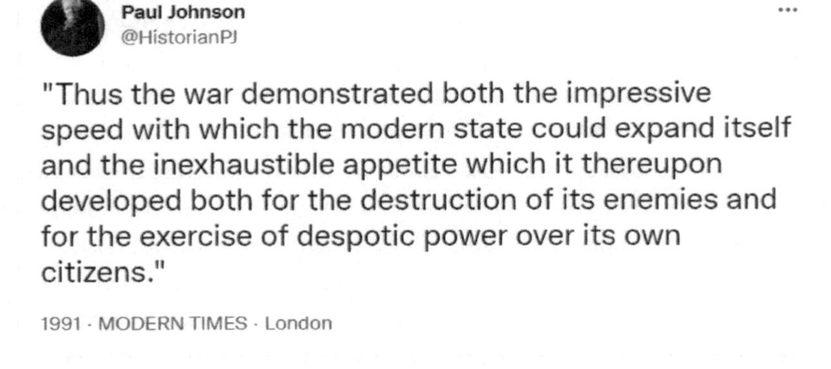

Never oblivious to public opinion, Woodrow Wilson ran his re-election campaign on a peace platform in 1916. All the while, he bore immense sympathy with the British and equally immense disdain for the Germans, as his conduct throughout the war shows.

Prior to the opening of hostilities, the Germans prepared for war with Britain by constructing numerous submarines (*Unterseeboote*—gotta love how literal the Germans are) so as to challenge the surface-based dominance of the British navy. The British had planned for naval conflict with Germany a decade prior to the war, and it was determined then that the British navy ought to enact a blockade of the North Sea should the two countries ever come to blows. In 1914, it was the job of the First Lord of the Admiralty, Winston Churchill, to bring that plan to fruition. Churchill's blockade was a rather heinous thing. Given the expanse of the North Sea, and the British navy's inability to take Northern German ports by force, this was to be a hunger blockade. The British mined the North Sea. Mines do not discriminate between ships containing soldiers and munitions for war, and those containing grain to feed a population. No matter. Even if a grain ship happened to evade the mines, should a British ship intercept it, the grain would still be confiscated and the ship destroyed. What a true humanitarian that Churchill!

As the British aimed to strangle the German economy and starve the German people, the British War Office printed propaganda at a speed equal to that of pound notes ('Bradburys' as they were known) from the British mint. The messaging cajoled and shamed Brits for not going into the armed forces as much as it simultaneously demonized the Germans as barbaric 'Huns.'

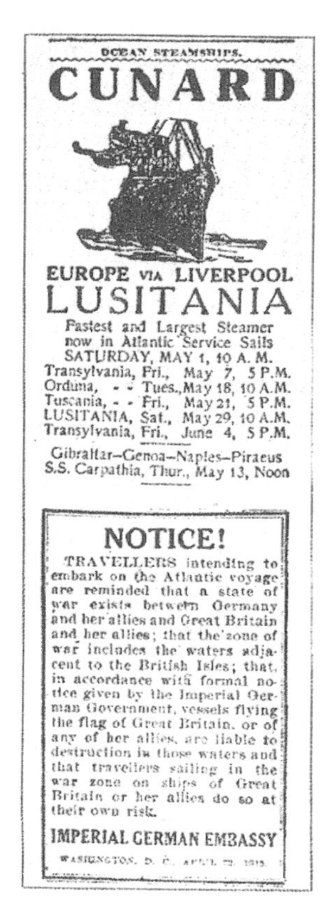

German treatment of the poor Belgians was an especially popular topic, as the War Office reported and then postered horrible atrocities perpetrated against the people of the Brabant. Belgian babies were, don't you know, routinely thrown into the air by German troops only to land atop German bayonets?

Governments appropriated mass media in order to create a narrative, mainly through carefully crafted images, of univocal nationalist tribalism and universal demonization of the enemy. States henceforth have yet to relinquish such power and influence. Of course, much of what the propaganda purported to be true represented a lavish and altogether inaccurate depiction of the causes of the war and the nature of the fighting. Principled and perceptive men and women saw through the all too carefully concocted drama, including—to their undying credit—people on the far left of the Western political spectrum. In France, socialist Jean Jaurès was assassinated by a French nationalist in July 1914, well before the war even began for France. Helen Keller and Jane Addams—socialists and American muckrakers both—campaigned for peace. Clarence Darrow, the famed Chicago attorney offered $1000 to anyone who presented evidence of supposed German atrocities against the Belgians. No one came forward. Turns out that the Germans saved their rage and directed it toward the numerous *franc-tireurs* (Belgian snipers) who picked off so many German officers that the German commanders took to hiding any insignia that might distinguish them from ordinary infantrymen. Such is the inferno of war. On the other end of the political and economic spectrum, in an effort to defend laissez-faire capitalism, Henry Ford funded an unfortunately ill-begotten trans-Atlantic voyage to argue for peace in 1915. It was all to no avail, as the nationalist, craven newspapers derided Ford's attempts as fanciful weakness. But, to my mind, Eugene Debs, the socialist labor leader in the United States, deserves the most credit for placing principle over comfort. Debs railed against the nexus of big capital and big industry and how both were producing and profiting from the armaments deployed by big government to kill millions. Debs's efforts went into high gear when the United States entered the war, so much so that Debs was thrown into prison for the crime of—if you can believe this—sedition (?!) because he urged draftees to evade capture by the government. Debs would run for president in 1920 from a prison cell, all the while rattling the government's cage from his own. He still garnered 3 percent of the popular vote despite being incarcerated. Warren Harding commuted his sentence in 1921. Wilson had preferred to see Debs rot in prison for ten years.

And enter World War I the United States did, in 1917; that is after a concerted campaign orchestrated by Wilson and Churchill to get the country on board for the slaughter.

In response to the British hunger blockade of the North Sea, German U-Boats sank ships carrying armaments to Great Britain. This was *discriminant* submarine warfare—at least much more discriminant than British war practices—in that the Germans did not target passenger and mercantile ships. Such avoidance did not fit the British War Department's narrative of the supposedly innate, Teuton penchant for barbarism. So, the British began shipping armaments, mainly from the United States, in ships flagged as commercial and passenger vessels. Churchill then, with Wilson's tacit approval, encouraged increased traffic into a virtual warzone, as the Germans had deemed some false-flagged vessels to be veritable combatant ships. Some were sunk. It was into this cauldron that the famous Lusitania met its fate in May 1915. The ship sank so quickly after the initial torpedo attack that the Germans themselves were shocked by the rapidity with which it went under. Subsequent claims that munitions were indeed on board were met with fierce and public denials from the British War and Foreign ministry, that is, until just recently. The fact is that the passengers on board the Lusitania were cannon fodder, placed there like fuses for war. Churchill and Wilson had hoped that the loss of the 126 American lives might trigger such public outrage that Wilson would have enough popular support for war to go before Congress with a call to mobilize. And yet, to the general American public's undying credit at the time, Americans remained obstinately non-interventionist.

Well, How 'Bout That?

Shocker. The British government lied through their poor teeth for almost a century. Papers from the Foreign Ministry reveal that in 1982, when divers aimed to probe the Lusitania, the British Foreign Ministry precluded such an expedition because of fear that the enormous number of known munitions on board could still explode! Public knowledge of London's scuttling of the 1982 expedition came as a result of papers that surfaced in 2014 to, sadly, little to no public scandal or even response. C.f. Alan Travis, "Lusitania Divers Warned of Danger from War Munitions in 1982, Papers Reveal" The Guardian, *30 April 2014.*

In order to be re-elected president in 1916, Wilson did everything he could to suppress his real urge to enter the war on the side of the Allies. He publicly proclaimed neutrality on the campaign and promised that American boys would not be dying in trenches on the Marne, only to, once re-elected in November of that year, engage in such hawkish and provocative behavior as to leave Germany in a state of bewilderment.

In the existential and relentless carnage into which World War I devolved, with desperate states and armies turning to everything from mustard gas to political subterfuge (Lenin was delivered to St. Petersburg by train, by the Germans), Wilson understood the transformative moment at hand. Nothing was to be the same as it once was. And, the notion that the United States, that *he*, would be excluded from the reshaping of the post-war world—well, that was anathema.

From November 1916 to April 1917, Wilson picked a fight with Germany. Senators and high- ranking members of Wilson's cabinet pleaded with the president to alter his aggressive positions toward Germany. This included the president's insistence that Germany's submarine warfare constituted some sort of surreptitious thus barbarous war act as opposed to Britain's more open and indiscriminate hunger blockade. This included a complete reversal of his position regarding Americans traveling into a war zone, one that warned Americans that they did so at their own risk in Mexico while American forces occupied that country in 1914. This included impossible demands placed upon Germany. So absurd and aggressive were Wilson's demands that his normally pliant, yes-man Secretary of State, Robert Lansing, even saw their incoherence. Wilson had sided with Churchill to require that German submarines emerge from the water and give warning to surface vessels which the Germans believed to be belligerent ships—*before* attacking. One need not be a graduate of Annapolis to figure out that such a practice defeats the central purpose of having a *submarine* at all. The whole reason for being underwater is to operate undetected by surface vessels! Regardless, Wilson treated any subsequent aggressions against American merchant ships—even those armed and ordered to shoot German submarines on sight as said U.S. ships headed to British ports—as German acts of war against the "neutral" United States. In the spring of 1917, four such ships were sunk by German U-boats, incidents which, when combined with the Zimmerman Telegram, provided Wilson enough cover to justify petitioning Congress for a declaration of war.

The Wilson Administration conducted the largest military mobilization in U.S. history in order to fight Germany, in France, an ocean away. The statistics are mind-boggling: 2.9 million men either volunteered or were conscripted, constituting about 6 percent of the entire American workforce. The overall, direct U.S. expenditure for the war would top 34 billion dollars, or about 750 billion dollars today. In order to fight, in 1918, about one-fifth of the country's resources were devoted to the war effort. To finance the war, Wilson and Congress relied upon massive tax increases (wild how quickly the income tax became an easy funding mechanism for war!), bond sales (borrowing), and currency creation (read: Fed printing). In other words, the United States found out very quickly what Europe had already long known: Modern, total warfare so destroyed the pre-war wealth of a nation that the only way to conduct and finance it was to bankrupt future citizens through massive borrowing and fiat printing. World War I belligerents eviscerated the international gold standard, that standard of currency banking that had so stabilized world markets and so prevented the wild global, boom-bust economic cycles experienced ever since. Inflation rates skyrocketed to 17.8 percent in 1917, 17.3 percent in 1918, and 15.2 percent, year over year, in 1919. That is to say that Americans at home saw the value of the dollars they were making and the value of the dollars they saved crushed by what amounted to war taxation without legislation.

Well, How 'Bout That?

In addition to immediate increases in the federal income tax, across wealth brackets, the War Revenue Act of 1917 levied sales taxes on everything from soft drinks and tobacco to musical instruments. The historically ignorant or simply historically detached Wilson, and his progressive lap dogs in Congress, even included a stamp tax. Wow.

Soapbox

Huge increases in inflation, like the ones experienced in the United States during World War I and its aftermath, are not without its moral and historical hazards. Set aside the fact that the federal government seized heretofore unimagined powers from American citizens; the economic turmoil wrought by American entrance into World War I set the stage for a biting (albeit short lived, thanks to Warren Harding and the post war Congress) recession in 1920-21. It goes still further: As I have argued and, indeed proven, the Black Sox Scandal of 1919, in which members of the Chicago White Sox threw the 1919 World Series at the behest of major gambling syndicates, was precipitated not by the supposed desperation and destitution of the players, but rather by the direct taxation and high inflation experienced by all Americans of the era. c.f. Gary Richied, "Fast Balls and Fast Bulbs: The Cause of Reckless Yet Rational Gambling Speculation on American Baseball 1917-1919 and Dutch Tulips 1636-1637" Mises Institute Libertarian Scholars Conference (2019): https://hoth2ohistory.com/product/fastballs-and-fastbulbs-paperback/

In Europe, American 'doughboys' arrived in France just in time to fight on the Western Front as Russia and her new Bolshevik government were exiting the war and ceding the Eastern Front (including vast expenses of European Russia) to Germany. The American entrance into the war bolstered already exhausted Britain and France, although without the

United States and left to face Germany alone, Britain and France might have been forced to enter negotiations to end the cataclysm. In essence, there is little doubt that American entry prolonged World War I.

American reinforcements suffered the same debilitating casualties as their Western European allies on the Front. In all, the United States sustained over 320,000 casualties; 116,516 American men died in Europe. Let that sink in: over 320,000 American boys and men died or came back seriously injured from a war in which the United States never felt any reasonable threat; from just over 12 months of actual fighting. Germany launched the "Michael Offensive"—St. Michael was considered the patron angel of Germany—in the spring of 1918. The Allies repulsed that incursion and then beat back the Germans in characteristically bloody battles along the then eastward moving Western Front. The Kaiser abdicated, and a battered and exhausted Germany sued for peace in November 1918.

Versailles Voodoo: Wilson Goes Mad

In 1919, representatives from the Allies and Central Powers met at Louis XIV's old playground to hammer out the details for the post-war world. Wilson earned his seat at the Versailles negotiating table by sacrificing those hundreds of thousands of American boys on the altar of what Wilson called democracy.

Outside of saddling Germany with causing the war and having to pay for all of its attendant effects, there really was no unifying theme behind the conference. Sure, the idea of national self-determination as opposed to reconstituting multinational states like the old Austro-Hungarian Empire had credence from the beginning, but practical matters and demands from Allied states like Italy and Japan rendered national self-determination null and void. In a myopic twist, even when national self-determination was to be held up as something of a principle, it was only to extend to the Mediterranean and the Ural Mountains; that is to say, only to Europe. Sure, the Czechs of Bohemia were going to get a state, but what of the old province-nations of the former Ottoman Empire? What about the German overseas colonies in the Pacific and Africa? Nope. There was to be no independent state for the Kurds in Mesopotamia, or for that matter the Shi'a Muslims toward the Persian Gulf. They couldn't possibly rule themselves, so Versailles granted Britain a "mandate" over a new multinational nation—one, in fact, conceived by Churchill himself—called Iraq. That would work out well... Just as there would be no independent Tanzania for the people of formerly German Southeast Afrika, there certainly was to be no independent Vietnam from French Indochina. The French won the war, after all; why should she relinquish an inch of her colonies? Against this notion stood a young, idealistic, Vietnamese nationalist, Nguyen Ai Quoc, traveled to Versailles and petitioned Wilson and Secretary of State Robert Lansing for an audience so that he might persuade them of the rectitude of his position that Vietnam ought to be freed from French colonial rule. He received no such meeting and no response from either American. Soon after Versailles, he traveled back to his native land, to

Hanoi in fact, where continued French domination radicalized him further. He became a communist and adopted the revolutionary name, Ho Chi Minh.

The German delegation left Versailles with as much, if not more disappointment and despair than the future North Vietnamese dictator. Not only was Germany ordered to surrender her overseas colonies to the Allies, but also Alsace-Lorraine was to go back to France, and much of the old German Empire's territory in the East would be swallowed up by a newly formed Poland. A large, German province known as the Sudetenland was given to the newly formed Czechoslovakia because the German speakers in the Sudetenland had always gotten along swimmingly with their Bohemian and Slovak neighbors to the south and east. No, as it turns out, not at all—they all hated each other. But into Czechoslovakia they all went. In fact, when a diplomat at Versailles informed Wilson that he was about to place 3 million Germans into Czechoslovakia, Wilson seemed completely and unapologetically unaware that such was the case. But, *qué será, será.*

Much worse, of course, were the war reparations payments foisted upon Germany and to a lesser extent, her Central Powers ally Austria. The war indemnities were designed to destroy the German economy, and provisions were made in the final documents to permit French occupation of Germany's industrial heartland should Germany be late with remuneration. Germany and Austria, in the following decade, tottered on the brink of economic destruction as various governments attempted to print their way out of debt. Unparalleled hyperinflation followed and living conditions in both nations became so poor as to produce a lasting, seething hatred of the parties to Versailles.

[3]

For Wilson, the new world map and treaty stipulations required a new global organization to oversee their implementation. He conceived of a League of Nations which would act as a forum with certain universal authorities to enforce his other Fourteen Points, a few of which, admittedly, were not half bad. For example, Points II and III called for freedom of navigation and a removal of trade barriers among nations. Other points strained the imagination, especially of David Lloyd George (Britain), Georges Clemenceau (France), and the majority of the United States Senate. The latter body remained so opposed to Wilson's new progressive order writ global that Wilson returned home to campaign to the point of exhaustion for the Senate to ratify the Versailles Treaty. It was in 1919 that Wilson's physical and mental health took a turn for the worse. He suffered a stroke that required the first lady to take on many of the executive functions. When mentally out of it, Edith Wilson and a cadre of close advisors kept the status of Wilson's condition a secret. When somewhat coherent, Wilson refused any concessions to the Senate regarding the Treaty. Led by Senator Henry Cabot Lodge, who was by no means an isolationist, opposition in the Senate focused on Article 10 of the treaty which obligated members of the League of Nations to "preserve as against external aggression the territorial integrity and existing political independence of all Members of the League." The United States should not be obliged to act, should, for instance, the Croats decide, per the Versailles Treaty's other declarations, that they no longer wanted to be a part of the artificially constructed, Serbian-dominated Yugoslavia. Wilson,

---

[3] https://commons.wikimedia.org/wiki/File:Europe_in_1923.jpg

in turn, dug in his heels and descended into a kind of mania regarding the Treaty. He ascribed divine connections to the Treaty, and his mental break from reality moved the United States ambassador to France, William Bullitt, to later collaborate with Sigmund Freud on a book detailing Wilson's flight to madness.

The Wilsonian Effect

The United States Senate never ratified the Treaty of Versailles. The United States, as a result, never became a member of the League of Nations. Wilson died in 1924 knowing (perhaps?) that his utopian progressive dream did not become a reality.

Or, did he? Note: I'm not suggesting here that Wilson didn't die—that would be weird. What I am suggesting is that Wilson's legacy has proven much more lasting and efficacious than even he could have appreciated. Of course, this has been disastrous for the country, but to say that Wilson's presidency was any less revolutionary because of his failure to get Versailles ratified is to miss the big, horrific picture.

To be sure, after the aggressive progressivism of the 19-teens, Americans pined again for a "return to normalcy" and, in turn, elected a Republican president and Congress in 1920. But, Wilson's progressive stamp remained on the country. Successive Congresses and executives never rolled back his domestic initiatives, including the Federal Reserve System. He segregated the U.S. Armed Forces and supported racist Jim Crow policy in the South, initiatives that would stand for decades to come. Few derided his open praise for the historicity of D.W. Griffith's apocryphal "Birth of a Nation."

But, the War itself, rather than invalidating government and its meddling in all aspects of American—and for that matter—human life, brought about no substantive, lasting revolution that returned the United States to a federal republic with provincial, humble ambitions.

As the great Murray Rothbard put it:

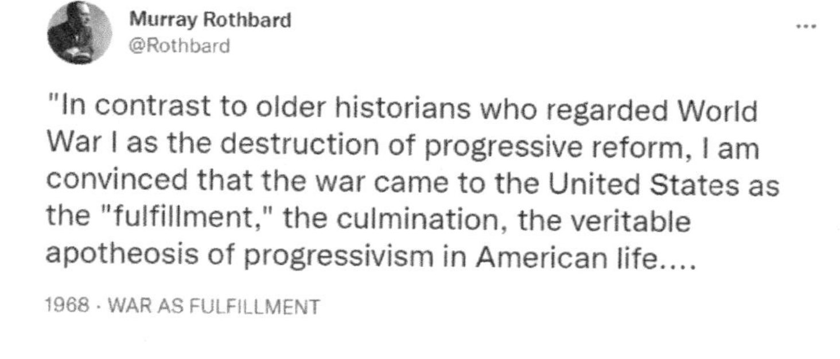

> ...I regard progressivism as basically a movement on behalf of Big Government in all walks of the economy and society, in a fusion or coalition between various groups of big businessmen, led by the House of Morgan, and rising groups of technocratic and statist intellectuals. In this fusion, the values and interests of both groups would be pursued through government.

Big business would be able to use the government to cartelize the economy, restrict competition, and regulate production and prices, and also to be able to wield a militaristic and imperialist foreign policy to force open markets abroad and apply the sword of the State to protect foreign investments. Intellectuals would be able to use the government to restrict entry into their professions and to assume jobs in Big Government to apologize for, and to help plan and staff, government operations. Both groups also believed that, in this fusion, the Big State could be used to harmonize and interpret the 'national interest' and thereby provide a 'middle way' between the extremes of 'dog-eat-dog' laissez faire and the bitter conflicts of proletarian Marxism.

I do not know of a better description of the modern American State. Despite the so-called 'return to normalcy' in the 1920s (which I will show is a dubious description for the decade), and for every Nye Commission or America First Committee that worked to raise the collective American eyebrow about government overreach and government schemes for foreign wars, the moment a "crisis" appears on the horizon, the reflexive reaction of the American populace has been deference to entrenched, elitist, corporate state operatives.

Crash. Depression. War. Poverty. Environment. Lab-created viral pandemic.

No matter.

Laissez Les Bons Temps Gueuler!

Let the good times return and roar!

That roar of the 1920s came as a result of the enormous pool of wealth generated during the decade following the rise of progressivism which culminated in the Great War.

Americans in the 1920s wanted to party, and partying became all the more attractive because the federal government made it illegal.

There was a healthy, rebellious spirit in the decade, so when Congress and the states finally buckled to the relentless, prudish petitioning of the teetotalers with the ratification of the 18th Amendment and then Volstead Act in 1919, prohibition prohibited little. Prohibition was a peculiar spasm, a strange holdover from the Progressive Era. It represented a typically progressive, idealistic, and sweeping social initiative that, in the end, proved how little the central government could do to enforce a law with which the vast majority of Americans refused to comply.

Americans had more time and disposable income than ever before. They worked less for higher wages, across class stratas.

[4]

The majority of American homes were electrified. Americans had new technologies and consumer products on which to spend that excess income, including refrigerators, vacuum cleaners, and radios. It was the era of thrilling audio detective dramas, which, given their high quality of writing and production, are making a comeback today with podcasts dedicated to that craft. The 20s were better than sliced bread for Americans across class lines—in fact, the decade was the era of sliced bread!

Loaves of bread will now be able to be sliced automatically by this machine that I created. Look for them in your local bakery soon!

Jul 1, 1928 · Saint Joseph, Missouri

98 Retweets 8 Quote Tweets 448 Likes

[4] N.B. "Molly Malone" is not a real historical figure. I chose the name because it sounded so prototypical and was also the name of one of my favorite bars in Chicago.

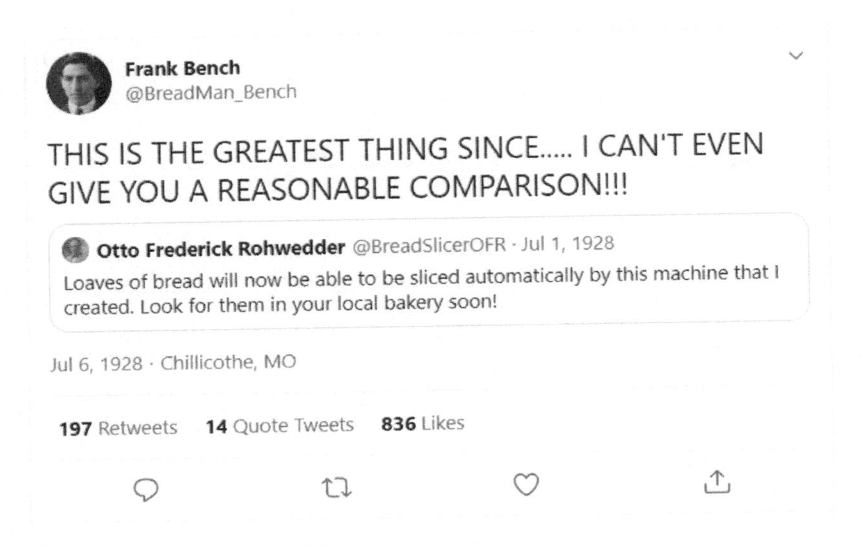

With all due respect to the automatic bread slicer, the most revolutionary product was the one that became available to more Americans than ever before: the automobile. In 1920, there were 7.5 million licensed cars and trucks in the United States; by 1929, there were 26 million on the roads. And yes, much of the credit for that belongs to Henry Ford.

Ford workers produced the Model T with such speed and efficiency that the car's price fell to the point that average Americans could put themselves behind the wheel. The Model T had no bells or whistles; it famously could be had in any color as long as it was black. But, it was affordable and dependable because it was the fruit of the labor of generally well-compensated autoworkers and Ford's own ingenuity. Way back in 1893, a young Ford attended the World's Columbian Exposition in Chicago and saw not only the internal combustion engines on display, but also availed himself of the side trip to the Chicago stockyards. With ruthless, gruesome efficiency, Ford witnessed how Swift, Armour, et al. had perfected the disassembly of livestock. It was said the only part of a pig not utilized by the Chicago meatpackers was the oink. Ford's Detroit factories reverse engineered the process for cars, and his assembly lines churned out a Model T every 93 minutes by 1914.

Cars became the primary means of conveyance for Americans seeking a good time. They attended massive sporting events, and the stadia and arenas of the era grew in size in order to accommodate them. Once they arrived, they were treated to Gene Tunney and Jack Dempsey boxing—and if one was really adventurous, one could jaunt off to exotic Havana or Ciudad Juarez to see the legend Jack Johnson fighting, into his 40s and 50s; that is, after he was released from prison for taking his white wife across state lines. No kidding, but we will get back to that in a moment. The legendary exploits of star baseball players grew, and they became household names as contests were broadcast over the radio. No one was bigger in the 20s than the Baltimore orphan who as a child was listed as "incorrigible"; when he turned to adulthood, George Herman Ruth joined the Boston Red Sox. In the most famous and decidedly one-sided transaction in professional sports history, "the Babe" was shipped off to the New York Yankees for cash considerations amounting to $25,000, possibly much less. The once star pitcher became the greatest hitter in the sport's history, as in both 1920 and 1927, he hit more home runs than any other *team* in the American League. He was the biggest sports star on the biggest stage, New York City, and like most other popular figures of the era, he possessed a wild air of accessibility and an equally apparent ability to relate to the everyday American. During the break between doubleheaders, while the Yankees visited Chicago's South Side to play the White Sox, Ruth ventured off to McCuddy's Pub for a roast beef sandwich and a beer. The "Sultan of Swat", the "King of Sting", the "Great Bambino" smashed any residual ill-will created by the Black Sox Scandal in 1919 with every home run and Yankees World Series Championship.

When urban Americans were not captivated by sports, they were off to dance clubs and speakeasies. Both venues featured the new, revolutionary music genres of the age: jazz and blues. Largely created by blacks and Italian immigrants (few 'nativists' saw a distinction between the two) in New Orleans and Chicago, jazz and blues were both innovative and improvisational in nature. Whites ventured to black neighborhoods like Harlem to see the best of the best play, like Bessie Smith and Duke Ellington. And, after the above ground shows, they frequented underground parties, imbibed bathtub gin, or when lucky, they got the good stuff, like Canadian whiskey smuggled in by bootleggers and crime syndicates. To drink was to break the law. Prohibition prohibited nothing, and that included the failure of government bureaucracies to enforce federal law. In point of fact, President Harding's Attorney General, Harry Daugherty, collaborated with and profited off of business with bootleggers. The whole thing was a boondoggle, as even the sporadic enforcement of prohibition naturally created a black market over which rival organized crime families battled it out for control of territories in the liquor trade. In many ways, prohibition was a prelude to the drug war of today. Rather than providing safety and security, government programs create the conditions by which violent crime results.

The licit and illegal, the mundane and the thrilling (and everything in between) in the Roaring 20s came as a result of first real, then later in the decade, ephemeral, prosperity. Americans turned away from the prevailing progressivism of the two previous decades in 1920. They elected Republican Warren G. Harding as president that November and sent a Republican Congress to Washington with him. Harding promised a "return to normalcy", and as a result, he practiced heroic inaction when the economic depression of 1920-21 hit. You read that correctly; Harding responded to the depression of that era by avoiding the modus operandi of his progressive predecessors. He prescribed *less*, not *more*, governmental intrusions. In so (not) doing, Harding charted a course for economic recovery that resembled a program that would have been favored by the best of the 19th-century presidents. Backed by his practical and experienced Secretary of the Treasury, Andrew Mellon, Harding recognized that the bubble-boom in American raw material and manufactures prices had ended with the war. Global demand for American agriculture and goods fell sharply in the war's aftermath. But, instead of enacting banking reforms, increasing protectionism, fixing prices or engaging in more welfare, Harding cut taxes so as to free up capital and incentivize investment away from municipal and governmental bonds and toward private equity. Harding slashed government spending nearly in half and reduced the national debt by one-third. In other words, the credit that was eventually extended to the market was not a result of fiscal stimulus nor intervention by the Fed (both institutions conspicuously sat on their proverbial hands in the early 1920s). Creditors had fought and worked hard for their capital; they were willing to risk it not for the foolhardy malinvestment of earlier years but rather sound and innovative outlets. As a result of the belt-tightening and laissez-faire oriented solution, unemployment went from 12% to 6.7% between 1920 and 1922. In 1923, it fell even further to a remarkable 2.3%. Those are numbers that future president Franklin Delano Roosevelt would kill for. And did...

Soapbox

Bring up Harding to any mainstream historian, and he's sure to bring up the "Harding Scandals". Hell, there are whole sections dedicated to Teapot Dome alone in major textbooks. Rarely if ever do said texts even mention Harding's idle achievements. This is because he does not fit the desired mode of credentialed micro-manager that the media and academia pine for today. Still some historians are more blatant in their enmity for Harding. For example, David Kennedy, Thomas Bailey, and Lizabeth Cohen—the same scholars who described Woodrow Wilson as a virtuoso gymnast as president—characterize Harding as possessing a "mediocre mind" who was not, "a bad man, just a slob." In truth, Harding was not a good guy, but a good president—though that is an admittedly very low bar. He conducted his time in the Oval Office with no conceit that government could or should solve peoples' problems. It needed instead to be throttled and ratcheted down. How wild.

So as to accommodate the rapid recovery and economic expansion, the construction of corporate skyscrapers matched that of new and reconfigured factories. The great metropoleis of America featured marvelous, ascendant skylines. Meanwhile, streets in New York, Philadelphia, and Chicago became synonymous with particular industries and sectors. LaSalle Street and Wall Street for finance. Broadway for theater. East Market Street, Michigan Avenue, and 5th Avenue for retail. Madison Avenue for advertising. Interestingly enough, under Harding and his successor, Calvin Coolidge, opportunities for rent-seeking and political entrepreneurship so dried up that K Street in Washington D.C.—so prominent today because of the massive political lobbyist firms operating there—was not a thing.

Harding died unexpectedly in August 1923. Coolidge took to the presidency and continued to head a government determined to get out of the way of entrepreneurship.

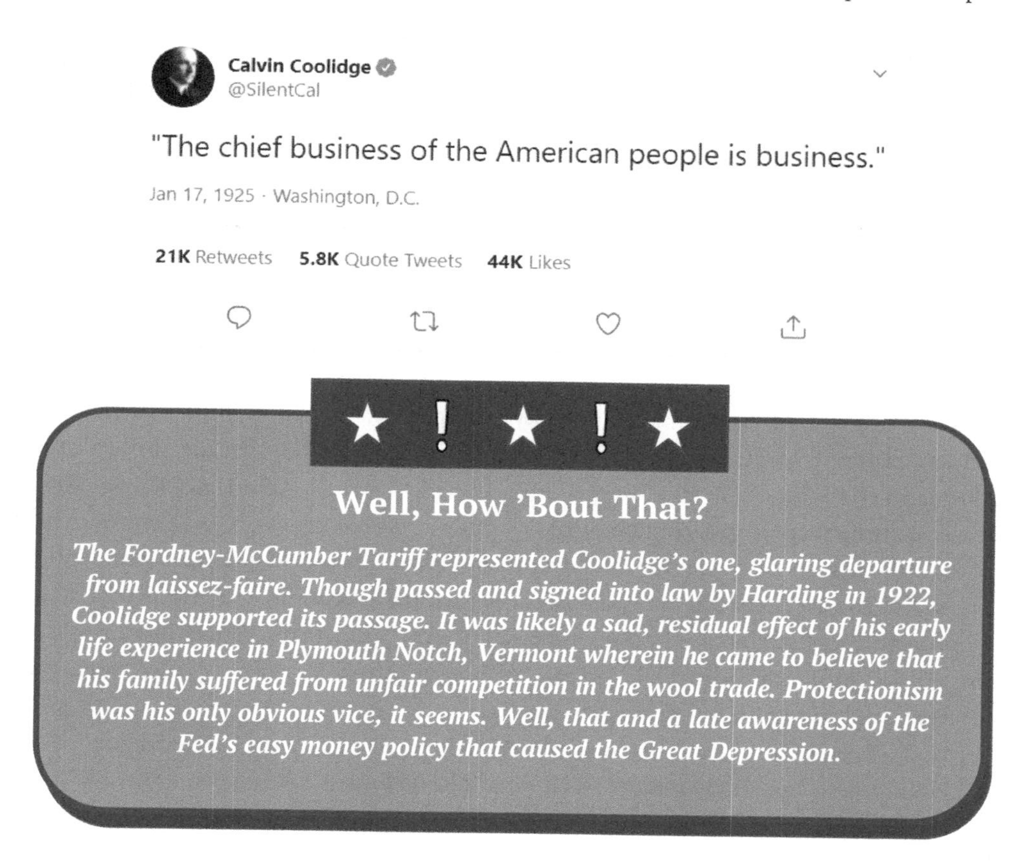

Always parsimonious with words, Silent Cal nonetheless possessed a humorous side indebted to his self-awareness. At a dinner in 1927, the President was seated next to a young Washington socialite. She addressed him and admitted, somewhat sheepishly, that she had made a wager that she could get him to say three or more words during dinner. He replied with stoic amusement: "You lose."

In the realm of foreign policy, both Harding and Coolidge charted a decidedly non-interventionist course. Secretary of State Charles Evans Hughes engaged in diplomacy that reflected the predominant mood—that is, outside of academia—of the American populace following World War I: Keep us the hell out of it. When the State Department did intervene in foreign affairs, it was to host the famous Washington peace conferences and endorse the Dawes Plan that allowed American credit to flow into Germany. The plan rescued Germany from utter impoverishment.

Under Coolidge, the national debt was reduced by another 25%. Real gross domestic product increased by over 21%.

But, to speak only of political economy is to miss the real essence of the American Roaring 20s. The common, generally lazy analysis provided in typical American texts from typical American historians is that the 20s represented a decade in which the country wrestled with two conflicting ideas and ways of life. It is repeated so often that it is almost the holy writ of American historiography: in the 20s, Americans were torn between tradition and modernity. Americans were wrenched out of their supposedly narrow, comfortable practices and mores and rushed into a life of secular and scientific modernity. To speak analogously, the skyscraper cast a tall and wide shadow over the cathedral; the city conquered the country; the village over the family. Certain events and trends are always cited as evidence of this tension. After all, the Scopes Monkey Trial pit evolution against creationism, did it not? It was all the rage in 1924 but seemed to lose Americans' attention as quickly as it captured them as the calendar year turned. Scopes—the Tennessee teacher who had unwittingly taught evolution in a government school—was convicted, but later the decision was tossed out on a technicality. After all, membership in the Ku Klux Klan reached an apex of 5 million in the 1920s. However, by the end of the decade, those numbers had fallen off a cliff. Were the 20s a unique period in which Americans struggled with nativist sentiment and open immigration?

The essence of the decade, better understood, can be found in a more familiar fight; namely the contest between the exercise of individual freedoms and the persistence of government constraints. Labor specialization, practical ingenuity, spirited entrepreneurship, and individual liberties won more often than not. Collectively, these victories served to repudiate the progressive era.

To be sure, prohibition was a colossal failure. Score one for the good guys. It was the illegality of booze that *made* Al Capone. The trumped up charges against Capone landed him in prison, only to have Joe Kennedy and others continue on to fill the keg, the barrel, the void. Americans wanted to drink, after all. Next, let's revisit legendary boxer Jack Johnson's story as an episode of clear racial injustice. In 1913, a federal court convicted Johnson of violating the Mann Act, which stated that it was a "felony to engage in the interstate or foreign commerce transport of any woman or girl for the purpose of prostitution or debauchery, or for any other immoral purpose." The only way that the law could be interpreted to have applied to Johnson was by the court defining consensual interracial sex as debauched. You remember that delegated power in the Constitution, right? Of course you don't—because it is not there. Johnson loved white women, and many white women loved Johnson. He was convicted. Terrible, because he committed no real crime, *pace* Freddy Mercury. Shortly after the trial, he and his second wife fled the country, and Johnson continued his career in Canada, Spain, Cuba, and Mexico. He went to Fort Leavenworth in Kansas to serve his year-plus prison term once he returned stateside. Because even in prison in the 20s, even with the clearly racist Mann Act acting as federal law, Johnson acted as though he were free. He wrote endearing love letters to his wife. His prowess and popularity as a fighter moved the warden to allow him to fight before crowds at the prison. For the rest of the decade, Johnson fought into his forties. Johnson raced cars. He traveled around the world. The government had taken a year of his life, but that was it—he took it back with a legendary vengeance.

That is not to say that racism in America died in the 1920s, and it certainly cannot be claimed that it diminished in the hearts and minds of men. It was virulent and unrelenting, especially to blacks like Johnson who lived boldly and refused to bow to racist restrictions. However, American culture in the 1920s impacted the political economy and policies of the country in such a way as to reduce those governmental intrusions that often exacerbated racial and class tensions. Numerous race riots occurred in the 19-teens and early months of the 20s. Some were sparked by the pure racism of whites reacting to Jack Johnson whipping white boxer after white boxer. But, the worst of the riots came in Chicago (1919) and Tulsa (1921). World War I veterans—many of them maimed physically and spiritually—returned home in those years to experience poverty, crippling inflation and a very loose labor market. Both cities enforced strict segregation that replicated that of the military under Woodrow Wilson; *de jure and de facto* segregation—that is, by law and in fact. Whereas those populations least affected by government policies like war, redlining, and Jim Crow mixed it up in Harlem, in speakeasies, and stayed busy bootlegging, those most disaffected by those destructive state policies suffered from the hazards they produced. Thus, as the decade continued, general prosperity and a general reduction in state intrusion reduced violence along racial and class lines. Racially motivated lynchings became increasingly rare. Large-scale strikes were equally as infrequent. In point of fact, during the decade, workers so demonstrated their general satisfaction with their jobs that they left unions en masse. Union membership fell by more than 40 percent in the 1920s.

It was the decade marked by the return of the rugged, pugnacious, American individual. The frontiers were different, yes, but they were conquered by the bold and the beautiful American man.

When Jack Johnson died, a reporter asked his last wife what she so loved about her husband. She responded:

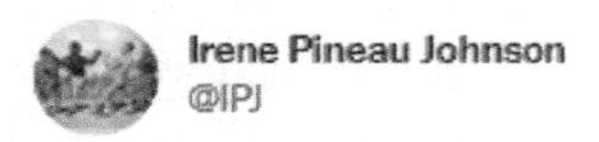

"I loved him because of his courage. He faced the world unafraid. There wasn't anybody or anything he feared."

June 1946 · Chicago, IL

8 Retweets **112** Likes

Well, How 'Bout That?

I can already hear the screeching, the howling, and the gnashing of teeth from those who have read of the atrocities committed by whites against blacks during the 1927 Mississippi Flood. Both John Barry and Bill Bryson have written great books about that year, 1927. It was the best of years. It was the worst of years. Irving Berlin and Ella Fitzgerald's tune "Blue Skies" hit the radio airwaves, and Charles Lindbergh and Robert Byrd flew nonstop over the Atlantic. Byrd would top (bottom?) that feat by venturing to Antarctica a year later. 1927 was also the year that heavy, constant rains battered the Delta and caused the Mighty Mississippi to crash over numerous levees from Cairo, Illinois down to New Orleans, Louisiana. Whites received government assistance to relocate while thousands of blacks were forced to reinforce the levees. Local oligarchs like Leroy Percy organized and supported what amounted to a systemized return of slave labor. The feds under Secretary of Commerce Herbert Hoover, were there to keep blacks in line, at times in literal chains, and ready to cover it all up with the help of—if you can believe this—propaganda from the American Red Cross which detailed the harmony with which the happy workers toiled! The incident would, at first glance, seem to disprove my analysis of a correlation between laissez-faire economics and laissez-vivre racial attitudes in the 1920s. On the contrary: It was only with orchestration by the government—local and centralized—that such racial crimes unfolded. It is true that Hoover's maleficence proved the catalyst for a black partisan shift from voting for Republicans to pulling the lever for Democrats in the century.

The Worst of Times

Next to the causes of the Civil War, the actual causes of the Great Depression remain utter mysteries to the vast majority of Americans. Blame for that falls on the usual suspects: teachers and politicians, as well as the many easily duped by both. I have encountered the predominant explanations of the Depression from students and scholars alike. Sparing the rare exception, they range from wildly apocryphal to obscenely absurd. There is no possible way that the United States as we know it today could have emerged from the 1930s and the experience of the Great Depression if those prevailing explanations were valid.

Allow me to list a few of them with some obligatory reactions. Warning: These explanations of the Depression make my ears and brain sting to this day. If you have the same symptoms while reading, do pause and even skip ahead if you know what is coming. I wish to not cause any unwarranted suffering.

1. "History has ebbs and flows. In the Roaring 20s, everything went up. Things were good. So, in the 30s, things had to go down to even out. The economy couldn't just keep going up after all."

I refer to this as the "mean reversion" or "what goes up, must come down" argument. These people are Hegelians, but don't really know it. Of course, there is really nothing analytical in this laziest of all explanations for the Depression. It relies on some strange, demiurge-like force that evens things out and recoils at extremes. It is pure superstition in that the length and degree of the improvement of standards of living appear extraordinarily random. Should we not, therefore, according to this explanation, now expect a return to feudalism since the Industrial Revolution of the 17th and 18th centuries lifted so many, so rapidly out of utter poverty? That would make things even, right?

2. "The Roaring 20s was a decade of excessive greed and decadence. There were no regulations on the stock market. The stock market crashed in October 1929. People panicked and spending went down. That led to a recession that turned into a decade-long depression."

This explanation sounds more sophisticated than the first, but when you scratch past the surface of it, it really is not much different. It depends upon a strange premise and logical fallacy; namely, that people in the 20s suffered from a bout of avarice more grave than the Spanish flu. People of previous eras were not very greedy, but Americans in the 20s were all fedora-wearing versions of Gordon Gekko.

At its core, this is the same pseudo-argument trotted out by the likes of American Senators Elizabeth Warren and Bernie Sanders when prices rise due to inflation. Instead of investigating fiscal and monetary manipulation by the government and Federal Reserve, they call for laws to set prices because those big oil companies and food producers are price gouging and suffering from malicious greed as though these enterprises want to make themselves less competitive by disincentivizing consumer purchases of their goods. They were not greedy a year or so ago when prices were low, but now they are greedy? The same point applies to the stock market. Were there more regulations preventing a stock market crash in 1900 than in 1929? The answer is no.

3. "People spent too much in the 1920s. They bought homes, cars, jewelry and stocks that they didn't need and couldn't afford, often on credit. This is the inherent failure of capitalism. It breeds 'keeping-up-with-the-Joneses' materialism. Overproduction to meet that demand then left farmers and workers unemployed when later, general demand fell."

There are some truths here. But, the moralizing is galling. It's quite something to hear modern Americans complain of the consumerism of others, from a century ago, as if a mirror is nowhere to be found! It is valid to point out that there were asset bubbles, particularly in the stock market. However, this argument begs two questions. First, what brought about the intense 'overspending'? If the answer is random 'greed', then see argument #2 above. If something else, then it ought to be indicated here. Second, why did the demand fall? Sounds like something was acting to artificially intensify demand, credit allocation and corresponding production. That something-monster then worked to suppress credit, reduce demand and quell production. What could that have been???

4. "The government did nothing and was asleep at the wheel as the economic downturn turned into a prolonged depression. Particularly problematic were laissez-faire Republican presidents like Coolidge and Hoover, then Congressmen and Supreme Court justices who blocked Franklin Delano Roosevelt's New Deal initiatives. Without the obstructionists, FDR's innovative policies would have gotten people

back to work, gotten the economy humming again, and ended the Depression. It would take World War II to finally get the country out of the Depression."

This is the line of argument that I have heard and read most often. It's a real doozy because it consists of a string of lies and counterfactuals. Coolidge was not a completely "laissez-faire" president, unfortunately. In truth, as much as Coolidge professed to be hands-off, he did favor tariffs, he restricted interstate lending, and he only pulled back on the reins of ever-expanding government. This is what economist Robert Higgs calls the 'ratchet effect'. Once a progressive government codifies sweeping interventions in American society and economy, history has proven that the subsequent 'conservative' reaction amounts to only a ratcheting back rather than full elimination of those programs and the bureaucracy created to impose them. Coolidge and the Republicans in Congress served only to stem the advance of big government and did nothing to eliminate the most odious initiatives of the previous progressive regimes. He did not get rid of the Fed. Antitrust laws remained in force. He was a trade protectionist. What is worse, when it became apparent that the economy was overheating, that credit was too easily available thanks to the Fed's policy of relatively low interest rates in 1926-1927, Coolidge resisted the urge to meddle with the Federal Reserve because of its supposed independence. He did, however, warn of economic bubbles and the turmoil ahead in 1929, all to no avail. As for Hoover—the guy was an interventionist and central planner from the beginning. Hoover did the exact opposite of what his former boss, Warren Harding, had done in 1921. Facing his own economic recession as president in 1930-32, Hoover committed to wage controls, higher taxes, and massive state expenditures. All of these actions crowded out private economic activity and intensified state larceny. Regarding the 'obstructionists' in Congress and the Courts, the Republicans in Congress were no more than minor speedbumps to FDR. The Courts did invalidate a number of FDR's more blatantly illegal measures, such as aspects of the Wagner Act, but left many more in place. But, even those acts ruled unconstitutional by the Courts wrought havoc for months or years before they were invalidated.

At first glance, the New Deal consisted of programs that did get some people back to work—sort of. An inconvenient fact about the programs was that they were designed to stunt unemployment, but unemployment never broke below 20 percent for the decade. Even those employed by the government programs labored on projects for which there was not nor would ever be, any true market demand. It was all folly, busy work and boondoggles. Inuits in Alaska made totem poles featuring U.S. presidents. The still vaunted Tennessee Valley Authority flooded more land than it protected. Perhaps the most infuriating of all were those actions undertaken by the Department of Agriculture. Secretary of Agriculture Henry Wallace, a Soviet sympathizer and apologist rivaling Walter Duranty, led his fellow apparatchiks and comrades in that bureaucratic cabal. Armed with the Agricultural Adjustment Act of 1933, they went out to destroy millions of tons of food. They ordered farmers to bulldoze lemon and orange groves. In Nebraska alone, the feds bought and then immediately slaughtered about 470,000 cattle and 436,000 pigs. They just buried the carcasses in mass livestock graves, because this savage reduction in supply would increase prices for foodstuffs and then help out American farmers. Ala Henry Hazlitt: Unfortunately, the cows and pigs were seen and then truly unseen. Sound economic thought, on the other hand, was wholly absent. All of this destruction of food in the revolutionary, planned economy occurred, just as, by the national government's own measurements, about 12 percent of the American population was so malnourished as to be defined as on the brink of starvation.

Even FDR's most ardent apologists today—such as historian Doris Kearns Goodwin—admit that there is no evidence that the WPA or the CCC or the National Labor Relations Board, or any of the 'alphabet soup' programs did a lick of good. Instead, they bleat something along the lines of, "Well, at least FDR did something," thus conflating activity with productivity, or they bloviate about how FDR's Depression fireside radio chats had a palpable psychological effect on the country. Please! FDR's own Secretary of the Treasury, Henry Morgenthau summed up the seven years of the New Deal in no uncertain terms:

Finally, World War II. This claim needs to be shot with a silver bullet laced with garlic and a crucifix shaped into a stake driven into its heart! It just keeps coming back again and again. American entrance into World War II did not rescue the country from the Depression. Wars are disastrously expensive, and World War II takes the cake. For almost four full years, the national government transformed a consumer economy, by force, into an industrial war machine. It required intense rationing at home. The war economy was a command and control, fascistic machine. The bill for it came in at $330 billion, or more money than *twice* all of the expenditures of the national government since 1776. All of that wealth, all of that value was expended, not on domestic needs but rather on the destruction of the Axis Powers.

Endnote here: If war was so recuperative to national economies, why would the nations of the world not favor total, unrelenting, and perpetual conflict? War resurrects economies; war rains prosperity on people after all! Back to reality: One should question why, throughout any other reading of world history, war is listed as a primary cause for the destruction of countries and the dissolution of empires. But, magically, World War II for the United States was the best thing ever; never mind, of course, the almost 300,000 dead American men! Stay tuned and alert to the later pages wherein I demolish the American historical myth of World War II. War prosperity is like a first-time heroin high: delusional, escapist, short-lived; ultimately debilitating and never matched.

Ok. The previous arguments are observably false. However, the greatest capitalist economist of the century—Milton Friedman—wrote with Anna Schwartz that the Fed is to blame for raising interest rates too quickly and at the most inopportune time. The rate increases took place as recession loomed, and in turn, this created a credit crunch. No credit was readily available for good companies to weather the downturn. Many of them failed as a result. Sustained unemployment, bank runs, and falling GDP resulted.

Friedman and Schwartz were great economists. On most things. Explaining the causes of the Great Depression was not one of them.

For that, we have to turn to the triumvirate of the truly greatest economists of the 20th century who left Friedman and Schwartz (and their surreptitiously Keynesian explanation of the Depression) in their brilliant dust: Ludwig von Mises, Murray Rothbard, and Friedrich Hayek.

"But, but Friedman won a Nobel Prize in economics?!" First of all, who cares? After all, so did Paul Krugman, Richard Thaler, and David Card. Barack Obama won the Peace Prize and then proceeded to drone bomb the shit out of the Middle East and expand the war on terror (whatever that is) into North Africa and beyond. The Nobel Committee in Oslo has yet to rescind the award. But, secondly, back when the economics crown did mean something, Hayek won it in 1974. Touché.

Armed with Mises's praxeology and Austrian business cycle theory, Rothbard and Hayek tore apart the above mainstream contention, which was more of an accounting of correlation as opposed to causation. To summarize, yes, the Fed did raise rates in the first half of 1928 as it was concerned with marked increases in asset prices, particularly in the stock market. The crash came in October 1929 and a necessary market correction followed because of all of the poor (or better, mal-) investment that occurred during the boom and bubble of the mid-twenties. The ensuing centralized, planned economy measures of the hyperactive Hoover and Roosevelt administrations plunged the economy into a long depression. It was not simply the increase in interest rates and resistance to lowering them, for, if it were, how could the market monetarists (Friedman's camp in Chicago) explain why even greater, even parabolic interest rate increases result in a decade long depression; for example, in the early 1980s when Fed chair Paul Volker raised rates to an incredible 20 percent? Simple: They don't.

The historical account of the 1930s further disproves the aforementioned arguments, and for that matter, any others that might contend with the proof that government intervention caused the Depression.

The alarming statistics of the era illustrate just how deep and sustained the Depression was. Non-farmer worker unemployment never fell below 14 percent for the decade; it reached a high of 38 percent in 1933. Between 1929 and 1933, real GDP fell by 30 percent. Corporate profits were *negative* from 1931 to 1933, and net *private* investment was negative as well. This meant that in the United States, which had been the dominant manufacturer to the world for the previous three decades, companies did not have the means by which to update and replace worn out machines nor outfit factories. In industry, therefore, innovation did not just stall—it went backward and contracted. The misery index, which consists of the consumer price inflation rate (CPI) and the unemployment rate, reached a still unmatched high of 23.2 percent in 1934.

What that all looked like at the time, just how destructive it all was for the American people—that is immeasurable. All the historian is left to do is to appeal to the historical imagination of those today, through visuals and accounts. Only through such a recounting can one attain an appreciation for the depths of impoverishment and despair, especially of an adult population that had experienced the heights of prosperity in the 1920s only to see most of it washed away.

With unemployment and the loss of savings through bank failures, desperation set in. Vagrancy skyrocketed. Men especially searched far and wide for gainful employment. They took to the rails as vagabonds, and mothers were often left alone to care for the family. Historian Robert Spinney recounts one of the most poignant stories of the Depression, one of the women in Cicero, a suburb of Chicago, picking through garbage at a local dump. When they discovered a discarded piece of meat, the women were seen picking maggots off of them and then handing the remnant to their children.

To be sure, many of the photos taken amounted to propaganda pieces for Roosevelt's regime. These just happen to be the ones most of us have seen because they are featured in U.S. History texts on the Depression. However dramatized to support New Deal interventions, that does not mean that the desperate situations of those depicted were hyperbolized. The Depression left a swath of Americans destitute and without any apparent way out.

JOBLESS MEN
KEEP GOING
WE CAN'T TAKE CARE OF OUR OWN

The Empty Suit

What, on the other hand ought to arouse righteous indignation, was the outright mendacity of the political class throughout the Depression. Roosevelt lied in his campaign against Hoover in 1932. In speech after speech, he hit Hoover for being *too interventionist* in the economy. Furthermore, as scholar and intellectual giant Lew Rockwell has pointed out, FDR's popularity with ordinary Americans soared, not as a result of his policy positions, but because of his campaign promises to end prohibition.

Roosevelt was a New York empty suit, the epitome of the Upper East Side establishment. He got his foreign policy from the war-mongering Council on Foreign Relations, and he got what might be called his economics (although identifying it as such would be too complimentary) from communists and Keynesians in his circle. He was an economic ignoramus who filled his speeches on the subject with empty platitudes and specious promises. He spoke of the "forgotten man" in America in a way generally unfamiliar to Americans from both his own time and bygone eras as well. Like his political hero, Woodrow Wilson, Roosevelt asserted that the forgotten man was the one who society had left behind.

In place of the invisible hand, the hand of government now needed to lift up those in the lower, working classes. To be sure, Roosevelt based his assertion on a blatantly false assumption; namely, that the lower class is permanent and fixed. In a true or close to totally free market, there is dynamic movement up and down the economic ladder. Roosevelt promoted, unsurprisingly, the notion of a static class structure which happens to be an essential feature of socialist regimes and not free ones. It is under socialist regimes that cronyism ensures that those connected to the state flourish while those independent of it remain downtrodden. Government oversight and hyperactivity create the injustices of which Roosevelt spoke. As a true progressive, Roosevelt proscribed more of it.

Back in the Gilded Age, the great William Graham Sumner identified who the real "forgotten man" was:

Poor "C." In Sumner's algebraic formulation, "A" and "B" represent interchangeably "concerned" government agents and agitated muckraker intellectuals. Neither group, one will notice, have any faith in emergent order or the natural flow of things. They leave themselves to their own messianic devices to fix the problem. Having convinced themselves of the righteous benevolence of their goal, "A" and "B" go the legislative route to remedy what they perceive is ailing "X." "A" and "B" determine—without hesitation—that they are not going to do this alone. We're "all in this together" after all. Hence, they enlist and impose upon "C" their particular remedy for "X." "C" always bears the brunt of their programs. "C" is too busy at work and life to think he can truly diagnose that from which "X" suffers, much less determine a cure for it. He is without pretension or presumption. Though he is seldom regarded and always victimized in the end, "C" might as well stand for "civilization" because, without "C," civil life is an impossibility.

But, that spirit that championed the entrepreneur, the innovator, and the free consumer was on life support by 1933. Sumner was dead and *this* Roosevelt was not. In his famous first Hundred Days, Roosevelt dispensed with the pretense that he was going to ratchet back his predecessor's economic interventions. Instead, he multiplied and intensified them.

Examine the table below which lists the most revolutionary acts and their effects.

LAW/ORDER	EXPLANATION	EFFECTS
Emergency Banking Relief Act (1933)	-enacted a four-day national banking holiday; government determined which banks were independently solvent, which needed government aid, and which were insolvent=forcibly closed.	*-amounted to a federal takeover of the banking industry; Congress empowered to arbitrarily determine winners and losers among banks; a bailout for government-connected banks by Federal Reserve printing.*
Emergency Conser-vation Work Act (1933)	-created the Civilian Conservation Corps (CCC) of federal, manual laborers to work to conserve and develop resources on government lands.	*-a boondoggle of epic proportions, the CCC removed tens of thousands of laborers from the private sphere to public work projects for which there was no demand in the consumer marketplace.*
Federal Emergency Relief Act (1933)	-created the Federal Emergency Relief Administration (FERA) which created new, unskilled jobs in local and state government, employing 20 million people at its height.	*-the "production" from the new government employees never approached the payouts (even then pejoratively called "the dole"); waste and fraud were rampant.*

Agricultural Adjustment Act (1933)	-begot the Agricultural Adjustment Administration and empowered the Department of Agriculture to decrease existing food stocks and limit farm production in the hope that lessened supply of foodstuffs would stabilize prices for farmers.	*-as a significant percentage of the country faced malnutrition and starvation, the Roosevelt Administration determined that low food prices indicated a fatal flaw of capitalism and thus sought to remedy said flaw by ruthlessly destroying food; the act benefitted large corporate agriculture firms and led to a rushed relocation of small farmers to cities.*
Tennessee Valley Authority Act (1933)	-established the Tennessee Valley Authority to modernize, mainly through electrification, the impoverished area. Dams were constructed and other utilities in the area were placed under the control of the TVA.	*-perhaps the most purely socialistic of New Deal programs, the TVA not just crowded out but eliminated all private investment and utility work in the Tennessee Valley. Henry Ford was blocked from developing the area. The resultant projects have resulted in ecological disasters (floods, toxic coal dumps) for which the federal government remains unaccountable. Over 125,000 Tennessee residents were displaced, by eminent domain, many of them disparaging to such an extent that suicides rose parabolically at the time. Remarkably, the TVA still exists and is still funded by federal tax dollars to this day.*

Banking Act (1933)	-also known as the Glass-Steagall Act, legally separated corporate from investment banking. In addition, the Federal Deposit Insurance Corporation (FDIC) was formed to back/guarantee deposits up to $5000 by 1934.	*-this Banking Act was to finance what the Hepburn Act (1906) was to railroads. Arising from populist sentiment and demagogic investigations, by stripping especially small banks of the flexibility to engage in open banking, the regulations in the law and FDIC itself institutionalized a government-enforced cartel which permitted and authorized commercial banks to earn high profits and avoid risk. It won for the Federal Reserve even greater control over credit markets.*

National Industrial Recovery Act (1933)	-codified what had been yet another Hoover administration policy; the bill authorized the executive branch to regulate industry wages and prices. It forced manufacturers to adopt government-approved codes for production. It provided sweeping protections for unions, including unheard of legal cover for collective bargaining.	*-written largely by Roosevelt adviser Hugh S. Johnson, an open fascist who proudly distributed Mussolini's writings to the Cabinet, the NIRA authorized central planning of the economy. Just like the Banking Act, the regulatory codes could only be implemented by large firms which could absorb or socialize the cost. Labor disputes and work stoppages increased. The act empowered Washington bureaucrats to arbitrarily determine what constituted "fair" prices and "fair" wages. The law even set prices for petroleum and related products. It was ruled unconstitutional by the Supreme Court in 1935.*
Executive Order #6420B (1933)	-formed the Civil Works Administration, a temporary work program for manual/construction laborers during the winter of 1933-34.	*-at enormous expense (a total of $800 million, or $175 billion today) thousands of laborers were put to busy work creating mostly hideous and useless buildings.*

Gold Reserve Act (1934)	-following Executive Order 6102, which prohibited the ownership or trade of gold by U.S. citizens, this act called for the seizure of all physical gold and gold certificates by the Treasury Department. It authorized the president to set the gold-dollar exchange rate by fiat proclamation.	*-with the dollar still nominally pegged to gold, the government moved to stop Americans exchanging their devalued dollars into gold, and using gold as an alternative currency. Owning gold became a crime. Roosevelt then set the gold-dollar exchange rate at $35 per troy ounce, up from around $20. More dollars were printed and circulated around the globe. Interest rates tanked, by design, in the hope that cheap credit would stimulate durable goods production. It increased modestly and only to then crater again in 1937-38.*
Securities Act (1934)	-regulated the purchase of stocks and other financial instruments; such power to do so, per the Constitution, was the jurisdiction of the states prior to the Act. The Securities and Exchange Commission (SEC) formed to oversee and police all exchanges.	*-yet another power that was usurped from the states and handed to Washington. The Act deemed all purchases of securities as acts of interstate commerce. The SEC provided a false sense of assurance to investors. SEC regulatory costs funds and value that might be otherwise allocated toward worthwhile goals. The SEC possesses a horrible record of actually uncovering market malfeasance. cf. Bernard Madoff et al.*

Communi-cations Act (1934)	-combined and organized the federal regulation of all telephone, telegraph, and radio communications. The Act created the Federal Communications Commission (FCC) to oversee, license and police these industries.	*-under the guise of safeguarding "national defense", and "for the purpose of promoting safety of life and property through the use of wire and radio communication," the Act effectively gave Washington the ability to determine the content of wire and wireless communication networks. The Act allowed AT&T to continue to operate as a regulated monopoly and protected the company from anti-trust suits. Major radio stations announced that they would no longer broadcast any content critical of the Roosevelt administration. Dissenters and critics had their licenses revoked. Per media historian Betty Houchin Winfield, radio allowed the president to be "the news gatherer, the reporter, as well as the editor," all at the same time. The Act has been used as legal precedent to justify abominations such as the "fairness doctrine" and "net neutrality".*

Executive Order #7034 (1935)	-one of the first acts of the Second New Deal. It established the Works Progress Administration (WPA) as a replacement to FERA. The WPA employed over 3.3 million people at its height.	*-at a ridiculous price tag of $4.1 billion ($201 billion today), the WPA paid everyone from construction workers to artists at rates well below private averages. Rife with waste, corruption and political angling, regions like the South – thought to be Democratic strongholds – were purposefully sent 75% less funding. Swing states and districts received heavy allotments of "the dole" to move the political needle. WPA workers were notoriously lazy owing to the recognized fact that few people desired what they produced. People in the 30s joked that WPA really stood for "We Piss Ants" and "Whistle, Piss and Argue". The crowding out effect hurt private businesses looking for work and labor.*

National Labor Relations Act (1935)	-otherwise known as the Wagner Act, the law guaranteed the right of private sector employees to form trade unions, to collectively bargain, and to strike. The National Labor Relations Board formed to police businesses that they might refrain from supposedly unfair labor practices.	*-the Wagner Act concluded the progressive vision of making laborers a legally protected and privileged class of citizens, albeit in select industries. Gone was the TR pretense of a Square Deal; the Wagner Act served as a declaration of the federal governments' dedicated preference of labor in labor/capital disputes – the presumption being that labor union leaders always acted on behalf of workers. Sit-down strikes and closed-shop activities became commonplace. Union membership became a near prerequisite in industries. Many black workers from the South who had moved to the North were shut out of unions and thus further shut out of work.*

Social Security Act (1935)	-created a social safety net, welfare program for the elderly along with unemployment insurance. Funds for the programs were to be collected in a novel way—directly through payroll taxes.	*-like with the Wagner Act before it, now elderly Americans were granted preferential class status. The Act created the (probably) intended consequences and moral hazards of destroying community and religious mutual aid societies as well as moving individuals and families to cede care of seniors to the government. It has amounted to a gargantuan transfer of wealth from generation to generation. Today, with its attendant Medicare programs, it accounts for an astounding 29.9% of the federal budget.*

Rural Electrification Act (1936)	-Roosevelt issued Executive Order 7037 which created the Rural Electrification Administration tasked with electrifying country districts. Congress codified the Order post hoc, through the passage of the Act. The Act amounted to a loan program to rural electric cooperatives. Rural residents, in order to receive service, needed to have formal membership in the cooperative.	*-the so-called "cooperatives" bore little to no distinction from the literal soviets, or workers syndicates, funded by the state in Bolshevik Russia. Head of the Communist Party of the United States, William Z. Foster, once proclaimed that cooperatives like those formed in the REA represented "the foundation stone in the socialist economic system". With rampant fraud and waste, rural homes were electrified by union workers through these REA cooperatives at the initial cost of $100 million. Taxpayers would continue to indiscriminately subsidize* the most connected Rural Electrification Cooperatives (RECs) with artificially low interest loans to the tune of tens of billions of dollars well into the 1990s. The public-private partnership model was only viable because of its reliance on government funds. The RECs became models for later Great Society Programs that proved to be equally ineffective and corrupt.*

United States Housing Act (1937)	-built upon the previous National Housing Act (1934) which provided funds for Americans struggling to pay their home mortgages. The Act instituted the Federal Housing Administration (FHA) which was charged with insuring private lenders against loan losses. It established a system of loans and grants-in-aid to local public housing authorities.	*-the housing and mortgage subsidies disproportionately went to middle class individuals and well-established developers who could buy and clear blighted areas with federal money, sell the land to private developers, and use the proceeds to cover the redevelopment costs. The federal payments prevented housing prices from clearing and locked out lower class and poor Americans from the housing market. Construction of new homes plummeted, which worsened unemployment in the construction industry. Finally, the Act laid the groundwork for the savings and loan scandal and crisis in the 1980s.*

Fair Labor Standards Act (1938)	-established a federally mandated minimum wage for any worker engaged in interstate commerce and delegated to the Congress the power to measure and determine the proper living wage of Americans, given the Act's assertion that the market had failed to provide labor conditions and pay conducive to the well-being of workers and the free flow of commerce.	*-the Act wars against basic economics in that an employer cannot pay his employee more than that employee's discounted marginal revenue product, i.e. the employee's contribution to the employer's company's revenues. As such, rather than ensuring mass employment at a fair or living wage, the minimum wage disincentivized hiring, especially at entry-level positions.*

★ ! ★ ! ★

Well, How 'Bout That?

What I mean by indiscriminate subsidy is that the Rural Electrification Administration provided low interest loan guarantees not just to fund the electrification of poor rural communities. As late as the 1980s, before the REA was disbanded and then replaced with a new bureaucratic monstrosity from Washington, the subsidies went out to large electrical distributors in such destitute areas as Hilton Head, South Carolina and Vail, Colorado. Those golf carts and ski lifts require a lot of electricity after all.

The Revolution Was

That is a lengthy table, but a necessary one. It spells out both the wishful but naturally doomed hyperactivity of the hapless Roosevelt administration and Congresses of the period. Propaganda spilled out of Washington to impress upon the American population that, regardless of what many were witnessing and experiencing in their daily lives, the government programs initiated at the time were working to quell the misery. They were not.

What was very much at work, was *a revolution*. It is not too much to call it *the revolution*. The New Deal eviscerated traditional American notions of what it meant to be free, that only with minimal, localized and constrained government could voluntary, mutual and cooperative action allow individuals within a society to live free and thrive. The central message of the New Deal read like this: Capitalism had failed due to its excesses; government therefore must humbly step in to rein in the system so as to correct and direct those passions into producing communal benefits and value to the nation. The messaging on this front—from fireside chats to WPA posters—ramped up as the Depression and its effects intensified and persisted.

To borrow from Ernest Hemingway, the revolution came gradually and then all of a sudden.

Notice the operative word included in the earliest acts of the New Deal: *emergency*. Roosevelt had not spoken of transformative executive orders and legislative acts on the campaign trail, at least in 1932. Sure, there were inferences to the forgotten man and a bottom-up rather than top-down recovery program, but who except Roosevelt himself and those in his close tow could have envisioned the Hundred Days? The speed and radicalism of it all was excused due to this state of emergency. It was largely permitted by a populace in despair and destitution.

Thus it was that Roosevelt assumed the role of president-tribune. Like the Gracchi brothers of the old Roman Republic, the more contemporary but nonetheless comparably flailing American Republic handed power to a populist despot who promised wealth redistribution from the rich to the poor, the privileged to the disaffected. Having secured power, Roosevelt had time—thanks to a compliant Senate and the persistence of the Depression—to transition into a president-dictator, more Caesar than Gracchi, because after all, the Gracchi did not stay in power very long. The Caesars sure did.

For the Rooseveltian-federal-establishment to maintain the immense and inescapable power their man and they themselves had won, the people had to be convinced—albeit subtly—that the emergency has never abated. It has to be perpetual. Sure, the nature and cause of the crisis might change over time, but the state of emergency cannot.

The title of this chapter comes from an eponymous essay by the great scholar Garet Garrett. It is a work that, in a just and curious world, would be featured reading in schools, as opposed to the sniveling and fawning drivel of establishment court historians like Arthur Schlesinger and Heather Cox Richardson.

In it, Garrett outlines exactly the course that the progressives took to bring the revolution to fruition and completion. *The revolution* had to be *a revolution* of great care and cunning, one in which the state had to be taken over from within, by a devout cadre of co-religionists determined to subvert individual rights to governmental authorities, all the while deploying double-speak like sacramental rubrics to fool the public into believing that the accidents, or shell of American society, reflected what was still truly taking place on the inside. The antecedent façade of constitutional self-determinism remained while the reconstruction from within was completed. Garrett opined back in 1938, that from 1933 onward, above the altar to the state read the "shibboleth that united them all: 'Capitalism is finished.'"

Garrett spelled out the program in nine ruinous steps. New Dealers aimed to:

1. Capture the seat of government.
2. Seize economic power.
3. Mobilize by propaganda the forces of hatred.
4. Reconcile and then attach to the revolution the two groups of workers who are normally enemies; namely, farmers and industrial wage earners. The government would pay off both.
5. Shackle business. Do not liquidate it Soviet style. Direct it toward state aims.
6. Domesticate the individual; make him dependent upon government.
7. Reduce if not eliminate all forms of rival authority.
8. Sustain popular faith in an unlimited public debt, and convince the public of the state's right to borrow and spend the wealth of the rich.
9. Make government the ultimate capitalist and enterpriser, forever transferring capital power from the hands of private enterprise to the all-powerful state.

"Each one of these problems would have two sides, one the obverse and one the reverse, like a coin. One side only would represent the revolutionary intention. The other side in each case would represent Recovery--and that was the side the New Deal constantly held up to view."

1938 · THE REVOLUTION WAS · New Jersey

2,860 Retweets **774** Quote Tweets **77.5K** Likes

The New Deal programs accomplished these specific steps amounting to the general triumph: Free markets ended in favor of a mixture of corporatism and syndicalism, and a free people surrendered their liberties in favor of security, even if that security was a delusion, it ended up being a very popular one.

So popular, in fact, was the New Deal taken as a whole, that it weathered the most serious storms. The Depression ground on in the absence of an actual economic recovery. Furthermore, when Roosevelt moved to pack the Supreme Court only for Congress to finally push back a little, the same population who had re-elected him to the tune of a 24.3 percent popular vote margin also stated, when polled, that 45 percent of them feared that the United States *was* devolving into a dictatorship. That is some scary overlap there. So be it: Whatever the governmental system, whatever the quantity and quality of economic interventions, at least the Depression *felt* like it was over. One can only stand amazed at the sway of a state over its captives, for whether it is a persistent economic depression, unending wars on amorphic themes, or a "pandemic", the state transitions to a new emerging crisis with the smoothest of ease and the total evasion of accountability. It is both Fred Astaire and Harry Houdini all at once.

Well, How 'Bout That?

The New Deal proved this corporatist-syndicalism possible. While at first glance, the marriage of the two appears to be a contradiction in terms and thus an impossibility. It turned out, on the contrary, to be the essence of the program. Under corporatism, the government picks corporate winners and losers, allotting subsidies, favorable regulations, contracts and other beneficences to certain companies. Those companies, in turn, become what Professor Michael Rectenwald has called the major social media and tech firms today—*governmentalities.* They are beholden to the dictates of Washington and function as extensions of the government, yet they retain the veneer of capitalist enterprises/private businesses. Syndicalism refers to the movement by which workers—thanks to preferential labor laws—come to demand increased control over the workplace, better pay and augmented benefits for less work, with the threat of a strike forever looming. Thus the federal government owned both: The favored and subsidized big businesses who could endure with collective bargaining, artificial wage hikes, and work stoppages and the appeased workers who felt protected by government should they petition it. The New Deal dealt a death blow to the old notion of contractual agreement between an employer and an employee. As such, the New Deal was rather indistinguishable from the contemporary economic aims of Mussolini and Hitler. cf. Rainer Zitelmann,* Hitler's National Socialism, *2022.

5

World War II, The Cold War, and the Warfare-Welfare State, 1939-1945

Running Toward Global War

If there was one unintended yet beneficial consequence of Roosevelt's obsession with the implementation of the New Deal, it was that, for the most part, he and his administration had little time to screw up foreign affairs as much as they were screwing up domestic affairs; that is, at least, early on in his presidency. Indeed, the foreign policy of the United States in the early 30s represented a sound continuation of the positions of his virtuously dovish predecessors since Wilson. The so-called "Good Neighbor Policy" resulted in the withdrawal of American troops from Haiti, for instance. Though selectively enforced because of the administration's continued obsession with meddling in Mexican and Cuban affairs, the "Good Neighbor Policy" featured an overall reduction of U.S. paternalism over Latin America and the Caribbean.

On the other hand, the consummation and then completion of the New Deal revolution only emboldened Roosevelt and fellow internationalists in his administration to do more on the world stage. In point of fact, the two developments track quite well: The more transformative and established the New Deal program, the more foolhardy and aggressive Rooseveltian foreign policy became. The isolationist mood, the general will, and the legislative acts of the Congressmen, posing as representatives of the people, be damned. *The revolution* was not intended nor designed to be limited to the borders of the United States after all. Seeing the rest of United States history through this historical lens makes things much, much clearer.

The foreign policy revolution came on gradually, and then, all of a sudden.

As early as 1935, Roosevelt committed the United States to an aggressive interventionist role in foreign affairs, and he did so in secretive circumvention of the law.

The truth of the build-up to American entrance into World War II remains so buried under anti-revisionist histories written by court historians and pseudo-journalists that even the bold and courageous who succeed in digging through the muck are left exhausted and disheartened—the latter feeling arrives when one notices how a more truthful and accurate account of what went into Pearl Harbor, for example, falls on willfully deaf ears. But, here we are, providing an account that serves as the finale to the historical fireworks show that is this book.

The first of two gigantic (mind) explosions: American entrance into World War II did not take place on December 8, 1941, the day after the Japanese attack on Pearl Harbor.

It started on September 2, 1940.

Not familiar with what happened on September 2, 1940?—well, don't feel bad about that—very few people are. On that day which ought to live in infamy, through an executive order, Franklin Delano Roosevelt transferred 50 American warships to Great Britain in exchange for port and base rights in several British colonies. Unlike in the post hoc, rubber stamp Congress days of the early New Deal, this fateful, unilateral act never received Congressional approval, but it amounted to nothing short of a declaration of war against Germany.

The destroyers-for-bases deal unveiled what had been really going on: As war had raged in Asia and Europe, the Roosevelt administration wished to maintain official neutrality while actively provoking Germany in the Atlantic and Japan in the Pacific.

Follow the logic in this thought experiment: If, for example, I was walking down the street, and I saw Taylor Swift and Katy Perry in a fistfight, my first inclination would be to hope that they would knock each other out so that they both would be unable to produce any more awful music. Sparing that outcome, if in this scenario, I walked up to Ms. Swift and gave her a gun and then tied one of Ms. Perry's arms behind her back, neither of the combatants would still believe that I was impartial and neutral within the fight. I gave Ms. Swift a lethal weapon, and I hampered Ms. Perry's ability to fend off an attack and continue living. By any definition, I am a belligerent on the side of Ms. Swift, as much as that pains me even to facetiously write.

One need not excuse the crimes or somehow defend the violence of the Japanese war machine nor the genocidal aggression of the Nazis to also note that Roosevelt's tact was aggressive and irresponsible, not to mention, illegal. Questioning U.S. foreign policy does not render someone some sort of neo-Nazi totalitarian or Axis sympathizer—leave that insipid and binary thought to the midwits all around us. Instead, look at the historical facts of how Roosevelt moved the American people into world war:

- Immediately following World War I, American officials in the War and State Departments constructed intricate, color-coded "rainbow" war plans in expectation of a military conflict with Japan, which they deemed as inevitable. Members of the Roosevelt cabinet developed these war plans with exacting detail and wild imagination.
- Thanks in part to the Nye Committee, which under the leadership of North Dakota Senator Gerald Nye, uncovered banking and war profiteering from World War I, Congress passed not one, not two, but four successive Neutrality Acts between 1935 and 1939. Though he was against them, for electoral and popular purposes, Roosevelt reluctantly signed the bills into law, noting that the country was in a decidedly non-interventionist mood.
- In 1937, Roosevelt moved to have British ships transport American arms to China in order to aid the Chinese in their war with Japan. Roosevelt stated that though the Neutrality Acts explicitly banned the sale of arms to "belligerent nations", because

neither the Chinese nor the Japanese government had officially declared war on one another, the arms deal was legal.

- In the famous "Quarantine Speech", October 5, 1937, on Chicago's newly completed Outer Lake Shore Drive Bridge, Roosevelt called for the isolation of nations which conducted war on other nations without a declaration of war(?!). Doing nothing would ensure that, sooner or later, the United States would be attacked.

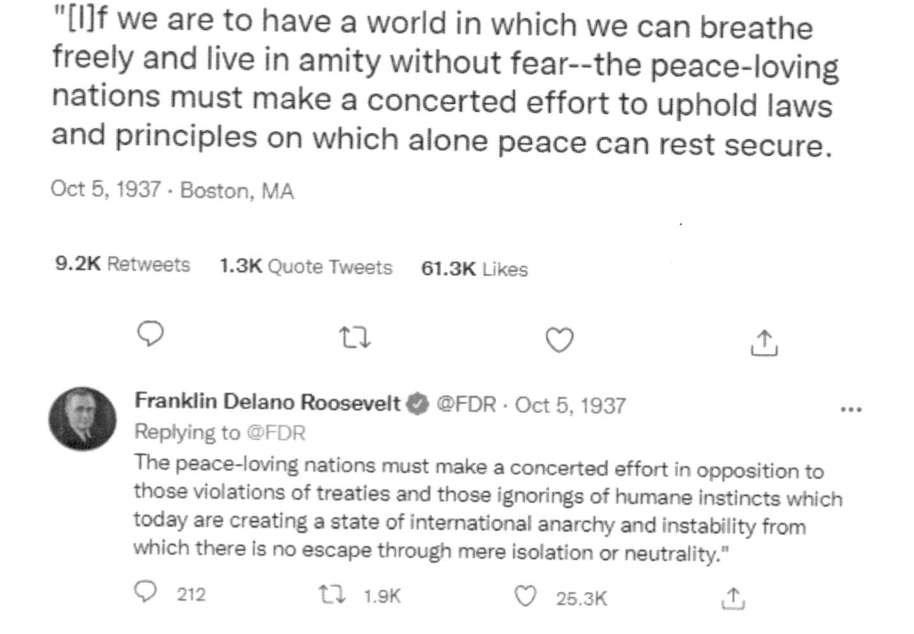

Oddly prescient, but of course, he erred regarding causality. The United States would do more than enough to ensure a war.

- In private letters after the speech, Roosevelt decried the stubborn isolationism of Americans. He wrote to his old high school headmaster at Groton Academy, Endicott Peabody, and admitted to him that:

Endicott Peabody @PeabodyGroton
Headmaster at Groton School
2,587 Following **8,134** Followers

"I am fighting against a public psychology which comes very close to saying 'peace at any price.'"'

Oct 16, 1937 ✓

- 1937 was a very busy year for subverting Congress. Late that year, Roosevelt secretly ordered the War Department to sell American warplanes to France. Congress was never notified or made aware of the act.
- Beginning in 1939, Roosevelt (think to yourself: "Where have I heard this recently?") imposed sanctions on Japan, an industrialized nation dependent upon fossil fuel and mineral resource imports. The sanctions ramped up to a full blown embargo on Japan by 1941. Finally, Roosevelt froze Japanese assets in American banks.

Meanwhile, in Europe, on November 9, 1938, the Nazi regime inspired *Kristallnacht* "the Night of Broken Glass"—a genuine pogrom against Jews in Germany and Austria. In response, Roosevelt moved to take the radical step of recalling his ambassador from Berlin. Those be fighting words! No long, drawn out official condemnation of Hitler followed from a president who never seemed unwilling to grandstand. Huh. The Roosevelt administration confirmed their deadly apathy for European Jews when just seven months later when Roosevelt himself refused safe harbor to Jewish refugees aboard the *SS St. Louis*. Facing no other option, the captain of the *St. Louis* turned his ship back around and returned the refugees to Europe. Britain, France and the Netherlands granted them asylum, but when the last two of those countries fell to Germany in 1940, more than 250 of the more than 900 former passengers on board perished in the Holocaust. Let us not pretend that the United States entered World War II so as to save Jews from Nazi genocide. During the war, officials repeatedly denied British and American bombers from destroying the railroads which ushered Jews from all over Europe to their deaths in Poland.

Well, How 'Bout That?

From the United States Holocaust Memorial Museum Encyclopedia: "In the summer and fall of 1944, the World Jewish Congress and the War Refugee Board (WRB) forwarded requests to bomb Auschwitz to the US War Department. These requests were denied. On August 14, John J. McCloy, Assistant Secretary of War, advised that "such an operation could be executed only by the diversion of considerable air support...now engaged in decisive operations elsewhere and would in any case be of such doubtful efficacy that it would not warrant the use of our resources." Yet within a week, the US Army Air Force carried out a heavy bombing of the I.G. Farben synthetic oil and rubber (Buna) works near Auschwitz III—less than five miles from the Auschwitz-Birkenau killing center.

This is not to say that Roosevelt harbored some secret affinity for Germany, its leader, *lederhosen*, or *schnitzel* for that matter. Rather, it is clear that—like his "political daddy" before him, Woodrow Wilson—Roosevelt *did* love everything British, from Churchill (oops, he did it again) to kilts and crumpets. It is simply that protecting Jews and other targets of Nazi totalitarianism never figured into Roosevelt's calculus as a cause for war.

Hitler invaded Poland on September 1, 1939, and that crossed the arbitrary red line that Britain and France had drawn. The major nations of Western Europe were at war again, the so-called "democracies" versus the fascist and totalitarian states of Italy and Germany.

France fell in May 1940. With Hitler doing a jig at Compiègne and German troops marching under the Arc de Triomphe in Paris, Britain was left as the sole democracy in Europe, and John Bull's solitude combined with Luftwaffe bombing during the Battle of Britain aroused the sympathies of internationalist interventionists in the United States. They ate up and spread afar the work of British propagandists. Meanwhile, British officials acknowledged that without American entrance into the war, Britain was doomed.

From late 1939 to Pearl Harbor, Roosevelt did everything he possibly could to get both reelected and to get the American people on board for global war. It was a surreal achievement of duplicity that would have made Machiavelli blush, given the decided penchant of the American public toward non-intervention. On the campaign trail, Roosevelt appeared decidedly dovish:

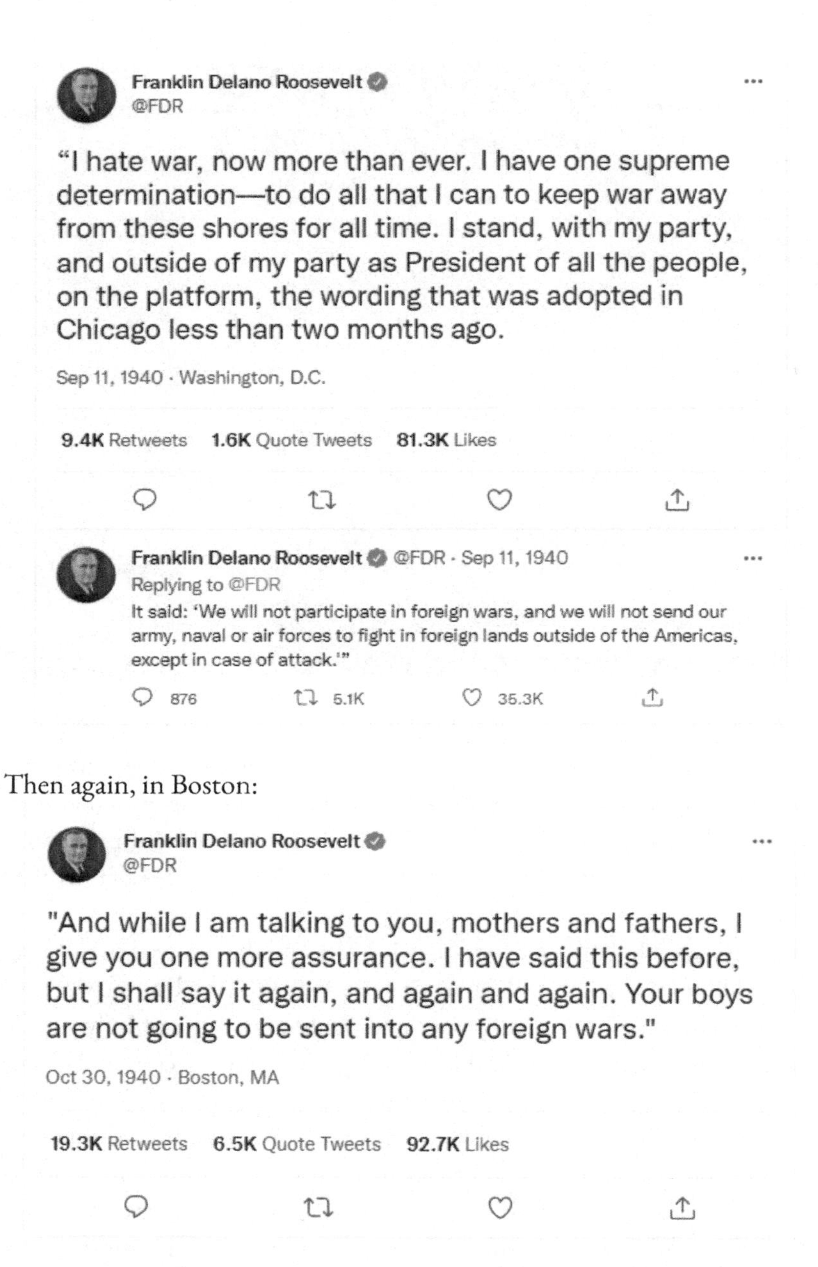

Mind you: Roosevelt made these pronouncements with full knowledge that he had followed 'Woodrow Wilson's How-To-Guide To Get Germany To Attack You' for months. Domestically, he smeared Americans far and wide who remained doggedly isolationist. The FCC revoked the radio licenses of dissenters. Members of the America First Committee like Charles Lindbergh drew the administration's intense ire. Even though Lindbergh had provided intelligence to Washington and London about German war capabilities throughout the 1930s—as such, Lindbergh had acted as a spy *for* the Allies, *against* the Nazis—Roosevelt and his army of apparatchiks in government and in the press branded him a spy *for* Hitler and a Nazi sympathizer!

Away from home, having already hit Japan with what amounted to an energy blockade, as stated above, the Roosevelt administration entered World War II on September 2, 1940 with the destroyer transfer. After the election over Wendell Wilkie in November 1940, escalations ramped up further. Roosevelt clearly felt that he had received a mandate from the American people to increase hostilities against the Axis powers despite adamantly denying that he would do so during the campaign—that is, "except in case of attack". And, it was that operative phrase that won the day. On December 29, 1940, Roosevelt declared what was already the United States's objective in a real yet undeclared war in a radio address:

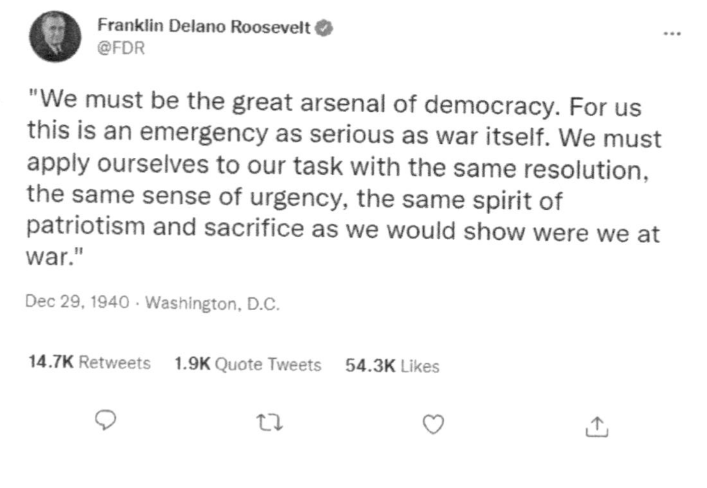

The war was about preserving democracy around the world, because, as Roosevelt had already shown in the New Deal, the United States was John Winthrop's 'City on a Hill'; it was the epitome of self-rule and enlightened government. If not America as the "arsenal of democracy", then who?

Next, Roosevelt pushed the Lend-Lease Act through Congress in March 1941. Always good for optics and a quip, Roosevelt declared that the act of loaning Britain guns, planes, tanks and artillery (which had already been underway for months) oddly ensured non-intervention:

The bodies would follow the billions, however, as they inevitably do. In July 1941, Roosevelt decided to allow U.S. warships to carry munitions to Iceland to be picked up by the British. This move put American sailors in harm's way. In August 1941, Roosevelt met in secret with Winston Churchill to hammer out what Roosevelt expected from Churchill in the aftermath of a war that the United States had not officially entered yet. The infamous 'Atlantic Charter' outlined the plan for the United States to replace Great Britain as the world's leading imperial power, albeit in different ways than the British had operated. Roosevelt was never in on the traditional, in-your-face imperialism. American imperialism postbellum would be less obvious but much more intrusive than simply having Old Glory replace the Union Jack from Harare to Hong Kong to Hawaii.

A month later, the USS Greer was attacked in the North Atlantic after the U.S. ship launched depth charges in order to destroy a German U-Boat. At that point, Roosevelt unilaterally ordered U.S. naval vessels to shoot German U-Boats on sight. On October 17, 1941, the USS Kearny was hit by a German torpedo after pursuing a German "wolfpack" of submarines *east of Iceland.* Eleven American sailors died. On Halloween, the USS Reuben James was torpedoed. In that attack, over 100 American servicemen perished.

Still, the big, dramatic attack for which Roosevelt clearly pined did not occur. Indeed, despite his best efforts to get Germany to strike in a decidedly "unprovoked" manner, the attack would not come. According to historian Harry Elmer Barnes, when it had become clear that Hitler could not be pushed into an act of war in the Atlantic, Roosevelt pivoted and further intensified hostilities with Japan:

In November, Japanese negotiators, including Ambassador Kichisaburō Nomura, submitted several proposals to their American counterparts in order to end the economic blockade imposed on them by the United States. Two of the proposals promised a reduction of Japanese troops in China and in formerly French Indochina. In return, the Americans would unfreeze Japanese assets abroad and allow the Japanese to acquire oil and other materials from the Dutch East Indies. Secretary of State Cordell Hull drew up additional conditions for the Japanese, conditions which the leadership in Tokyo deemed as ultimata and, subsequently, utter capitulations. Roosevelt himself scuttled the process. He favored an unyielding trade embargo and, as State Department official Dean Acheson advocated, a "full-blooded financial warfare against Japan."

The Japanese high command concluded that there was no bend, no compromise in the American position. The American high command knew of their decision because American agents had broken the Japanese "Purple" diplomatic code dating back to August 1940. The Japanese knew the Americans had cracked the code in April 1941. Why did the Japanese insist on using a code known to be broken by their adversaries? Measured, controllable and calculated transparency. A cracked code is a fantastic way to convey the intent and gravity of a country's positions in diplomacy. By the end of November, with negotiations at a standstill, both governments, long adversaries in the Pacific, understood war to be imminent and made plans accordingly.

Pearl Harbor. Forever...

It was the attack that need not have been.

For Americans, it started the war that need not have been. Their president had provoked the attack that convinced them otherwise.

Only because of 'the revolution that was' in the 1930s could the entrenched Washington establishment drag the country into World War II, yet another global conflict with which Americans, by and large, wanted no part. The war and its aftermath for the United States cemented in place the putrid, statist regime. With war came the American totalitarian state's proving ground and the state of emergency served as a perfect excuse to let state power grow unabated. It was necessary to suspend individual liberties, freedom of exchange, civil rights, and normal American life so as to, in the end, preserve those things for Americans and their posterity. War fever, xenophobia, and propaganda served as proper sedatives to any independent thought that might challenge the inherent contradiction there.

Roosevelt and his closest advisors knew that the Japanese attack was coming by early December. The Administration kept both the American public and U.S. military commanders in the dark about the impending conflict. This produced the desired scenario, even if that meant the death of thousands of sailors and soldiers in Hawaii. This was the price of Roosevelt getting his war: We know that this was in the President's calculation because he said it. Upon hearing of the attack, according to his own administrative and press secretary, Roosevelt exclaimed: "No!" but that the president quickly qualified his reaction by saying, "The blow was heavier than he had hoped it would necessarily be... But the risks paid off; even the loss was worth the price."

Well, How 'Bout That?

The blackout was not complete. Some newspapers and their reporters—many of them of the non-interventionist penchant—did investigate and convey the most important news of their time. For example, Colonel Robert McCormick's Chicago Tribune *exposed some of the intricate war plans that the Roosevelt Administration had ready to launch—just three days prior to the attack on Pearl Harbor. The Tribune writers were correct in asserting that American entrance into World War II was a* fait accompli.

The next day, he had the audacity and mendacity to utter words that live in infamy:

Suddenly, no. Deliberately? Yes. By the way, how exactly does a military regime deliberate and then act suddenly? The Japanese aimed to incapacitate the U.S. navy in the Pacific before the United States could build up American forces there and initiate its own war plans against the Japanese. The Roosevelt administration was quick to blame General Walter Short and Admiral Husband Kimmel for the disaster at Pearl Harbor. Both were kept ignorant of the true danger, and they were just the fall guys. The truth of the matter was that Roosevelt had clearly used Pearl Harbor as bait, and the Japanese bit. Roosevelt's Secretary of War, Henry Stimson, who had taken the job in June 1940 to ensure American entrance into the war, stated after the attack:

With Pearl Harbor and Washington's apocryphal framing of it to the country, peaceful non-interventionism died. Charles Lindbergh himself favored American entrance into the war. Garet Garrett did too. It is a curious thing, however, to see how little commentary or pushback there was on what Roosevelt himself admitted in the subsequent fireside chats, namely that the United States aimed to engage and defeat the Axis in Europe before devoting the bulk of its forces against Japan. This was a necessary war because it was *defensive*, was it not? That said, a decided effect of nationalistic propaganda is monomaniacal thought: It precludes and forbids nuanced inquiry and considerate doubt. The United States was the hero-victim that looked to vanquish all of the sinister, anti-democratic forces raging throughout the world. In summary, the Japanese and their (somewhat) indistinguishable allies had attacked the United States because of our freedoms. If only a book could include a laugh track.

That last claim needs to be qualified though: Americans—particularly the government in Washington—did draw some distinctions, not so much pertaining to who were "enemies to the nation"—but rather regarding how to treat those enemies. Just by virtue of national origin, all German and Italian-Americans' right allegiance was placed under suspicion. The Japanese, due to their more apparent racial distinctions, immediately lost the tenuous presumption that white Americans might have held of their proper loyalties. The federal government—never one to work to quell racial and ethnic enmity and fear—took to the old Lincoln formula of obviating the Bill of Rights. Roosevelt ordered the compulsory relocation of tens of thousands of German and Italian Americans, and federal agencies restricted the movements of hundreds of thousands more in Executive Order #9066. More intense evisceration of civil liberties were in store for the Japanese. Mainly located along the West Coast, per the executive order, American agents ushered Japanese nationals and Japanese-American citizens off to rural, deserted concentration camps from Idaho to Arkansas. Their homes and often thriving businesses were seized. Americans in Seattle and San Francisco absconded with the personal belongings that the Japanese were forced to leave behind. All of this was done in the name of preserving human rights and government of, by, and for the people in a supposedly propositional nation created so as to preserve them. What a sham.

As American boys, both volunteers and those conscripted, went off to fight in Europe and the Pacific, World War II became the justification and excuse for the government to engage in a revolution within *the revolution*; that is to say, the revolutionaries in Washington changed the country's Depression-era, soviet-syndicate political economy into full blown corporatist political economy. In short, the American economy got Nazi-fied. Roosevelt and Congress replaced many of the exceedingly pro-labor New Deal initiatives with ominous and Orwellian programs under the auspices of the new War Production Board and War Labor Board. The ostensible mission: Washington meant to ensure that, while strikes and sit-downs in private companies had been officially promoted and protected, now that the war economy was to be governed by the federal government, labor disturbances were to be anathema. Traitorous even. Those planes, tanks, guns, and ships needed to be built.

After Pearl Harbor, the United States became not only the arsenal to the Allies but also their main spear and ultimate financier. Modern, total warfare demanded nothing less. No military battles took place in the continental United States and yet Americans on the home front became essential contributors to the war effort. They did not have a choice. Those who were convinced of the just and noble cause of war tended to equate sacrifices in the forms of significant rationing, working overtime, reduced real income, and dead sons, brothers, and husbands, with proof of patriotism. They imbibed the messaging from Roosevelt whole. That is not to say all Americans bought into the war. Black American men—particularly those who did not pledge their allegiance to the Black establishment, one represented by institutions like the NAACP and Urban League—rightly draft-dodged and protested against the war in the most effective ways possible. According to the great Thaddeus Russell, when Malcolm X had to present himself for the draft, he dressed up in a zoot suit and played the role of crazy black man willing to go and "kill some crackers" over in Europe. The army psychiatrist dubbed him "4-F" or unfit for service. Win. Jazz great and ultimate legend John "Dizzy" Gillespie won his 4-F status by telling his army recruiter:

Other black and Latino men objected to the draft by donning zoot suits which featured excessive clothing at the very time in which the government had demanded cloth rationing. They danced. They partied. Their collective rebellion and cultural disobedience made them a target of the so-called "patriotic" white Americans. In June 1943, when the press in Los Angeles played up an incident in which zoot suiters supposedly assaulted a group of white sailors, the "patriots" took to the streets of Mexican neighborhoods and violently stripped men of their clothes and shaved their long hair. More than one hundred people were injured in the "zoot-suit riots".

From normie, "patriot" to dramatic dissenter, and everyone in between: all Americans suffered due to the yoke that was World War II. The consumer price index, then a more accurate depiction of real inflation, rose by an incredible 26.4 percent during the war, despite the fact that the government artificially reduced demand—by law. Unemployment was low, to be sure, but that came as a result of sending more than 20 million men off to war. War, as it turns out, is the worst of economic dislocations. During it, the state allocates resources and human capital in the form of actual humans to the destruction of other humans. It is the ultimate malinvestment; it is the ultimate malevolent investment. Just as insidious is that the productive necessities of war, which take the forms of new jobs and seemingly productive work, in reality, exist as aberrations. Consumers never line up for warships and tanks in peace. War produces perverse economic demands and equally perverse incentives. For example, when G.I.s returned home from war they were greeted to an economy that was shrinking at a rate of 11.6 percent year-over-year. The total price tag for the war for the United States came out to over $330 billion—in 1945 ($5.2 trillion today). That final figure was twice the amount of money expended by the federal government in its entire existence up to 1941. Allow that to sink in: World War II cost two times the spending of the national government from 1789 to 1941.

Of course, the price was much higher—indeed much more incalculable—than all that. Over 400,000 Americans died in the war. Total U.S. casualties numbered over 1 million. And all for a war that the United States lost in the end.

The United States Lost World War II

That is radical, controversial, revisionist-but-true statement number two. I assert it again: The United States lost World War II.

Perhaps it is unfair to leave that bombshell/tease hanging there sans explanation, but first, let me briefly chronicle what transpired in the war and assess the status of the world after it. Keep in mind that the ostensible causes for war, as FDR had articulated them before Pearl Harbor and expressed them in his addresses during the war, included that the United States was fighting a defensive war to preserve the American way of life and a war that aimed to preserve liberal democracy, in the face of fascism and totalitarianism, across the globe.

- From late 1941 to mid-1942, the Allies suffered stunning military losses. Nazi armies fortified their acquired territories in France, and in the East, the blitzkrieg had advanced so far into the Russian interior that Soviet cities Leningrad and Stalingrad were under siege and on the brink of collapse. Meanwhile, in the Pacific theater, the Japanese invaded and occupied Hong Kong, Singapore, the Dutch East Indies (they needed that oil), Burma (through which the Allies had been supplying the Chinese), and the Philippines. It was there where famed American General Douglas MacArthur fled the islands promising, "I shall return."

- By May 1942, the United States, aided by Australian forces, halted the Japanese advance at the Battle of Coral Sea, and in June, U.S. forces repulsed the Japanese advance at the Battle of Midway. This was important because it was from Midway's airfields that further attacks could be launched upon Hawaii and even West Coast positions. American commanders adopted the war plan with the worst of monikers: island hopping. It was not as though the American advance toward Japan necessitated taking every Japanese occupied atoll in the Pacific. A better name for the policy is island-leapfrogging. Admittedly, it does not have the same ring to it. Certain islands like Saipan, Iwo Jima, Guadalcanal and Okinawa were deemed essential. They would become the focus of the American war in the Pacific.
- Meanwhile, in Europe, the Allies launched furtive air raids into German cities such as Cologne. North Africa became a hot spot as British General Bernard Montgomery halted the Erwin Rommel-led German advance into Egypt. Soviet troops held out at Stalingrad, in gory, bloody fighting. By the end of the war, 20 million Soviet subjects lay dead. In November 1942, the Allies launched the largest amphibious assault in human history (up to that point)—Operation Torch. Troops landed in Morocco and faced Vichy French(!) and Nazi resistance. For the next 18 months, the British in the East and Americans in the West acted like a vice in North Africa, squeezing Rommel's Afrika Korps until the Maghreb was liberated.
- After the success of Operation Torch, Roosevelt and Churchill met at Casablanca. It was there that the Allied leaders agreed upon pursuing the unconditional surrender of the Axis Powers. This would require the near total destruction of Germany and Japan, followed by Allied occupation. Roosevelt and Churchill excluded the possibility of compromise and negotiation. Roosevelt said on the last day of the conference that occupation was necessary to carry out American war objectives:

"The elimination of German, Japanese and Italian war power means the unconditional surrender by Germany, Italy, and Japan. That means a reasonable assurance of future world peace.

Jan 24, 1943 · Casablanca

13.8K Retweets **2.3K** Quote Tweets **101.8K** Likes

Franklin Delano Roosevelt @FDR · Jan 24, 1943

Replying to @FDR

It does not mean the destruction of the population of Germany, Italy, or Japan, but it does mean the destruction of the philosophies in those countries which are based on conquest and the subjugation of other people."

432 3.1K 45.9K

- Roosevelt alluded to the fact that during the Civil War, Ulysses S. Grant was referred to as "Unconditional Surrender" Grant, and since a merciless war of attrition worked in the 1860s, the same should apply to war in the 1940s. Quite the tenuous connection; that is, a tenuous and murderous connection. Hundreds of thousands of more people—many of them civilians—would perish in horrific ways in an unnecessarily prolonged war based on Roosevelt's unfounded assertion that only by complete surrender could democracy and self-government persevere. But just like his Depression-era policies, his strategies in the war were based on hunches, and these gut feelings always ended up backfiring at the tremendous cost of people in the United States and, then, across the globe. For generations.
- American forces moved ever closer to mainland Japan, after seizing Guadalcanal in February 1943. Shortly after securing North Africa, Allied forces moved into Sicily and Italy, with the aid of the Mafia in the United States and their partners in Southern Italy. In August 1943, Mussolini was deposed as the Nazis had taken over control of Italy. Roosevelt, Churchill and Stalin met at Teheran in November-December 1943 wherein the Western Allies acceded to Stalin's emphatic demands that they open up a Western front in order to relieve the pressures Stalin faced in the East.

Well, How 'Bout That?

You might have wondered in the past how the Federal Government—particularly the Central Intelligence Agency—got so chummy with organized crime. The marriage of convenience and natural similarities began after Prohibition when mob families could no longer concentrate on bootlegging, so they relied on the old, tried and true crimes of racketeering, prostitution, and gambling. Along with those standbys, organized crime found a new growth crime industry in organized labor. Mob bosses became the heads (in name but also de facto) of enormously powerful and graft-ridden unions, especially those associated with transport, like the Longshoremen's Association. Mobsters Joseph Lanza, Charles "Lucky" Lucciano, and Albert Anastasia could, at any time, halt the transport of legitimate goods while simultaneously utilizing ships, trains and trucks to deliver their overpriced and smuggled goods throughout the country. Their power ran so deep that the Office of Naval Intelligence (ONI)—which along with the Office of Strategic Services (OSS) was a forerunner to the Central Intelligence Agency (CIA)—reached out to the mob during the war to ensure that no strikes or labor unrest would take place. In Detroit, Italian and Jewish mobsters worked closely with Teamsters' Union boss Jimmy Hoffa. The mobsters and their union allies crushed any whiff of strikes or labor unrest. In return, mobsters had federal cases against them dropped, and, most profitable in the long run for organized crime, the eventual CIA (1947) facilitated the mob monopoly on the production and then importation of heroin into the country after the war. So long as organized crime rackets concentrated distribution to black communities, they could operate unimpinged by the feds. What synergy.

- Rome was liberated on June 4, 1944. Just two days later, American, British and Canadian forces launched Operation Overlord, the still-largest amphibious assault in human history. Operation Torch held that distinction for less than two years. From bases in England, Allied troops stormed onto Norman beaches wherein the Germans inflicted heavy losses. Once Allied positions were established, Allied forces moved eastward to liberate Paris. Some of the GIs were astute historians: It was reported that as they made their way through France, many chanted "Lafayette, we're here again!"
- In the Pacific theater, American forces captured Guam and reoccupied the

Philippines. General MacArthur, always one for historical drama, did indeed declare, "I have returned." Back in Europe, Hitler and the rest of the German High Command unleashed a concentrated, last-ditch effort to beat back the advancing Allied forces at the Battle of the Bulge, in December 1944. At the same time, the Soviet Red Army continued to advance into Eastern Europe. Warsaw was occupied by the Red Army in January 1945. American and British bombers unleashed enormous payloads on the center of Dresden which bore little to no military significance. The purpose was retribution for the bombing of British cities earlier in the war. When the Soviets urged the British to continue to bomb other German cities so as to ease Soviet occupation of eastern Germany, British and American bombers readily complied.

- The peoples of Eastern Europe, which the Nazis had taken hostage, then pillaged, then raped and then enslaved as part of the Wehrmacht's workforce, were then pillaged further, raped and ravaged by the invading Red Army. Stalin's order to his advancing armies was to treat Eastern Europe as Soviet spoils of war, and though officially it was not to be condoned, Stalin excused what he believed to be inevitable if not natural. The Red Army obliged to the tune of *millions* of women, many gang raped and then killed by Soviet troops. They raped women "liberated" from the extermination camps in Poland. 110,000 women in Berlin alone were raped. To be sure, the British, French and American occupying forces did much of the same, but the satanic rate of rape and murderous cruelty of the Red Army prompted Western Allied commanders to confront Stalin on the issue, to which he once responded to a Serbian reporter/politician:

- Hitler probably, likely committed suicide in his bunker on 30 April 1945. Supposed Soviet "misinformation campaigns" post-war advanced the theory that Hitler was still alive and cooperating with Western Allied powers. Victory in Europe (V-E Day) followed eight days later.

- In the Pacific, the Japanese government remained resolute in refusing to surrender, despite the fact that 67 Japanese cities had been destroyed by relentless, conventional bombing campaigns by the end of summer, 1945. In March 1945, over 100,000 people—largely Japanese citizens—had perished in a two-day campaign over Tokyo. New president of the United States, Harry S. Truman, committed to using up to four newly crafted atomic bombs on Japanese cities that had remained largely untouched by the previous bombing raids. This was to better understand the destructive scale of what the Manhattan Project had wrought. On 6 August 1945, the United States government dropped an atomic weapon on Hiroshima. On 9 August 1945, another was dropped on Nagasaki. Kyoto had been rejected as a target because Secretary of War Henry Stimson had spent part of his honeymoon there. Estimates vary, but anywhere between 130,000 and 226,000 people were either instantly vaporized or died up to several months later due to radioactive burns and poisoning.

Soapbox

The dropping of the atomic bombs constitutes, at once, one of the most evident and heinous war crimes in human history. Dwight David Eisenhower himself declared the bombings to be totally unnecessary, since Japan was already defeated. The targeted cities possessed economic and military importance, but in both Hiroshima and Nagasaki, American pilots dropped the bombs on civilian centers away from the Mitsubishi works on the outskirts of Hiroshima and the seaport of Nagasaki. Suspiciously, both cities had sizable Japanese Catholic populations; in point of fact, Nagasaki had long been the capital of Japanese Catholicism, and the atom bomb landed in close proximity to the Catholic cathedral there, then the largest in Asia. The attacks epitomized how far afield from Western *standards for what constitutes just war (crafted mostly by St. Augustine and St. Thomas Aquinas) the* Western Allies *had gone. The whole affair was designed to kill as many innocent civilians as conveniently and technologically possible. On his news-comedy show, non-Catholic, American comedian Jon Stewart declared in April 2009 that Harry Truman was a war criminal due to his decision to drop the bombs. Sadly, someone absconded with Stewart's backbone two days later when he returned to the air to sheepishly retract his utterly valid assertion.*

- The Japanese government signed the instrument of surrender on 2 September 1945. Japan was to be occupied, under the prescribed conditions of unconditional surrender, by Allied forces just as Germany, Italy and Austria already had. The bloodiest war in human history came to its end.

Or did it? Sadly, just as in the case of the aftermath of the First World War, the official end to the Second World War left a global political mess that remains unresolved to this day. The residual effects and conditions stemming from a conflict that left upwards of 85 million people dead, that was, approximately 3 percent of the global population at the time, ought to have purchased some semblance of peace and stability. The opposite emerged. Nations that suffered from the demographic and economic destruction have yet to recover and probably never will. Moreover, the chaos of the war proved to be an excuse, a means by which sinister and nefarious forces and interests first conceived of a new world order and then profited immeasurably from the perpetual instability that resulted from it. In other words, the United States government especially begot a post-war framework wherein the relentless sense of existential threat would justify both Washington's hegemony over the globe as well as the creeping diminishment of individual liberty and individual rights at home.

Dating back to the Atlantic Charter in 1941, Roosevelt had already laid out the preconditions for the United States' entry into the war: The old, colonial empires were to be replaced by a new, American economic dominance. Sure, it was not to be a blatant transferral of power—the Union Jack and *le Tricolore* were not to be lowered over Nairobi and Saigon and replaced with Old Glory—but American dominance would be even more present and inescapable. The meetings and agreements that transpired during the war ensured that this reconfiguration emerged.

Three meetings and occasions prove this reality beyond any reasonable doubt: Bretton Woods in 1944, Yalta in 1945, and Winston Churchill's "Sinews of Peace" speech in 1946.

In July 1944, economic ministers and emissaries the world over assembled in Bretton Woods, New Hampshire to complete the job that governments in both world wars had begun; namely, to transform the world economy—and nothing short of that. Turns out that world economic elites who wish to maintain their wealth and status permanently through state protection really do live by the mantra of never letting a crisis go to waste—it matters not the time nor place. One can recall that the brief (Theodore) Roosevelt Panic of 1907 was used to justify the subterfuge undertaken at Jekyll Island to beget the American Federal Reserve. Now, as the great Henry Hazlitt indicated at the time, and the great Lew Rockwell has reiterated, World War II cemented (or at least those elites and their governments would like the world to believe that it had cemented) the apparent need "to [coordinate and to] promote global economic growth, encourage macroeconomic stability, and rein in inflation"—especially since, yet again, governments had spent themselves into near oblivion. Thus, the same mandates that seemingly justified the existence of an all-powerful American central bank were offered as justifications for a world bank and a monetary system divorced from clunky, old gold, and wed instead to a gold dollar standard; or better, "a phony gold standard".

Bretton Woods was the hideous offspring of hideous men; namely John Maynard Keynes and his ilk. As Rockwell describes:

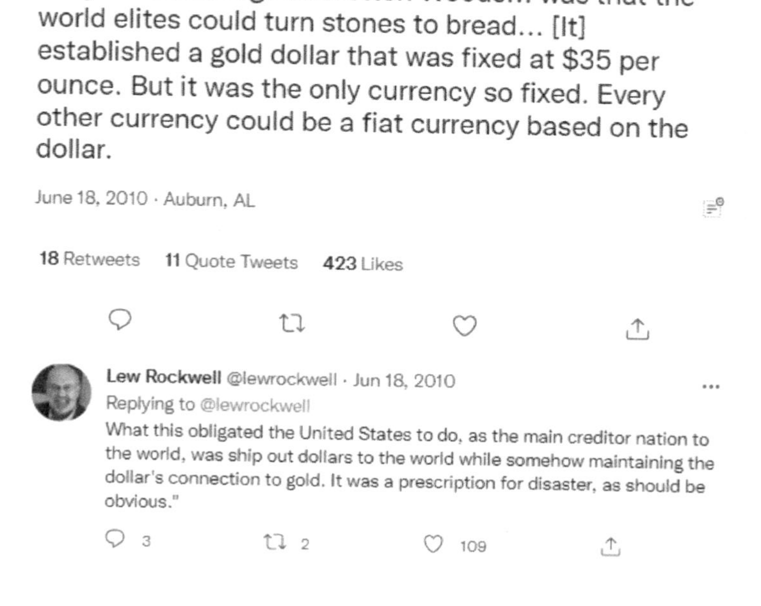
Lew Rockwell
@lewrockwell

"Keynes's message at Bretton Woods... was that the world elites could turn stones to bread... [It] established a gold dollar that was fixed at $35 per ounce. But it was the only currency so fixed. Every other currency could be a fiat currency based on the dollar.

June 18, 2010 · Auburn, AL

18 Retweets 11 Quote Tweets 423 Likes

Lew Rockwell @lewrockwell · Jun 18, 2010
Replying to @lewrockwell
What this obligated the United States to do, as the main creditor nation to the world, was ship out dollars to the world while somehow maintaining the dollar's connection to gold. It was a prescription for disaster, as should be obvious."

3 2 109

In order to drill it down even further: Bretton Woods unleashed governments to spend at will. No individual nor corporation could exchange their cash for gold, but governments could. In turn, the United States encouraged foreign governments to exchange and redeem their currency units in dollars, feigning that it was the only truly stable currency tied to gold. The dollar was to be the world's reserve currency, or the principal medium of exchange used whenever credit, debt, materials or goods crossed borders. When countries (inevitably) printed more money to expend themselves, the United States would provide credit to these countries, effectively bailing them out and concurrently making them more dependent on the dollar. The U.S. Treasury and Federal Reserve played the role of drug dealer, incentivized to get more peers hooked on a drug, with the high progressively wearing off as the addiction worsens.

Soapbox

Bretton Woods killed and buried the international gold standard. It had been on life support since World War I, and Keynes and company pulled the plug in 1944. The phony, dollarized gold standard emerged as the next target, as its collapse was just as inevitable. The first shock to its system spelled doom. That stress test arrived in the 1960s. Under the weight of enormous expenditure during the Great Society and Vietnam years, the dollar itself collapsed to such an extent that foreign governments demanded redemption in gold instead of dollars. The Treasury did not have the reserves, so Richard Nixon unpegged the dollar to gold, and rendered the dollar—truly and entirely—valued based on the "full faith and credit" of the U.S. government as legal tender. In short, this whole scheme can be summarized as the process by which legal tender itself became universal, legal plunder. At the height of irony, the Soviet delegate, Mikhail Stepanovich Stepanov, signed the Bretton Woods Final Act only to, a few months later, have his country refuse to ratify it on the grounds that the whole scheme made the world beholden to the monied interests of Wall Street. Leave it to Bolsheviks to point out how absurdly undemocratic and inequitable a system would be! And another thing... When the United States engages in enormous monetary expansion, for example, as Washington did during the government-manufactured Covid crisis of 2020-22, those nations who have fixed their currencies to the dollar (most of them in the developing world), suffer from the intense inflation associated with it. The money in their people's pockets lost tremendous value in very short order. Meanwhile, none of the financial bailouts and federal welfare approved by Washington to soften the blow of shutting down the economy went out to non-Americans. Thus, the people of El Salvador were doubly-impoverished—devalued currency and no support. No wonder then that their prescient president, Nayib Bukele, elected to make bitcoin legal tender in 2021.

It amounted to, and still amounts to, American economic imperialism, and as the United States has manipulated its own currency and continued to insist on the supremacy of the global dollar, the American people have incurred the wrath of others worldwide.

At Yalta, in the Russian Crimea, American and British officials took a much more conciliatory tact with another devil who they knew, Josef Stalin. Conciliatory is an understatement; Roosevelt and Churchill bent over backwards and forwards to appease and accommodate Stalin. FDR believed deep down—I suppose very deep down, below all of the apparent genocidal and sociopathic character traits—that Stalin was a Christian gentleman. A Christian gentleman, who had already engaged in forced collectivization, the Great Purge of political opponents, and the systematic starvation of the Ukraine? A Christian gentleman who had already shown such wanton disregard for the lives of his own people during World War II that he engaged in a complete war of attrition, valuing human beings as more expendable than natural resources and war materiel? Indeed, at Yalta, Roosevelt expressed misplaced sympathy to Stalin for the loss of so many (over 26 million) Soviet subjects. Stalin could not have cared less, but he was a savvy and observant negotiator, so he read his pliant inferiors well.

In return for relenting on his insistence that all of the Soviet republics have individual representation in the new United Nations, and in return for his assurances that the Soviet Union would finally declare war on Japan, Stalin won every concession from Roosevelt and Churchill that he could have ever imagined and more. "Uncle Joe", as FDR affectionately called Stalin, promised free and fair elections in the vast swaths of Eastern European territories controlled by the Red Army—after all, the American cause of the war was to defend self-determination and liberal democracy. Instead, as a fourth-grader could have predicted, Stalin installed autocratic Soviet-puppet Communist regimes throughout Eastern Europe post-war. In Asia, FDR ceded total control over Manchuria and Northern Chinese railways and ports to the Soviet Union. Recall—this is the very region which, when the Japanese invaded it dating back to 1931, served as the cause for Britain and the United States (under FDR back then as well) to fund and weaponize Chinese nationalists in their fight against the Japanese occupation! What was the purpose of all of that if, after World War II, the United States was ready to grant that same area to the Soviet Union and not to Chinese nationalists allied with the United States! Soviet domination of that region ensured that Stalin could then arm and support Chinese and Korean Communists in Asia. It took all of four years and 25 million dead for the Communists under Mao Zedong to take control of China. Three years after that and 3 million dead (including over 36,000 more Americans), a hardline Communist regime reigned in North Korea.

The capitulation to Stalin went, incredibly, even further. Stalin had insisted at Yalta that Soviet defectors and prisoners of war, whom the Western Allies had liberated from German prisoner camps, be shipped back to the Soviet Union. Roosevelt and Churchill agreed. Problem here: Unlike the British and American POWs who happened to have been liberated by the Red Army from enemy camps, many of the Soviet detainees wanted nothing to do with returning to the Soviet Union. Whether labeled as failures or traitors, their unavoidable fate—as the Soviet POWs themselves knew well—ranged from life in a Siberian gulag to immediate torture and death. A good number of them had donned the uniforms of dead German soldiers along the eastern front in order to escape the Red Army into which they had been forcibly conscripted. In addition to the Red Army defectors, several hundred thousand anti-Bolshevik White Russians, including several generals who fought against Lenin, Trotsky and company back in 1918 and had even earned British military honors; they too were extradited back to the Soviet Union. Stalin especially prized Bolshevism's old enemies.

Soapbox

Is it not astonishing that the Soviet Union, by February 1945, had not declared war on Japan? How about the fact that Stalin had to be compelled to do so, after the Allies had caved to his demands that the Western Allies open up a Western front in 1943 and 1944? What an honest and committed ally! The United States had funded the Soviet war effort to the tune of over 1 billion dollars, and in return the Soviet Union declared war on Japan just six days before Hiroshima. The Soviets did nothing to expedite the end of the war in the Pacific. The Soviets would do everything in the aftermath of the war to render swathes of Asia under communist regimes sympathetic to the Soviet Union. Great...

Allied commanders and soldiers alike reported that, in the process of handing over the defectors/POWs to the Soviets in Austria, the Soviets immediately tortured and executed thousands of them. Some were hung from trees; others were mowed down en masse with machine gunfire.

Stateside, U.S. military officials enacted Operation Keelhaul, an outright war crime. At Fort Dix, New Jersey, the approximately 200 Soviet defector/POWs refused to board ships destined for the Soviet Union. According to historian Tom Woods, on one occasion in which American military police forced them on board a vessel, the defector/POWs damaged the ship's engines to such an extent that it was no longer seaworthy. So, the American guards spiked the prisoners' coffee. While asleep, they were placed upon other ships and returned to the Soviet Union. They met the same fate as their peers in Europe.

In the dark shadow of Yalta, Winston Churchill delivered his version of the Gettysburg Address in Fulton, Missouri in March 1946. It bore all the marks of a post-mortem, post-slaughter speech, by a man who was still searching for a reason for it all. It also meets the criteria of a speech that has received far too much acclaim—and for all the wrong reasons.

Churchill seems to have been channeling his departed countryman, Charles Dickens. The address is unnecessarily long. It features elegant language in parts, but it is also riddled with inconsistencies and unaddressed questions.

Most people know it for Churchill's famous, at once, insight and admission that an "iron curtain had descended over Europe", so much so that few know it by its actual title: 'The Sinews of Peace'.

He stated what was already abundantly clear in less than a year since V-E Day: Half of Europe had traded occupation by one totalitarian, National Socialist power for domination by another totalitarian, Communist power. From Hitler's Germany to Stalin's Soviet Union.

Churchill admitted to no delusions regarding Stalin's intent; in fact, he lamented that, with each mile that the Red Army advanced into the center of Europe, it was to be admitted that the iron curtain advanced with them, and freedom was extinguished behind it.

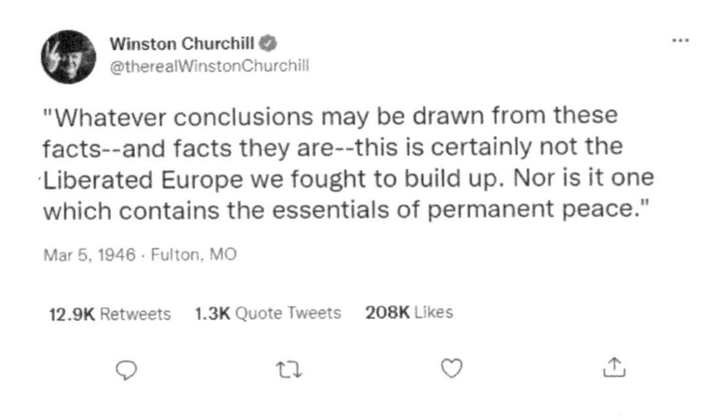

Just let that sink in for the moment: Churchill conceded in 1946 that for all of the death, all of the destruction, all of the carnage—to use his phraseology—all of the blood, sweat and tears; for all of that sacrifice, the world was left in essentially the same straits it had been in 1940. No peace. In fact, Churchill argued that the English-speaking world needed to unite in an effort to confront the Soviet threat. He recognized the dawn of the Cold War, a global, ideological, economic, and sometimes hot conflict whose dusk would not come until 46 years later.

This is startling, but a close reading of the speech does explain a lot that is lost in a traditional analysis of the end of the war, one that invariably ends with a declaration that the United States had won World War II. How could the United States have won World War II when the former Prime Minister of the country's foremost ally in that conflict delivered what for all intents and purposes (look at Churchill's own words) amounted to a concession speech 11 months after the war? Recall too, Roosevelt's stated objectives at the start of the war. The Allies intended to use their overwhelming manpower, economic wealth, and productive capacities to rid the world of fascistic and totalitarian regimes for the purpose of preserving liberal, representative democracy. Well, that did not turn out so well. If any power won World War II—albeit at an enormous cost of human life, again a price Stalin was more than willing to pay—it was the Soviet Union.

Call me old. Call my views arcane. Whatever the case, I hold that victory in any endeavor amounts to attaining one's initial objectives in a contest. In golf, it is to hit the ball into the holes with fewer strokes than your opponents. In baseball, it is to score more runs than the other team. In soccer, more goals. If we are to take Roosevelt at his word; if we are to take the overall messaging of the government propaganda at the time, the United States went into World War II so as to protect and defend the right of peoples to self-government—or what FDR referred to as democracy—then the war effort was an abysmal failure. The geopolitical reality evinced a near total loss, not a victory in any real sense.

That being said, Churchill's admission that the Cold War had emerged provided the perfect justification for the emergence of the totalitarian state in the West. After all, a divided world represented the ideal environment for the continuance and perpetuation of the American warfare-welfare state/empire due to the perceived, continual and relentless emergency at hand. Successive regimes, at will, could then intensify the suppression of dissent, of free speech, of a free press, of individual liberty with the weapons of ideological rhetoric, indirect conflict, proxy wars, and corresponding propaganda.

The tragedies live on today as one considers that the United States has not, in any real sense, moved off of that status. We are stuck in a perpetual emergency state, one that the ever-growing, ever-metastasizing national government utilizes to justify new wars, unabated spending, limitless imperialism, domestic welfare (to sedate we, the captives, here), population control, a police state, and the state's own continued existence.

Who will keep you safe from that dangerous world out there? Who will provide your job, food, education and shelter? Who will ensure your economic security? Who will keep you safe from disease? Who will build the roads? Indeed.

The best Americans of the colonial era, the best Americans today and of every era in between could not and cannot tolerate the interminable despotism of the security state.

The *revolution that was* made it all possible; the only way to resolve it, to break the chains, is to fight for the *revolution that is to be.*

Hasten the day.

In Gratitude

The past two years spent writing this book coincided with the sharpest, most ubiquitous, and most immediate decline of human liberty in history. Across the globe, governments caught the bug of totalitarianism, ostensibly and supposedly in order to stop every individual from dying from a bug whose creation and spread most certainly came about through state coordination and obfuscation. To our own shock and horror, subjects of developed nations fell especially prey to the various public health agencies, within their respective, behemoth bureaucracies, who came to act as de facto dictators. Superstitious fear reigned. As the great artist, commentator, and all-around brilliant guy, Zuby, has stated on Twitter: Before the Covid pandemic, most of us were of the mindset that 80 percent of our fellow citizens preferred to live free and have others live free among us; that is, without strictures or impositions that would render one another conformists, social prisoners to the predominant institutions and powers of the day. The other 20 percent preferred such conformity, and if that had to be attained with masks for your kids, a boot to the neck, jail bars in front of your face, or a bayonet tip to the back--so be it. What the pandemic showed was the reciprocal: in reality, 20 percent want freedom and will die to live and to enjoy it, while 80 percent prefer the illusory safety blanket of state conformity and embrace the virtue-signaling, vicious elation of socially reprobating the free. What once had been hallmarks of Western Civilization, or for that matter, just civil society, were so quickly discarded that one was left with the impression that they were never really there. Or, at the very least, we now know just how fragile they are. Justice. Science. Morality. Consent. Bodily autonomy. Agency. Love. Without them, the person walking down the street transforms into a threat, an opportunity, or an insult; they certainly do not retain the dignity and respect of a fellow human being made in the image and likeness of God.

If this book illustrates or proves anything, it is that without the gradual and then all of a sudden erosion of liberty that began in the Progressive Era and then culminated in the New Deal and World War II, Americans would never have succumbed to the Covid hysteria that provided cover for the real effects: The largest transfer of wealth from the American middle class to the rich in history; The government contrived culture wars that move Americans to resort to base tribalism; The unremittent growth of state and corporatist power and the concomitant evisceration of individual rights and market freedom; The demonization of those who dare dissent. And this is no counter-factual argument, for just as we can look at North and South Korea from space at night in order to determine by the lights which is free, so too American history shows that when cholera or typhoid epidemics ravaged American cities in the 19th century, or the Spanish flu struck in 1919, statism had not yet taken such a hold over them so as to allow the government to determine who could work, and who could not; what medical treatment you could take, and that which you could not; where you could go, and where you could not; who you could see, and who you could not; what you could think and say, and what you could not. Bygone Americans understood trade-offs well--perhaps better than that, they understood that government ought not to have a say in any of those matters. In fact, without exception, those Americans were either themselves or were descendants of others, who had fled places that had entertained or embraced notions that governments, to various degrees, ought to have such authorities. Americans moved so often and with such intensity of purpose that they "barely let the rain dry on their heads" before they were off to the next place, the next opportunity.

From the NATIONAL CHARACTER OF AMERICANS — First Impressions (1831):

> ***Né sous un autre ciel, placé au milieu d'un tableau toujours mouvant, poussé lui-même par le torrent irrésistible qui entraîne tout ce qui l'environne, l'Américain n'a le temps de s'attacher à rien; il ne s'accoutume qu'au changement, et finit par le regarder comme l'état naturel à l'homme; il en sent le besoin; bien plus, il l'aime: car l'instabilité, au lieu de se produire à lui par des désastres, semble n'enfanter autour de lui que des prodiges...***
>
> Born often under another sky, placed in the middle of an always moving scene, himself driven by the irresistible torrent which draws all about him, the American has no time to tie himself to anything, he grows accustomed only to change, and ends by regarding it as the natural state of man. He feels the need of it, more he loves it; for the instability; instead of meaning disaster to him, seems to give birth only to miracles all about him.

When the going got too tough, to the point of being unbearable, American ancestors got going. De Tocqueville recognized a healthy restlessness in the American character, and that preference for the adventure of itinerancy over the inertia of control struck him as being prototypically American. He wished his fellow Frenchmen had more of that spirit. He wished, like the Americans, they had a quick and easy and freer place to go.

Time to run again; likely not in an expatriate, spatial sense--where are we to go, after all, to places like Canada or New Zealand?! Better to uproot to Florida, Alabama or New Hampshire, or to the free enclave project in your city, your town, or your church. It might be as small as your home. Wherever you have to go to be free, no matter where you end up, run *from* or *against* statism; that is the true infection. If we do so fast enough, and with enough numbers and conviction, we will see the *revolution that is to be*.

On that more hopeful than dour note, we wish to express the utmost gratitude to you, the reader. As promised, this book is a wild ride, and you stayed on for all of it. A great concern of ours is that you not be left in a depressed state of inertia, but rather more knowledgeable and therefore convicted of the truth. The revolution for freedom that is to be cannot be accomplished in ignorance. We're honored if you consider this work part of a first step.

We extend extra special praise and thanks to those who donated to this effort in order to bring this book to market. We will always remember your generosity and your encouragement. Thank you, because without all of that, no one would be reading a word of this.

Of particular note, we thank our families, especially our parents who helped us to become good men. Our friends, who aided us in so many ways, including through creative insights, impassioned argumentation, and constant encouragement, deserve so much credit. To the great T.k. Coleman, our brother and friend whose love of people and desire for them to live free surpasses anyone else we know. Our respective colleague and teacher, Rick O'Connor, provided encouragement and very efficacious prayers. Robert Schneider and Jason Skvarenina enlightened us with fantastic debate, usually over a text stream, a book and/or pints. Big thanks to the creative Isabelle Kroeker, for her availability in the 11th hour to assist us in finalizing our illustrations. The man most essential to bringing this book to form is the ingenious and equally generous "Bookmaker" Brett Hoffstadt. What a beautiful mind and soul! Thank you for all of the hours you poured into this project. We enjoyed every minute of working with you. Finally, to Father Thomas Aschenbrener, our friend and the pastor of the best church, St. Mary of Perpetual Help in Bridgeport on the South Side of Chicago; a neighborhood home to the Daley's, a lot of sinners, a lot of saints, and a very holy priest: Thank you for your spiritual guidance and unwavering faith.

Until our temporal end... let not the rain dry on our heads.

Bibliography

Alpers, Benjamin L. *Dictators, Democracy & American Public Culture: Envisioning the Totalitarian Enemy, 1920s-1950s*. Chapel Hill, North Carolina: The University of North Carolina Press, 2003.

Ammous, Saifedeen. *The Bitcoin Standard: The Decentralized Alternative to Central Banking*. Forward by Michael Saylor. Hoboken, New Jersey: Wiley, 2018.

Axelrod, Alan and Phillips, Charles. *Portraits of the Civil War: In Photographs, Diaries, and Letters*. New York: Sterling, 2001.

Bailey, Thomas A., Cohen, Lizabeth and Kennedy, David M. *The American Pageant*. 13th ed. New York: Houghton Mifflin, 2006.

Bailey, Thomas A. and Kennedy, David M. *The American Spirit: United States History as Seen by Contemporaries*. 10th ed. Vols. 1-2. Boston: Houghton Mifflin, 2001.

Baptist, Edward. *The Half Has Never Been Told: Slavery and the Making of American Capitalism*. New York: Basic, 2016.

Barnes, Harry Elmer. (Ed.) *Perpetual War for Perpetual Peace: A Critical Examination of the Foreign Policy of Franklin Delano Roosevelt and Its Aftermath*. Westport, Connecticut: Greenwood, 1969.

Barry, John M. *The Great Mississippi Flood and How It Changed America*. New York: Touchstone, 1998.

Beard, Charles A. *President Roosevelt and the Coming of War, 1941*. New Haven, Connecticut: Yale University Press, 1948.

Beito, David. "FDR's War Against the Press." *Reason Magazine*, May 2017. https://reason.com/2017/04/05/roosevelts-war-against-the-pre/

Bellerue, A.R. "REA Co-ops, a Compulsory Political System." *The Rampart Journal* (Winter 1966): 25-81.

Bovard, James. "American Tariffs and Wars From the Revolution to the Depression" *Mises Institute Wire*, last modified November 1, 2018, https://mises.org/library/american-tariffs-and-wars-revolution-depression.

Bryson, Bill. *One Summer: America, 1927*. New York: Knopf Doubleday, 2014.

Bullitt, William C. and Freud, Sigmund. *Thomas Woodrow Wilson: A Psychological Study*. New York: Houghton Mifflin, 1966.

Bureau of Labor Statistics. *Union Scale of Wages and Hours of Labor, May 15, 1916 : Bulletin of the United States Bureau of Labor Statistics, No. 214*. Washington: Government Printing Office, 1917.

Calhoun, John C. *Union and Liberty: The Political Philosophy of John C. Calhoun*. Edited by Ross M. Lence. Indianapolis, Indiana: Liberty Fund, 1992.

Carnes, Mark C. and Garrity, John. *The American Nation: A History of the United States, Combined Volume*. 13th ed., New York: Longman, 2007.

Carney, Judith. *Black Rice*. Cambridge: Harvard University Press, 2001.

Channing, Steven. *Crisis of Fear: Secession in South Carolina.* New York: W. W. Norton & Company, 1974.

Congress of the United States. *Hearings Before the Joint Committee on the Investigation of the Pearl Harbor Attack*, 79 Congress, 2 Session. Washington, D.C.: Government Printing Office, 1946.

Delaney, Carol. *Columbus and the Quest for Jerusalem*, Glencoe, Illinois: Free Press: 2011.

Denevan, William M. "The Pristine Myth: The Landscape of the Americas in 1492." *Annals of the Association of American Geographers* 82, no. 3 (September 1992): 369-385.

Donoghue, John. *Fire under the Ashes: An Atlantic History of the English Revolution.* Chicago: University of Chicago Press, 2013.

Duffy, James P. *Lindbergh vs. Roosevelt: The Rivalry That Divided America.* New York: MFJ Books, 2010.

Eisenhower, John S.D. *Go Far From God: The U.S. War with Mexico, 1846-1848.* New York: Random House, 1989.

Federal Trade Commission. *Federal Trade Commission Decisions: Findings, Orders, and Conference Rulings of the Federal Trade Commission, March 16, 1915-June 30, 1919.* Vol. 1. Washington: Government Printing Office, 1920.

Flynn, John T. *The Roosevelt Myth* (1948). 50th ed. New York: Fox & Wilkes, 1998.

Folsom, Jr., Burton W. *The Myth of the Robber Barons: A New Look at the Rise of Big Business in America.* Reston, Virginia: Young America's Foundation, 2018.

_______. *New Deal or Raw Deal?: How FDR's Economic Legacy Has Damaged America.* New York: Threshold Editions, 2009.

Forret, Jeff. *Race Relations at the Margins: Slaves and Poor Whites in the Antebellum Southern Countryside.* Baton Rouge, Louisiana: Louisiana State University Press, 2010.

Fredrickson, George M. *The Inner Civil War: Northern Intellectuals and the Crisis of the Union.* New York: Harper and Row, 1965.

Friedman, Milton and Schwartz, Anna J. *A Monetary History of the United States, 1867–1960.* Princeton, New Jersey: Princeton University Press, 1963.

Fromkin, David. *The King and the Cowboy: Theodore Roosevelt and Edward VII, Secret Partners.* New York: Penguin, 2009.

Garrett, Garet. "The Revolution Was (1938)." In *Ex America: The 50th Anniversary of the People's Pottage.* Fwd. Bruce Ramsey. Caldwell, Idaho: Caxton Press, 2004.

Glass, Carter. "The Opposition to the Federal Reserve Bank Bill. Proceedings of the Academy of Political Science in the City of New York." In *Banking and Currency in the United States. The Academy of Political Science* 4, no. 1 (October 1913): 12-19.

Greaves, Jr., Percy L. *Pearl Harbor: The Seeds and Fruits of Infamy.* Edited by Bettina B. Greaves. Auburn, Alabama: Mises Institute, 2010.

Greene, Jack P. *Understanding the American Revolution: Issues and Actors.* Charlottesville, Virginia: University of Virginia Press, 1995.

Gutzman, Kevin R.C. and Woods, Jr., Thomas E. *Who Killed the Constitution?: The Fate of American Liberty from World War I to George W. Bush*. New York: Crown Forum, 2008.

Haight, Jr. John McVickar. "Roosevelt as Friend of France." *Foreign Affairs* 44, no. 3 (April 1966): 518-526.

______. "Roosevelt and the Aftermath of the Quarantine Speech." *The Review of Politics* 24, No. 2. Cambridge University Press (April 1962): 233-259.

Hazlitt, Henry. *Economics in One Lesson* (1946). Reprint. Foreword by Jeff Deist. Auburn, Alabama: Mises Institute Press, 2011.

______. *From Bretton Woods to World Inflation: A Study of Causes and Consequences*. Edited by George Koether. Auburn, Alabama: Ludwig von Mises Institute, 2012.

Hamilton, Alexander, Madison, James, and Jay, John. *The Federalist Papers: The Classic Original Edition*. New York: SoHo, 2011.

Hattikudur, Manesh, Pearson, Will and Sass, Eric. *The Mental Floss History of the United States: The (Almost) Complete and (Entirely) Entertaining Story of America*. New York: HarperCollins, 2010.

Henderson, Jr., Irvine H. "The 1941 De Facto Embargo on Oil to Japan: A Bureaucratic Reflex.". *Pacific Historical Review* 44, no. 2 (May 1975): 201-231.

Higgs, Robert. *Crisis and Leviathan: Critical Episodes in the Growth of American Government*. New York: Oxford University Press, 1987.

______. "Regime Uncertainty: Why the Great Depression Lasted So Long and Why Prosperity Resumed after the War." *The Independent Review* 1, No. 4 (Spring 1997): 561-590.

______. "Why Grover Cleveland Vetoed the Texas Seed Bill" *Independent Institute* (July 1, 2003): https://www.independent.org/publications/article.asp?id=1329.

Hiles, Charles C. "Roberta Wohlstetter's *Pearl Harbor: Warning and Decision:* A Candid Appraisal". Introduction by Harry Elmer Barnes, *The Rampart Journal*, Winter 1966: 82-95.

Hillenbrand, Laura. *Seabiscuit*. New York: Ballantine, 2002.

Hoppe, Hans-Hermann, *Democracy, The God That Failed: The Economics and Politics of Monarchy, Democracy, and Natural Order*. New Brunswick, New Jersey: Transaction, 2001.

______. *A Theory of Socialism and Capitalism*. Auburn, Alabama: Ludwig von Mises Institute, 2010.

Inal, Tuba. *Looting and Rape in Wartime: Law and Change in International Relations*. Philadelphia: University of Pennsylvania Press, 2013.

Jenkins, Philip. *The New Anti-Catholicism: The Last Acceptable Prejudice*. New York: Oxford University Press, 2003.

Johnson, Paul. *A History of the American People*. New York: Harper & Collins, 1997.

______. *Modern Times : A History of the World from the Twenties to the Nineties*. New York: Harper, 2001.

Kunitz, Stephen J. "Hookworm and Pellagra: Exemplary Diseases in the New South." *Journal of Health and Social Behavior* 29, no. 2 (June 1988): 139-148.

Larson, Erik. *The Devil in the White City: Murder, Magic, and Madness at the Fair that Changed America*. New York: Vintage, 2004.

______. *Thunderstruck*. New York: Broadway, 2007.

Lash, Kurt T. "'Tucker's Rule': St. George Tucker and the Limited Federal Power" Vol. 47, No. 4, *William and Mary Law Review*, (2005-06): 1343-1391.

Lautner, David. "REA's Tenacity Shows Why Some Government Programs Never Die". *Los Angeles Times*, October 1, 1989. https://www.latimes.com/archives/la-xpm-1989-10-01-mn-1088-story.html

Lea, Henry Charles. *A History of the Inquisition of Spain: And the Inquisition in the Spanish Dependencies*. Revised Ed. London: I.B. Tauris, 2011.

Lewis, Nathan. "The Federal Reserve in the 1920s 2: Interest Rates" *New World Economics*. last modified November 5, 2012. https://newworldeconomics.com/the-federal-reserve-in-the-1920s-2-interest-rates/.

List, Friedrich. *National System of Political Economy (1841)*. trans. G. A. Matile. Ann Arbor, Michigan: University of Michigan Historical Reprint, 2005.

Lockley, Timothy J. *Lines in the Sand: Race and Class in Lowcountry Georgia, 1750-1860*. Athens, Georgia: University of Georgia Press, 2001.

Mahon, Alfred Thayer. *The Influence of Sea Power Upon History, 1660-1783*. Dover Military History, Weapons, Armor. Mineola, New York: Dover, 1987.

Malice, Michael. *The Anarchist Handbook*. New York: self-published, 2021.

McCullough, David. *1776*. New York: Simon & Schuster, 2003.

______. *The Greater Journey: Americans in Paris*. New York: Simon & Schuster, 2011.

McLear, Patrick E. "William Butler Ogden: A Chicago Promoter in the Speculative Era and the Panic of 1837," *Journal of the Illinois State Historical Society* Vol. 70, No. 4, November 1977: 283-291.

McMeekin, Sean. *Stalin's War: A New History of World War II*. New York: Basic Books, 2021.

Mises, Ludwig von. *Human Action: A Treatise on Economics, The Scholar's Edition* (1949). Auburn, Alabama: Ludwig von Mises Institute, 2010.

______. *Nation, State, and Economy* (1919). Translated by Leland B. Yeager. New York: New York University Press, 2000.

______. *Socialism: An Economic and Sociological Analysis* (1962). Eastford, Connecticut: Martino Fine Books, 2012.

Morgenstern, George. *Pearl Harbor: The Story of the Secret War* (1947). Fountain Valley, California: Institute for Historical Review, 1987.

Morris, Edmund. *Theodore Rex*. New York: Random House, 2001.

Milgram, Stanley. *Obedience to Authority: An Experimental View*. 3rd Ed. Intro. Philip Zimbardo, New York: HarperPerrenial, 2009.

Millard, Candace. *Destiny of the Republic: A Tale of Madness, Medicine and the Murder of a President*. New York: Anchor, 2012.

Miller, Donald L. *City of the Century: The Epic of Chicago and the Making of America.* New York: Simon & Schuster, 1996.

Mueller, John D. *Redeeming Economics: Rediscovering the Missing Element*. Wilmington, Delaware: Intercollegiate Studies Institute, 2010.

Murphy, Robert. *Choice: Cooperation, Enterprise, and Human Action*. Oakland, California: Independent Institute, 2015.

Murrin, John M., Hamalainan, Pekka, Johnson, Paul, et al. *Liberty, Equality, Power: A History of the American People*. 7th ed. Boston: Cengage Learning, 2016.

New York Sun. "The King of Frauds: How Credit Mobilier Bought Its Way Through Congress." September 4, 1872.

Novick, Peter. *That Noble Dream: The 'Objectivity Question' and the American Historical Profession.* Cambridge: Cambridge University Press, 1988.

Oakes, James. *The Radical and the Republican: Frederick Douglass, Abraham Lincoln, and the Triumph of Antislavery Politics*. New York: W.W. Norton, 2007.

Orwell, George. *1984*. New York: Signet Classic, 1961.

Ostrowski, James. *The Libertarian Devil's Dictionary*. Buffalo, New York: Cazenovia Books, 2021.

______. *Progressivism: A Primer on the Idea Destroying America*. Buffalo, New York: Cazenovia Books, 2014.

Oswald, Alix. "The Reaction to the Dred Scott Decision" *Voces Novae* 4 , Article 9 (2008). https://digitalcommons.chapman.edu/vocesnovae/vol4/iss1/9.

Parker, Rachel R. "Shays' Rebellion: An Episode in American State-Making" *Sociological Perspectives* 34, no. 1 (Spring 1991): 95-113.

Powell, Jim. "How Big Government Infrastructure Projects Go Wrong" *Cato Institute*, last modified March 2, 2009, https://www.cato.org/commentary/how-big-government-infrastructure-projects-go-wrong.

Prendergast, Mark. *For God, Country, and Coca-Cola: The Definitive History of the Great American Soft Drink and the Company That Makes It*. 3rd Ed. New York: Basic Books, 2013.

Puleo, Stephen. *The Caning: The Assault That Drove America to Civil War*. Yardley, Pennsylvania: Westholme, 2012.

Raico, Ralph. *Classical Liberalism and the Austrian School.* Forward by Jörg Guido Hülsmann. Preface by David Gordon. Introduction by Llewellyn H. Rockwell, Jr. Auburn, Alabama: Ludwig von Mises Institute, 2012.

Rectenwald, Michael. *Google Archipelago: The Digital Gulag and the Simulation of Freedom*. Nashville, Tennessee: New English Review Press, 2019.

Richied, Gary. *A Catholic Prep School Teacher's Guide to European History*. Chicago: Marooned Friar Press, 2016.

______. *Fastballs and Fastbulbs: The Cause of Reckless Yet Rational Gambling Speculation on American Baseball 1917-1919 and Dutch Tulips 1636-1637*. Chicago:

HotH20History.com, 2019, https://hoth2ohistory.com/my-work/fastballs-and-fastbulbs/.

Rockoff, Hugh. "Until It's Over Over There: The U.S. Economy in World War I" *National Bureau of Economic Research,* June 2004, https://www.nber.org/system/files/working_papers/w10580/w10580.pdf.

Rockwell, Jr., Llewellyn H. "Hazlitt's Battle with Bretton Woods," *Mises Institute,* June 18, 2010, https://mises.org/print/5682

_____. "Prohibition's Repeal: What Made FDR Popular," *Mises Institute Wire,* February 18, 2021, https://mises.org/library/prohibitions-repeal-what-made-fdr-popular

Rothbard, Murray N. *A History of Money and Banking in the United States: The Colonial Era to World War II.* Introduction by Joseph T. Salerno, Auburn, Alabama: Ludwig von Mises Institute, 2002.

_____. *Anatomy of the State.* Ludwig von Mises Institute. Auburn, Alabama: BNPublishing, 1974.

_____. *Conceived in Liberty (1979).* Vols. 1-5. Forward by Andrew Napolitano. Edited by Patrick Newman. Preface by Thomas E. Woods, Jr. Auburn, Alabama: Mises Institute Press, 2019.

_____. *The Progressive Era*. Forward by Andrew Napolitano. Edited by Patrick Newman. Auburn, Alabama: Ludwig von Mises Institute, 2017.

_____. "War as Fulfillment" In James Weinstein, *The Corporate Ideal in the Liberal State, 1900–1918.* Boston: Beacon Press, 1968.

Russell, Thaddeus. "How 'Crazy Negroes' With Guns Helped Kill Jim Crow." *Reason Magazine* August/September 2014, https://reason.com/2014/07/22/how-crazy-negroes-with-guns-he/.

_____. *Out of the Jungle: Jimmy Hoffa and the Remaking of the American Working Class.* Philadelphia: Temple University Press, 2003.

_____. *A Renegade History of the United States*. New York: Free Press, 2010.

Salonia, Matteo. *Genoa's Freedom: Entrepreneurship, Republicanism, and the Spanish Atlantic*. Lanham, Maryland: Lexington, 2017.

Schlesinger, Sr., Arthur. *The Rise of the City, 1878-1898.* Columbus, Ohio: The Ohio State University Press, 1999.

Shlaes, Amity. *Coolidge*. New York: HarperCollins, 2013.

_____. *The Forgotten Man: A New History of the Great Depression*. New York: HarperCollins, 2008.

Smith, Adam. *An Inquiry into the Nature and Causes of the Wealth of Nations (1776).* Introduction by George Stigler. Edited by Edwin Cannan. Chicago: University of Chicago Press, 1976.

Solzhenitsyn, Aleksandr. *The Gulag Archipelago 1918-1956: An Experiment in Literary Investigation, Parts I-II.* New York: HarperCollins, 1974.

Sowell, Thomas. *Basic Economics: A Common Sense Guide to the Economy*. Philadelphia: Basic Books, 2011.

_____. *Intellectuals and Society*. Philadelphia: Basic Books, 2009.

Spinney, Robert G. *City of Big Shoulders: A History of Chicago*. DeKalb, Illinois: Northern Illinois University Press, 2000.

Spooner, Lysander. *A Letter to Grover Cleveland: His False Inaugural Address, The Usurpations and Crimes of Lawmakers and Judges, and the Consequent Poverty, Ignorance and Servitude of the People*. Boston: Tucker, 1886.

______. *No Treason. Nos. I, II and VI*. Boston: self-published, 1867.

Stephanson, Anders. *Manifest Destiny: American Expansion and the Empire of Right*. New York: Hill and Wang, 1996.

Stinnett, Robert B. *Day Of Deceit: The Truth About FDR and Pearl Harbor*. New York: Free Press, 2001.

Stoll, Ira. *Samuel Adams: A Life*. New York: Free Press, 2009.

Sumner, William Graham. *Protectionism: The -ism Which Teaches That Waste Makes Wealth*. New York: Henry Holt and Company, 1888.

Swanson, Michael. *The War State: The Cold War Origins of the Military-Industrial Complex and the Power Elite, 1945-1963*. Scotts Valley, California: CreateSpace, 2013.

Thornton, Mark. "Slavery, Profitability, and the Market Process." *The Review of Austrian Economics* (February 1994): 21-47.

______. "The War on Drugs Was Born 100 Years Ago" *Mises Institute*, https://mises.org/library/war-drugs-was-born-100-years-ago, December 17, 2014.

Tocqueville, Alexis de. *De la Démocratie en Amérique. Et Augmentée d'Un Avertissement et d'Un Examen Comparatif de la Démocratie aux États-Unis et en Suisse*. Tome Premier. Paris: Pagnerre, 1848.

______. "Impressions of America: Three Letters", Trans. Frederick Brown. New England Review, Vol. 30, No. 4 (2009-2010): 141-153.

Tracy, Joseph. *The Great Awakening: A History of the Revival of Religion in the Time of Edwards and Whitefield*. Charleston, South Carolina: Arcadia, 2019.

Travis, Alan. "Lusitania Divers Warned of Danger from War Munitions in 1982, Papers Reveal." *The Guardian*, 30 April 2014: https://www.theguardian.com/world/2014/may/01/lusitania-salvage-warning-munitions-1982.

Tucker, Henry St. George. *View of the Constitution of the United States: With Selected Writings (1803)*. Forward by Clide N. Wilson. Indianapolis, Indiana: Liberty Fund, 1999.

United States Holocaust Memorial Museum. *Holocaust Encyclopedia*. https://encyclopedia.ushmm.org/

Valentine, Phil. *Tax Revolt: The Rebellion Against an Overbearing, Bloated, Arrogant, and Abusive Government*. Nashville, Tennessee: Nelson Current, 2005.

Van Cleve, George William. *A Slaveholders' Union: Slavery, Politics, and the Constitution in the Early American Republic*. Chicago: University of Chicago Press, 2011.

Wheelan, Charles. *Naked Economics: Undressing the Dismal Science*. New York: W.W. Norton, 2002.

Williams, Walter. *American Contempt for Liberty*. Palo Alto, California: Hoover Institution Press, 2015.

Williamson, Kevin. *The End is Near and It's Going to Be Awesome: How Going Broke Will Leave America Richer, Happier, and More Secure*. New York: Broadside, 2013.

Wood, Gordon S. *The Creation of the American Republic, 1776-1787*. Chapel Hill, North Carolina: University of North Carolina Press, 1998.

Woods, Jr., Thomas. *33 Questions About American History That You're Not Supposed to Ask*. New York: Crown Forum, 2007.

_____. *Nullification: How to Resist Federal Tyranny in the 21st Century*. Washington, D.C.: Regnery, 2010.

_____. "The Forgotten Depression of 1920". The Intercollegiate Review, Fall 2009, accessed on Mises Daily Articles: https://mises.org/library/forgotten-depression-1920.

_____. *The Politically Incorrect Guide to American History*. Washington: Regnery, 2004.

Zinn, Howard. *A People's History of the United States*. New York: HarperPerennial, 2005.

Zitelmann, Rainer. *Hitler's National Socialism*. Oxford: Management Books, 2022.

Index

A

B

C

D

E

F

G

H

I

J

K

L

M

N

O

P

Q

R

S

T

U

V

W

X

Y

Z

About the Authors

Gary Richied wasn't always a shit-starter; he grew into the role with adulthood. Prior to writing this book, Gary served as an Adjunct Professor of History at Loyola University-Chicago and taught American and European History at Fenwick High School in Oak Park, Illinois. Despite being an alumnus of both schools, he managed to get himself fired from both institutions--simultaneously--for his professed and open libertarianism/anarcho-capitalism as well as his dogged criticism of Pope Francis and other apostates and bad actors within the Catholic Church. He might be the only person in the world to have achieved such a distinction and honor. Gary is a published author in the fields of history, economics, theology, philosophy and social science, addressing subjects ranging from the economics of the Chicago Black Sox Scandal of 1919 to the patristic theology of the fourth century. He holds his B.A. in History and French from Loyola University-Chicago, his M.A. in Social Science from the University of Chicago, and his M.A. in Theology from the Aquinas Institute of Theology in Saint Louis.

By the grace of God and with the inspiration of his Guardian Angel, all of that schooling failed to close his mind to the beautiful simplicity and abiding truth of the Austrian school of economics and attendant liberty movement; he is a devoted student of both. Most of his insights and thoughts are owed to giants of the past and present, including Ludwig von Mises, Murray Rothbard, Joseph Salerno, Guido Hülsmann, Hans Hermann Hoppe, Ron Paul, Lew Rockwell, Tom Woods, Dave Smith and Rob Bernstein.

The Good Lord willing, he'll continue unnerving people in his writing and on his website and podcast, hoth2ohistory.com, that is, until that same Good Lord calls him home.

Charlie Westerman was writing for fun on Medium when the idea for this book came to him. Charlie proposed the book concept to Gary during the height of Covid lockdowns. The vision was to create a book that would not only be innovative but also challenge the unchecked historical narratives passed down from generation to generation. As someone who was let down by the lack of intellectual openness at university, Charlie's vision and curiosity has led to the intellectual thunderstorm that is *A Twisted History of the United States.*

Charlie is currently a member of the business apprenticeship program Praxis, co-host of the Hot Water History Podcast with Gary, 2006 Time Magazine person of the year, and the most 5'10" person to ever live.